FROM PLANTATION TO *Paradise?*

FROM PLANTATION TO *Paradise?*

CULTURAL POLITICS AND MUSICAL THEATRE IN FRENCH SLAVE COLONIES, 1764–1789

David M. Powers

Michigan State University Press | *East Lansing*

∞ The paper used in this publication meets the minimum requirements of
ANSI/NISO Z39.48-1992 (R 1997) (Permanence of Paper).

Michigan State University Press
East Lansing, Michigan 48823-5245

This publication was made possible in part thanks to a grant by the Lloyd Hibberd Endowment of the American Musicological Society, funded in part by the National Endowment for the Humanities and the Andrew W. Mellon Foundation.

Printed and bound in the United States of America.
20 19 18 17 16 15 14 1 2 3 4 5 6 7 8 9 10

LIBRARY OF CONGRESS CATALOGING-IN-PUBLICATION DATA
Powers, David M.
From plantation to paradise? : cultural politics and musical theatre in
French slave colonies, 1764–1789 / David M. Powers.
pages cm
Includes bibliographical references and index.
ISBN 978-1-61186-120-4 (pbk. : alk. paper)—ISBN 978-1-60917-410-1 (ebook)
1. Theater and society—France—History—18th century. 2. Theater and society—West Indies, French—History—18th century. 3. Musical theater—West Indies, French—History—18th century.
4. West Indies, French—Social life and customs—18th century. I. Title.
PN2633.P69 2014
792.0944'09033—dc23
2013024388

Book design and composition by Charlie Sharp, Sharp Des!gns, Lansing, MI
Cover design by TG Design
Cover image is "Nègre et Négresse Ballet" and is used with permission
of the Bibliothèque nationale de France.

Michigan State University Press is a member of the Green Press Initiative and is committed to developing and encouraging ecologically responsible publishing practices. For more information about the Green Press Initiative and the use of recycled paper in book publishing, please visit *www.greenpressinitiative.org.*

Visit Michigan State University Press at *www.msupress.org*

IN MEMORIAM

The Styles

CONTENTS

LIST OF ILLUSTRATIONS

PREFACE

P*aradise*? In all colonial theatres, an upper section, *Paradis pour les gens de couleur* ("Paradise for Colored People"), was reserved for a select portion of the free nonwhite population who seemed to have been absorbed into French culture.[1] To receive permission to attend the theatre was regarded as a very high privilege for any nonwhite. However, in order to avoid any mixing of the races, it was required that these "select" persons had to enter and leave the theatre by a special door. Nevertheless, attendance at the theatre was seen by some of them, such as the rich planter elite, as a sign of acceptance by white society. Regardless of the view taken, authorities used this cruelly provocative institution as one of the most effective means of control over this sector of the population, mentally as well as physically. This so-called *Paradise* promoted and encouraged division among nonwhites; and whites encouraged such stratification, for they regarded such free peoples, many of whom were their own sons and daughters, as allies against threats of slave revolt.

The present study is intended for persons interested in black history, French Caribbean studies, and musical theatre in slave colonies during the height of colonization of the Americas. The study explores the strong bonds between music, society, and the French concept of the sub-Saharan African Other—all of which were nourished within an environment consumed with the complexities of colonization. Uniquely, my study illustrates that those bonds also provided a venue in which nonwhites (enslaved and freed) were able to excel in the performance of classical genres produced in the colonies.

Thus, I approach the subject from a very unique position—one that focuses on classical art forms (operas and concerts) produced in slave colonies and performed by nonwhites who achieved high acclaim in these genres.[2] While the present study is not intended to be an all-inclusive history of French opera or of French colonization in the Americas, I do explore several French colonial policies, rules of conduct, and other legal documents to determine the relationship between the ruling class, those being ruled, and theatre production.

Historians and other scholars have studied colonization of the Americas for centuries, and many of the various cultural traditions involved therein have received extensive treatment—with the exception of performances of classical theatre (musical and spoken) in slave colonies. Several musicologists have examined the cultural significance of operas performed in France during the seventeenth and eighteenth centuries; however, they omit any study of similar performances in French colonies. Thus, the various musical dramas (or sections thereof) that reflect and glorify colonial policies and practices of France have received little or, in most cases, no attention. My project will complement such studies, for it will demonstrate the various ways in which musical theatre illustrated the degree of sub-Saharan African influence, socially as well as economically, on colonial lifestyles, and therefore will also help to close unfortunate lacunae in the annals of black history, of Caribbean studies, and of opera. Further, the study can be a valuable source for graduate readings, as well as for more advanced study in some very important areas: social status and the economic role of women (enslaved and freed) in Caribbean colonial society; African-Caribbean musical theatre; world music; and the influence of *le Code Noir* (the Black Code) on various sectors of the population.

Eyewitness accounts of operas produced in the colonies, and other contemporary opinions presented in the present study are those of government officials, missionaries, slave owners, and other white authorities, since formal education was forbidden to the enslaved and only a few successful free nonwhites were allowed to send their children to France for this purpose (generally with the approval and support of a white benefactor). While such accounts generally present limited points of view, they do, however, provide useful descriptions of dances, costumes, *mise-en-scène* (staging), and types of instruments used in these productions. For a view of different approaches, I refer the reader to several works by modern Antillean musicians and scholars cited frequently in the present study. Of these, the most thorough studies were prepared by Jean Fouchard, the noted Haitian historian;[3] Jacqueline Rosemain, musicologist;[4] Maurice Nicolas, music historian;[5] and Moreau de Saint-Méry, one of the most-quoted contemporary historians on culture and politics in French colonial society.[6] Each author focuses primarily—but not exclusively—on her or his own island. From them, we gain valuable knowledge about types and function of dances, concert music, and opera repertoire. Their brief biographical sketches of several artists imported from France are surpassed in content only by the extremely detailed discussions of the physical appearance (shape, size, capacity, decor, etc.) of some of the theatres.

For those operas performed in the colonies, I focus primarily on literary components, making use of colonial newspapers, eyewitness accounts, an abundance of French regulations, and other documents as bases for facts and conclusions presented in the study. With regard to musical styles, rarely did the music in works that dramatize cultural aspects of non-European peoples differ from those operas devoid of such references. Further, I have not included music examples of performances in the colonies because, unfortunately, such documents suffered the same fate as theatres in the colonies—total destruction resulting from fires, hurricanes, slave uprisings, and volcanic eruptions. Rather, music examples are included in the present study, primarily, to reflect the *types* of pieces performed in the colonies and, for the most part, are excerpts from operas that premiered in France and subsequently were performed in the colonies in the same manner as in Paris (elaborate staging, costumes, and décor; excellent vocalists, instrumentalists, and dancers, etc.). Excellent recordings of some of these operas are available commercially, and, in order that the reader may acquaint herself/himself easily with the sound of this music, I have provided sources in appendix 6, "Discography." It is hoped that these materials will help readers, particularly non-musical persons, to attain a better understanding of the nature of French colonial musical theatre.

The book is composed of two parts. The first part (Introduction and chapters 1 and 2) explores the special significance of the dates cited in the title (1764–1789), defines the monarchy's efforts to control cultural activities, and provides the reader with a general understanding of French opera and of French colonial society, with particular emphasis on the environment in which nonwhite artists emerged. It also examines both negative and positive contributions of the Catholic Church to colonial society, particularly the types of musical training the enslaved received from priests—the results of which can be linked to the first appearance of black violinists on the concert and opera stages. Musical functions and official responsibilities of the military that relate specifically to operas and concerts produced in the colonies are also explored.

The second part of the study (chapters 3–7 and epilogue) examines the function and types of operas produced in each island colony and the level of participation by nonwhites. Chapter 3 discusses theatre architecture, décor, repertoire, seating arrangements, and types of audiences. (Descriptions of theatres discussed in this study are provided in appendix 4.) Chapters 4–6 thoroughly explore the status of nonwhite artists in colonial society; the types of operas in which they performed; accomplishments, praises, criticisms, etc.; and the various ways in which *créole* texts were used in several productions. The study concludes with an examination of the ways in which colonial opera was affected by slave uprisings, the French Revolution, the emergence of "patriotic theatres" and their role in fostering support for the king at the onset of the French Revolution, as well as the impact of these events on performers and on subsequent operas produced in the colonies and in the United States (chapter 7).

The present study includes a myriad of terms; some are musical, but a much larger portion consists of nonmusical terminology that was used to underscore and promote class distinctions within the nonwhite population. To provide the reader with more clarity and understanding of the complexities of social stratification in French colonial society, I have included a glossary (appendix 1).

In addition to exploring and presenting an enormous amount of operas and other documents, the author repeatedly asks the reader to keep in mind that all French and *créole* texts, dances, and music were composed by whites (French and *créole*); titles applied to the dances are also those of whites. Thus, such pieces reflect *perceptions* of white composers, white librettists, and other white authorities as to what constitutes cultural elements of sub-Saharan Africa.

ACKNOWLEDGMENTS

The journey of research for the present study was far-reaching, leading me down an ever-winding path, and I am extremely grateful for the support of several individuals and institutions during this long voyage. I am especially indebted to three music scholars who gave me their unwavering support, constantly and freely: the late M. Elizabeth C. Bartlet, an exceptional musicologist, who was always generous with her time and advice—professionally and personally—from the beginning of the study until her untimely death in 2005; Samuel A. Floyd Jr., founder and director emeritus, Center for Black Music Research, whose encouragement and guidance from the beginning of my study were immeasurable; and Cheryl Keyes, professor of ethnomusicology at University of California-Los Angeles, and composer-arranger, whose sage advice, support, and knowledge of ethnomusicology were invaluable.

For examination of primary resources, the staff of several archives and libraries provided invaluable assistance in locating librettos, scores, and other pertinent documents for the project. In the French Antilles and in France, the institutions are Archives Départementales de la Martinique; Archives Départementales de la Guadeloupe; Bibliothèque Schoelcher, Martinique; Archives Nationales, Paris; Archives Nationales, Centre des Archives d'Outre Mer, Aix-en-Provence; Bibliothèque de l'Arsenal, Paris; Bibliothèque Nationale, Paris; Bibliothèque-Musée de l'Opéra, Paris; and Bibliothèque Municipale de Versailles. In the United States, I was able to examine several libretto collections and other documents at the Pusey Theater Library, Harvard University; Bancroft Library, University of California-Berkeley; University of California-Los

Angeles; University of California-San Diego; Stanford University Music Library; New York Public Library (Schomburg Center, the Research Division, and Performing Arts at Lincoln Center); and public libraries in Oakland, San Francisco, and Escondido, California.

In the very early stages of research, I was fortunate to receive financial assistance from the College of Art and Architecture, University of Illinois at Chicago, consisting of a three-year research grant and a Faculty Fellowship in the Institute for the Humanities, for which I am extremely grateful. A few years later, I was awarded a Resident Fellowship by the Camargo Foundation (Cassis, France) that enabled me to conduct invaluable research at the Archives Nationales in Aix-en-Provence. I am also grateful for additional financial support from The John Nuveen Center for International Affairs, University of Illinois-Chicago, for foreign travel awards to present papers on my project at Université de la Sorbonne Nouvelle, Paris, in collaboration with the W.E.B. Du Bois Institute for Afro-American Research, Harvard University, and at the Second Conference of the International Centre of African Music and Dance, University of Ghana, Accra, West Africa.

I am particularly grateful to two scientists, Paul Huber and Father James Foster, University of Notre Dame, for their guidance in my attempts to understand the various scientific hypotheses regarding skin color in the eighteenth century. It is with great pleasure and admiration that I acknowledge the Zéphirs, the incredible family that I always stayed with while in Martinique and in Guadeloupe. Their warmth and hospitality, as well as their vast knowledge of the history and current trends of these two islands, were simply amazing. I also wish to thank scholars and other professionals in Paris who provided invaluable suggestions and assistance: Catherine Kintzler, a Rameau scholar; Catherine Massip, Bibliothèque Nationale; Ghislaine Macret; Colette Le Dolédec; Mabrouk Bekkouche, Jacques Emsalem, and Brigitte Steinmann. I am thankful to Nancy Wright, Nimia Ramos, Esq., and Dorothy Figueira for their meticulous reading of certain portions of the manuscript, and, especially, to Angelina Gault for her assistance during my last trip to Martinique. Through all of this, a very, very special gratitude goes to Edward Larry and Sheri, my two wonderful and extremely supportive children.

INTRODUCTION

Is it possible that the color barrier in opera was broken over two centuries ago—and in a slave colony? The concept is quite amazing, for how and why did such a phenomenon occur in a place in which the institution of slavery was such a thriving enterprise? To what extent did the politics of a European empire impact the cultivation of opera in its colonies? The concepts, theories, and attitudes presented in travel narratives, and those propounded by the *philosophes*[1] significantly impacted musical activities in France and in the colonies. We know from past research that European colonial powers in the Americas maintained an active concert life modeled after that of their own country, and that this included a lively tradition in theatre (musical and spoken) and in dance. However, such research also demonstrates that these events occurred in the nineteenth century—more than a century after the first appearance of sub-Saharan African personages in operas performed in Paris, and at least five decades after productions featuring some type(s) of sub-Saharan African elements were launched in French colonies. Opera productions in France cast sub-Saharan Africans as main or (more frequently) secondary characters. In fact, no other national opera up to and including the eighteenth century reflected such fascination with sub-Saharan African culture. Through a closer look at the preoccupation of the French with their musical theatre and its positive influence on the individual (according to them), we can begin to understand why the same standards of musical performance were extended to the colonies.

The time is 1764–1789, covering two and one-half decades prior to the onset of the French Revolution. The year 1764 marks the establishment of the first printing press in the colonies, the beginning of official documentation of operas and plays performed there, and the inauguration of the first theatre in the colonies. The year 1789 refers to the beginning of the French Revolution. Several events encompassed within these boundaries ignited and prepared the way for what happened prior to, during, and after the French Revolution. Among these were the increasing antipathy toward the enslavement of human beings, the beginning of the breakdown of the vast French colonial empire, and, ultimately, in the mid-nineteenth century, the abolishment of slavery in the French Antilles.[2] The subject era also coincides with the twilight years of the *siècle des lumières*, the Enlightenment, a movement in which the concepts of liberty and justice rendered the institution of slavery intellectually indefensible, for Enlightenment tenets defended individual rights and equality as the primary bases of natural law.

The place is the French colonial empire in the Antilles, with a focus on the islands of Guadeloupe, Martinique, and Saint-Domingue (now Haiti). The total area of Saint-Domingue is 10,579 square miles, approximately the size of the state of Maryland (10,460 square miles). Guadeloupe and Martinique are much smaller, with a total area of 687 square miles and 436 square miles, respectively. Although several territories in the Caribbean were under French control, all references to "colonies" in the present study pertain to these three islands unless specifically noted otherwise. If an event pertains to only one of these islands, such occurrence will be indicated in the text.

The earliest indigenous people on the three islands were the Tainos, members of the Arawakan language family and a peaceful, agricultural people. The Tainos were the first natives Columbus encountered when he arrived on the coast of their island, later called Saint-Domingue. However, it seems that the Arawakan tribes in Guadeloupe and Martinique were not able to withstand constant attacks by the Caribs, a more aggressive and warlike tribe. The Caribs drove most of the Arawaks out of Guadeloupe and Martinique shortly before the arrival of Columbus in 1493. Several Caribs remained in Martinique and occupied more than half of that island up until 1658.[3]

With the colonization of these islands, there was a huge and continually increasing need for labor. The warlike, independent Caribs refused to be enslaved, and as a result, the Europeans wiped them out in a few years. It was during this period also that the Spanish and Portuguese, the first colonizers of the New World, also began to capture, bring to the Americas, and enslave thousands of Africans. The French acquired slaves from their European neighbors for about two decades. By the third quarter of the seventeenth century, however, they were purchasing slaves directly from several sub-Saharan African countries. The origins of the enslaved in the French colonies are very diverse. In each island colony, there were at least fifteen different tribal groups from several different countries, including—but not limited to—Angola, Dahomey, Ghana, Guinea, Ivory Coast, Liberia, Mali, Nigeria, Senegal, Sierra Leone, and Togo.[4] In sum:

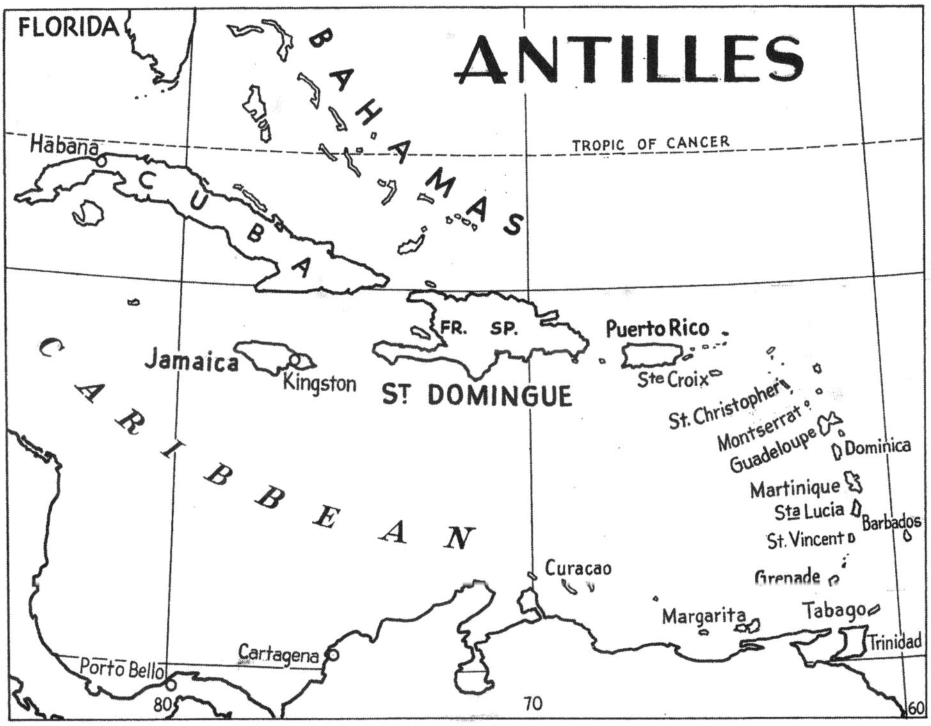

MAP 1. *Antilles*

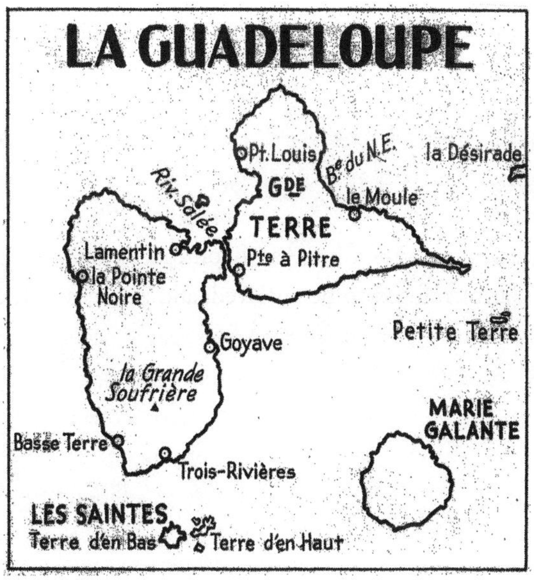

MAP 2. *Guadeloupe*

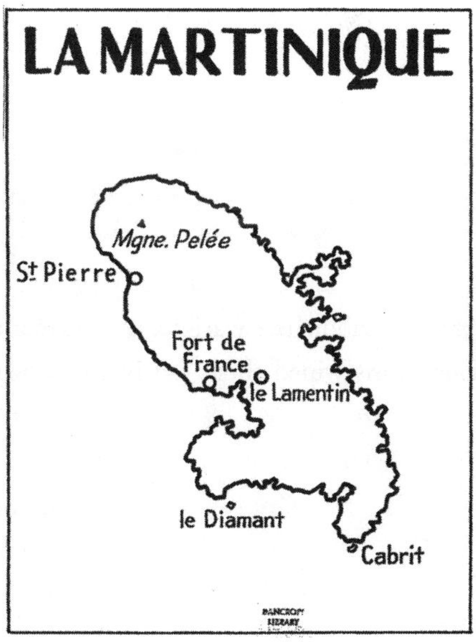

MAP 3. *Martinique*

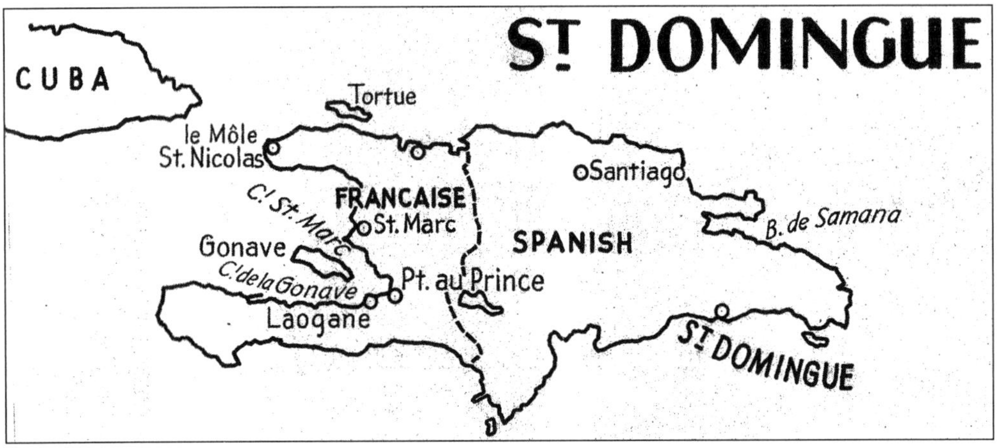

MAP 4. *Saint-Domingue*

> Slavers scoured the coasts of Guinea. As they devastated an area they moved westward and then south, decade after decade, past the Niger, down the Congo coast, past Loango [now Republic of Congo] and Angola, round the Cape of Good Hope, and, by 1789, even as far as Mozambique on the eastern side of Africa. Guinea remained their chief hunting ground.[5]

The French took possession of Guadeloupe and Martinique in 1635, and for almost four decades, the islands were managed by private companies appointed by the king. Due to immense financial problems and other complications confronting the companies, the two islands were officially annexed by Louis XIV in 1674. After several battles and other turmoil between Spanish and French settlers on the island of Hispaniola, Spain ceded the western portion of the island to France in the Peace Treaty of Ryswick in 1697, at which time that territory officially became the French colony of Saint-Domingue.

It was in these three island territories that history recorded one of the most fascinating events of that period—the emergence of extremely talented nonwhite musicians, singers, and dancers of sub-Saharan African descent performing in lavishly produced French operas. While this fact alone is amazing, it is also quite astonishing that such phenomena could occur under the stringent racist policies of eighteenth-century French colonialism and, particularly, when most Western nations were entangled in the throes of the Atlantic slave trade.

The above events and attitudes were reflected in several operas produced in France, for it was here—not in the colonies—where we see the beginning of an extraordinary trend: dramatization of the *presumed* notion of superiority of French culture over that of sub-Saharan Africans and their descendants. Subsequently, many works were transported to and elaborately staged in Guadeloupe, Martinique, and Saint-Domingue. These productions were a reflection of the times, for they offered the audience an escape from the stark realities of a nation exhausted—financially and emotionally—from decades of war with European neighbors, social unrest among the impoverished masses, famine, and endless struggles between the royal family and various factions of government. In the colonies, the theatre became a refuge from the many complexities of colonization—particularly the growing unrest throughout the colonies as the number of slave revolts and runaways continued to increase. Officials viewed the theatre as one of the primary ways to appease citizens' mounting fears of the burgeoning black population, coupled with the enactment of several laws to regulate every facet of daily existence of the nonwhite population.

In order to specifically address the "how and why" of the second question posed at the beginning of this introduction, one must take a close look at Western European societal values with regard to New World explorations, which were firmly entrenched in ethnocentrism. Modern scholars have examined the presumed "qualitatively different" status of Indians[6] and imported sub-Saharan Africans, a societal trend that promoted the concept of *the Other* and "became a counter in the making of modern European identity."[7] The Bulgarian philosopher Tzvetan Todorov, who emigrated to France in the early 1960s, examined the concept by focusing on age-old perceptions in modern France regarding *Us* (his own cultural and social group) versus *the Others* (those who do not belong to it).[8] Todorov emphasized that in such a society, where tolerance for true diversity was lacking, *the Others* had to be confined to the "purely relative category of otherness."

> No one is intrinsically other; an individual is "other" only because he is not myself.... I know nothing about him and do not want to know anything, since any positive characterization of him would keep me from confining him to the *purely relative category of Otherness*.... The best candidates [for this category] are the peoples and cultures that are most remote from us and least known to us.... [Such attitudes are] almost always accompanied by an attraction for certain contents *at the expense of Others*.[9]

Those persons confined to the "purely relative category of Otherness" in French colonial society were sub-Saharan Africans, their descendants, and Indians.

Initiation of Cultural Politics

One of the most distinctive characteristics of French colonialism is that from the early part of the seventeenth century onward, the nation implemented an elaborate system of class distinction not seen in any colony governed by other European nations. Class distinctions between whites and nonwhites and within the two groups were integral parts of French colonial society. Therefore, I must point out here that the use of certain terms in the present study—such as colored people (*les gens de couleur*), mulatto (*mulâtre*), and quadroon (*quarteron*)—while rather pejorative, is necessary; for it is important to keep in mind that such terminology was created in a climate of *presumed* white superiority over the *presumed* inferiority of persons of sub-Saharan African descent and applied to the latter during every second of their existence. Thus, my use of these terms is designed not only to expose such colonial misconceptions, but also to allow the reader to realize—and possibly to experience—the impact of such negativisms on various sectors of colonial society.

Such classifications were inevitable, however, for beginning with the reign of Louis XIII (1601–1643; reigned 1610–1643) and lasting throughout the subject period, the kings of France continuously waged a campaign to promote French culture throughout France, in the colonies, and elsewhere. Goals of this *cultural* political campaign of the monarchy were threefold: to maintain the peace, to ensure absolute respect for the established social order, and to promote theatre (musical and spoken) and other forms of French culture. In this regard, the monarchy felt that its citizens in the colonies should be able to enjoy "the fruits of peace"[10] as did those in France; and what, the French deemed, could be a more delightful diversion than their own musical theatre!

It is important to note that during the initiation of cultural politics, the French crown instituted regulations to maximize control and domination over its subjects in the colonies and in France. Specifically, in March 1685, the government enacted the *Code Noir*, a set of sixty articles that forced Catholicism on its subjects and regulated every facet of daily existence of nonwhites in French colonies in the Americas and in Africa.[11] A few months later (October), the Edict of Nantes, a law that had given the Protestants a large measure of religious and civil liberties for almost a century, was revoked.[12] Nevertheless, during this period, composers and librettists, who knew little or nothing of the actual horrid state of the enslaved, consistently cast sub-Saharan African personages speaking in the most glowing terms of love and devotion for the "benevolent" Louis XIV (1638–1715; reigned 1643–1715). Therefore, using the theatre to promote the *cultural* political campaign can be viewed as an attempt by France not only to lessen the emotional drain on its citizens, but also to strengthen and to accelerate the internal propaganda machine. Furthermore, despite the negativity associated with colonization of the Americas, the curiosity for knowledge of faraway lands spurred the advent of a new literary phenomenon, the travel narrative, at the dawn of the seventeenth century. Tales of experiences of explorers, missionaries, government officials, and other visitors to the colonies found an avid audience in the French educated public. Patrons of the arts, composers, librettists (authors of opera texts), and other writers relied primarily on these eyewitness accounts to form opinions of the sub-Saharan African Other.

The *Philosophes*

The same reliance can also be applied to the leading *philosophes*, who never ventured outside Western Europe, but had a profound influence on operas produced in the colonies. The subject matter for these works was based, primarily, on their concepts of individual rights and liberty. The *philosophes* believed in a social contract that identified liberty with equality; they opposed absolutism, advocated political freedom, and defended individual rights and equality as primary bases of natural law. They reinterpreted and, in some cases, rejected traditional Christian values and searched for a natural, or rational, religion. In their lofty form of social organization, natural rights and democratic ideals were of paramount importance. As the most influential proponents of such concepts during the eighteenth century, their "civilized world" must be explored against the backdrop of their country's heavy involvement in the institution of slavery—an extremely *de*humanizing phenomenon.

In Rousseau's vision of the civilized world, man's greed for money, property, and other instruments of power had plunged society into the depths of moral degradation, leaving it devoid of natural freedom and equality.[13] For one who advocated so eloquently and forcefully the concepts of individual rights and liberty in three of his most important political writings,[14] Rousseau's discussions on slavery are rather perplexing. He spoke of slavery in terms of "voluntary servitude" and of "agreements [as] the basis of all legitimate authority among men."[15] It is evident that Rousseau was totally ignoring French colonial policy, for the two terms "voluntary servitude" and "slavery" are contradictory, because there was certainly no "agreement" between European slave owners and sub-Saharan Africans forced into slavery. The "slavery" to which Rousseau referred concerned men of his own society—their loss of natural freedom as they succumbed to greed, immorality, and other vices of an illegitimate government that, through laws it had set down for its citizens, deprived them of natural freedom. At a time when France held hundreds of thousands of individuals in human bondage, this great thinker did not just sidestep the issue; he ignored it.

Absolute domination and dehumanization were the norm in the colonies; and, as a result, native populations and imported sub-Saharan Africans were considered inferior beings—incapable of intellectual growth and, therefore, unworthy of philosophical thought. This concept is evident in the so-called "exotic" dramas and novels of the great *philosophes*—not by references to the French Antilles, but by the exclusion of any subject matter based explicitly on the arts and customs of the peoples of these lands. Rather, the *philosophes*, in their critiques of contemporary society, chose other European colonies or more positive exotic locales. In *Candide*, Voltaire satirizes European cultural and political institutions, such as the Church and the military, as we follow the hero's travels through Europe, South America, and Turkey.[16] However, in this novel of thirty chapters, Voltaire devotes only a few lines to abuses of slavery—not in a French colony, but in Surinam, a Dutch possession. He illustrates the horrors of that system through Candide, shocked at the sight of a crippled slave (his left leg and right hand missing), sparsely clothed, and lying on the ground. The slave pointed out how Europeans benefited from his "*situations*" ("That is the price of the sugar you eat in Europe").[17]

Diderot,[18] inspired by the travel narrative of Louis Antoine de Bougainville,[19] chose the idyllic land of Tahiti to emphasize his concept of a free society based on tolerance and mutual understanding between different cultures, as well as to develop his views of sexual freedom in the state of nature, a place where the ascetic repressions of European religious institutions are nonexistent. In his *Supplément au voyage de Bougainville*,[20] Diderot opines that Europeans and Tahitians are brothers, for they are both "children of nature and neither has a right over the other." Unfortunately, he suggests, Europeans have "burdened the conjugal state with too many conditions [and] subjected the institution of marriage to endless formalities; [for, to civilize man] is to poison him with a system of morality that is contrary to nature."[21]

Montesquieu[22] satirized French (especially Parisian) society as seen through the eyes of two Persians visiting Paris.[23] In "letters" to friends back home, the two Persians relate their impressions of French society (theatre, opera, the passion of French women, Parisians' reactions to their Persian dress, etc.) and government, particularly the enormous power of the king (Louis XIV) as well as the weakness and gullibility of those around him. This is not to suggest that Montesquieu viewed Persian attitudes as correct, or even valid. Rather, considering the contemporary political atmosphere in France, it was undoubtedly one of the safest and most imaginative ways to criticize his own society while pretending to ridicule Persian culture and politics. In fact, the *philosophes* frequently used characters from a foreign, yet enticing and strangely beautiful, locale to critique their own government, society, and religion.[24]

Despite a host of theories with regard to political and social equality and the laws of nature, there were pitifully few attacks on the slave trade and the institution of slavery in French territories. In fact, French writers portrayed their own colonists as men of honor and sensitivity who, "less arrogant and less disdainful, [grant] to sub-Saharan Africans a type of morality."[25] On the other hand, they showed no hesitation in criticizing their European neighbors for slavery abuses. Accordingly, the enslaved were "playmates for the indolence" of the Spaniard, "instruments of seduction" for the Portuguese, "victims of the greed" of the Dutch, and, for the English, "purely physical beings to use or destroy at will, . . . never smiling nor speaking to them."[26] Voltaire, equally critical of the "arrogant" and "greedy" Spanish colonizers, focused on the sufferings of the Peruvians under the reign of the Spaniards. He pointed out that "these tyrants, seduced by gold found in the Americas, think the heavens made America [especially] for them."[27] Montesquieu held Portuguese and Spaniards in such contempt that, to him, these people "who despise everyone only honor the French by hating them."[28]

Although the *philosophes*, for the most part, were ambivalent or even silent about France's involvement in the Atlantic slave trade, their incessant attempts to promote concepts of liberty and equality rendered the institution of slavery intellectually indefensible. In this regard, the *philosophes* exerted a positive influence on the growing antipathy to slavery in the eighteenth century.

The *philosophes* also extended their influence to a very different arena, the performing arts. Diderot was an ardent supporter of tolerance and reform in the theatre (musical and spoken), and this is reflected in his monumental output of musical essays and treatises, plays, and poems. They range from the function of instrumental accompaniment (*Lettre sur les aveugles*, 1749 [Letter on the Blind], and *Lettre sur les sourds et les muets*, 1751 [Letter on the Deaf and Dumb]) to musical criticism in the form of literary dialogue that focuses on the relative merits of French music versus the "shallow" music of the Italians (*Le neveu de Rameau* [Rameau's Nephew], written between 1761 and 1774).[29]

Voltaire's musical interests were confined to opera, which seems to have held a fascination for him. He wrote texts for seven operas, and during the late eighteenth and early nineteenth centuries, more than seventy operas were based on his tragedies (*Zaïre*, 1732; *Alzire, ou les Américains*, 1736; *Mahomet, ou le fanatisme*, 1741; *Sémiramis*, 1748; *Tancrède*, 1760; and *Olympie*, 1764).

Rousseau also made significant contributions to the field of music. He wrote several vocal and instrumental pieces and works for the stage. Of the latter, two were very successful. *Le Devin du village* (The Village Soothsayer), an *intermède*,[30] premiered at Fontainebleau in 1752, and *Pygmalion, scène-lyrique*, premiered in Lyons (1770). Both works were performed numerous times in France and in Saint-Domingue. As indicated above, Rousseau was a strong critic of his own society and their moral degradation. The composer underscored these same views in *Le Devin du village*, for the work focuses on the triumph of rustic simplicity and virtue (the original state of nature) over corruption and moral degradation (deviation from that state). Rousseau presented his philosophy of music in several articles. The *Lettre sur la musique française* (1753) reflected his dislike for French opera and contributed to the *Querelle des Bouffons* (War of the Buffoons), a literary debate centering on the respective merits of French and Italian operas.[31] Rousseau also contributed several articles on music for the monumental *Encyclopédie* that were later included in his *Dictionnaire de musique* (1768).

Emergence of Musical Theatre

As indicated above, dramatization of the concept of the sub-Saharan African Other was initiated in France and then extended to the colonies. The transporting of a form of classical music, opera, to slave colonies was indeed an elaborate French innovation. The reasons for such a unique societal event stem from the close relationship between music and society in France and the high esteem with which the French regarded musical theatre. The Académie Royale de Musique, under the direction of Jean-Baptiste Lully, composer and adroit administrator,[32] became the primary cultural showcase of the monarchy. The repertoire included several works in which the reigning monarch was glorified through pronouncements from the mouths of ancient deities, while, in contrast, the sub-Saharan African Other was presented as racially inferior. We can observe the early stages of this trend in Lully's first *tragédie lyrique* (1673), *Cadmus et Hermione* (III, 1). Arbas, an African servant, boasts of his strength and bravery—killing a dragon—to two princes, who do not, however, believe a word he says, and scornfully refute his claims:

> One believes your bravery from your word;
> But the color of your face
> Does not agree with such valor.[33]

Arbas, although trembling and very meek, responds with a question that still weighs heavily on Western society today:

> Is it by color
> That one's courage must be judged?[34]

Although French opera remained deeply embedded in native traditions, Italian influences gained a strong foothold by the mid-eighteenth century, particularly in public theatres such as the Fair Theatres (*Théâtres de la Foire*), which became the venue for satire and parody.[35] They catered to the public's appetite for gaiety and crude humor and, thus, were very successful. *Vaudevilles* (popular airs) replaced the courtly airs, the serious plots, dramatic construction, and versification of Lully's *tragédie lyrique*. Singers at the Académie were treated with humor and ridicule by stock characters from the Italian *commedia dell'arte*.[36]

In 1715, the Fair Theatres were granted the title Opéra-Comique,[37] and later, in 1762, merged with another public theatre, the Comédie-Italienne.[38] Under the guidance of some of the best French composers and librettists of the eighteenth century, the Opéra-Comique and the Comédie-Italienne gradually abandoned *vaudevilles*, satirical buffoonery, vulgarities, and physical stunts.[39] These artists created a serious musical drama infused with social commentary and bourgeois morality. The characterizations, plots, and settings were greatly influenced by the *philosophes*. These works generally characterize the aristocracy as morally corrupt. Love continues to be a primary theme, as in the *tragédie lyrique*, but now main characters are peasants or village people leading a simple, natural life; they are generous, courageous, and devoid of the corruption, greed, and jealousy of the court (or city) society that Rousseau denounced so eloquently. It is this lighter type of musical theatre—not the serious panegyric *tragédie lyrique*—that we will see produced in the colonies with great success.

With the abandonment of *vaudevilles*, these composers wrote some of the most creative, inspiring music of the period. One of the favorite vocal forms was the *ariette*, a virtuoso solo piece with flexible and diverse rhythms. Characteristically, the *ariette* was set in ABA form and accompanied by the full orchestra. Most notably, however, were the virtuoso melodies and the large degree of musical expansion. Composers accomplished the latter through the use of numerous phrase repetitions in the vocal line, punctuated with or separated by dramatic *symphonies*.[40] In addition, numerous techniques were applied within phrases (individually to the vocal line, to the orchestra, or to both simultaneously), such as chromatic harmonies, melodic pauses, accented phrases, verses of varying lengths, and rapid (and sometimes abrupt) modulations.[41] *Ariettes* of this new group of composers were extremely popular forms in Paris and in the colonies. An example of an *ariette* that includes all the above-mentioned techniques (and was performed several times in the colonies) is provided in appendix 2.[42]

It was also in the *récitatif accompagné*[43] that the musical skills and creativity of this new group of composers came into prominence. It was delivered by a main character, generally in a highly emotional state caused by the injury or presumed death of a lover, or some other dreaded fate; or it could be the words themselves that provoke sudden changes in the action, such as a rival's angry outburst after being rejected. The orchestra assumes a highly descriptive and expressive role in these situations, particularly to reinforce the inner turmoil of a character. Generally, the setting for such events is the *monologue scene*, for the character is alone on stage and can give free rein to his or her thoughts and emotions. The focus on the concerns of one character can reflect several contrasting affections—anxiety, solitude, joy, sadness, or tenderness—and thus provide the composer with several opportunities for creative expansion of musical ideas.

An example in which many of these events are brought together in a single piece occurs in *Titon et l'Aurore*, a *pastorale héroïque* by Jean-Joseph Cassanéa de Mondonville (1711–1772), one of the most successful and prolific composers of pastoral operas.[44] Titon, a handsome young shepherd, and l'Aurore, goddess of dawn, are in love with each other, but each innocent has a jealous and vengeful rival. The two rivals (Palès, goddess of shepherds, and Eole, god of the winds) unite to punish the handsome young Titon (the mortal) with a curse: the ravages of old age. In a monologue scene, Titon looks at his reflection in a fountain and is horrified at his appearance, the result of Palès's revenge:

> What do I see? Am I ready to end my life?
> My feet are unsteady. I tremble, I am pale.
> A frightful cloud conceals the daylight from my weak eyes.
> By what disastrous enchantment,
> Oh, Fate, why do you shorten the passage of my years?
> Barbarian! Finish, destroy, for pity's sake,
> The deplorable remainder of my days.

> The evil that you make me suffer feels crueler than death itself.
> Ah! How happy it is to die
> When one has lost the one he loves." (III, 2)[45]

The composer applies a highly dramatic form, the *lament*, to reflect the emotional turbulence in which Titon finds himself. The score and original French text of this scene are provided in figure 1. The short prelude sets the tone, the gravity of which is dramatized by descending chromatic lines in all parts and a repetitive bass pattern. The anguish of Titon is brought out in the melody through affective intervals, descending chromatics (occasionally followed by ascending chromatic melodies), and short-breathed phrases punctuated by the orchestra. The orchestra provides reinforcement with scale rushes in sixteenth and thirty-second notes and chromatic harmonies. Effective pauses in all parts—vocal and instrumental—underscore the miserable state in which Titon finds himself.

Anti-Slavery Sentiment

As indicated above, the primary tenets of the Enlightenment espoused so eloquently and forcefully by the *philosophes* were the concepts of individual rights and liberty as primary bases of natural law. Their incessant attempts to promote these concepts rendered the institution of slavery intellectually indefensible and, thus, exerted a positive influence on the growing antipathy to the enslavement of human beings. Opinions on both sides of this issue were subjects of heated debates among Parisian society. Various aspects of antislavery sentiments were dramatized by both court and public theatres. Some productions were closely related to the institution of slavery, such as the first *entrée* of *Les fêtes, ou le triomphe de Thalie* (1714),[46] set in Marseilles, one of the main ports of the slave trade (see table 1). As the plot unfolds, Acaste, the hero and captain of the ship, finally wins the hand of his virtuous beloved. Then, in a magnanimous deed befitting his heroic stature, Acaste frees all Algerian slaves on board his ship, telling them that they owe their newly found freedom to the power of love, and encourages them to live in peace with everyone (I, 6).

Another example of the *philosophes'* influence on French opera can be seen in the use of non-French characters and settings in order to critique one's own society.[47] One of the most unique examples of how they dealt with this issue as well as that of antislavery sentiment occurs in *La Négresse, ou le pouvoir de la reconnaissance*, produced by the Comédie-Italienne in 1787 (see table 2). The setting is "an African island." Dorval, a young French captain, and his valet, Frontin, were shipwrecked by a storm. He fears that his father, captain of a companion ship, did not escape the storm that had separated the two ships. The source of Frontin's fright, however, is "those damned Negroes who [inhabit this place and] have vowed to kill all whites

PARIS: MONTULAY, 1753

FIGURE 1. Monologue scene, *Titon et l'Aurore*, III, 2 (1753)

PARIS: MONTULAY, 1753

PARIS: MONTULAY, 1753

Table 1. *Performances by the Court Theatre, Académie Royale de Musique*[*†]

TITLE/PREMIERE/LENGTH/ COMPOSER/LIBRETTIST	SOURCE OF PLOT AND MAIN CHARACTERS	REMARKS (PURPOSE, SECONDARY ROLES, AND ELEMENTS OF THE OTHER)
Ballet Royal de Flore, ballet February 13, 1669 15 *entrées* Jean-Baptiste Lully (1632–1687) Isaac de Benserade (1613–1691)	Mythology Flore, goddess of flowers and gardens, accompanied by goddesses of Beauty, Youth, Abundance, and Felicity	Glorification of Louis XIV and "the peace, abundance and happiness that he bestows on his subjects." Africans sing, dance, and play castanets.
Cadmus et Hermione, tragédie lyrique April 27, 1673 prologue and 5 acts Jean-Baptiste Lully (1632–1687) Philippe Quinault (1635–1688)	Mythology Cadmus (heroic warrior prince) Hermione (daughter of Mars and Venus)	Presumed inferiority of the African Other and celebration of victory in war with Holland. Arbas and "two other Africans"—all servants of Cadmus. Africans dance and play guitars.
Roland, tragédie lyrique Versailles, January 18, 1685 prologue and 5 acts Jean-Baptiste Lully (1632–1687) Philippe Quinault (1635–1688)	History Roland (French knight and nephew of Charlemagne) Angelique, Queen of Cathay	Presumed inferiority of the African Other and celebration of war victory (surrender of Luxembourg, 1684). Médor (African soldier).
Le Temple de la Paix, ballet Fontainebleau, September 12, 1685 6 *entrées* Jean-Baptiste Lully (1632–1687) Philippe Quinault (1635–1688)	Celebrates contemporary events (*entrées* 5 and 6) No specific characterizations; consists of chorus, dances, vocal airs, and recitatives	*Entrées* 5 and 6 focus on glorification of Louis XIV, inferiority of the Other, and a celebration of peace (Treaty of Regensburg, 1684). Choruses: American and African savages.
Théagène et Chariclée, tragédie mise en musique February 3, 1695 prologue and 5 acts Henry Desmarets (1661–1741) Joseph-François Duché de Vancy (1668–1704)	Contemporary view: inferiority of the Other Love triangle of: Chariclée (Ethiopian servant) Théagène (Greek prince) Meroébe (Ethiopian prince)	Conflict between Egypt and Ethiopia is used as a backdrop. Ethiopian dancers and chorus and Arsace (sorceress).

Les Fêtes, ou Le triomphe de Thalie, opéra-ballet August 14, 1714 prologue and 3 *entrées* Jean-Joseph Mouret (1682–1738) La Font (1686–1725)	Contemporary event: anti-slavery sentiment Acaste (ship captain) Cléon (captive of Acaste) Bélise (wife of Cléon) Léonore (daughter of Cléon and Bélise)	The composer dedicated the work to his patroness, the Duchess of Maine, daughter-in-law of Louis XIV and Mme de Montespan. Algerian slaves.
Les Romans, ballet héroïque August 23, 1736 prologue and 3 *entrées* 4th *entrée* added Sept. 23, 1736 Jean-Baptiste Niel (1690?–1775) Michel de Bonneval	Contemporary view: process of "refinement" Ismène (princess) Lindor (lover of Ismène) Minerve (goddess of wisdom and patroness of arts and crafts)	*Entrée* 4 reflects contemporary practice of taking or sending slaves to Paris to be "educated" properly. Such "refinement" was dramatized by personages representing the Arts (*Génies* of Opera and Comedy) who demonstrate the calming effect of a "sweet *symphonie*" on "savage hearts." Paints savages of America as "blood-thirsty barbarians." Grand priest of savages and choruses and dances by savages.
La Caravane du Caire, opéra-ballet Fontainebleau, October 30, 1783 3 acts André Ernest Modeste Grétry (1741–1813) Etienne Morel de Chédevelle	Contemporary view: heroic and superior qualities of the Frenchman Florestan (French ship captain) Zélime (slave and daughter of an Indian chief) Suitors of Zélime: Saint-Phar (slave and son of Florestan) Pasha of Egypt	Contrast is drawn between the corruption and greed of slave merchants compared to the power of virtuous love. Almaïde (lover of Pasha), Husca (chief of slave caravan), choruses of slaves, Arabs, harem women, Turks, French, and guards of the harem.

*All works performed in Paris unless indicated otherwise.

†Numerous libretti, scores, and a variety of sources were consulted for this table, including, but not limited to, Théodore de Lajarte, *Bibliothèque musicale du théâtre de l'Opéra*, 2 vols. (Paris: Librairie des Bibliophiles, 1878); *Recueil general des operas représentez par l'Académie Royale de Musique depuis son établissement*, 16 vols. (Paris: Christophe Ballard, 1703–1745; reprint, Geneva: Slatkine Reprints, 1971); Théâtre de l'Opéra, Journal, 1671–1790, 6 vols., MS Usuel 201, Paris, Bibliothèque de l'Opéra; *Bibliothèque du théâtre françois depuis son origine* (Dresden, 1768); Claude and François Parfaict, *Dictionnaire des théâtres de Paris*, 7 vols. (Paris, 1756); and François Parfaict, "Histoire de l'Académie Royale de musique depuis son établissement jusqu'au présent," MS Fr. 12355, Bibliothèque de l'Opéra, Paris.

who come on their island." Dorval, however, reminds Frontin that the white man is at fault, and compares the exploitation by the cruel Europeans to the kindness, hospitality, and natural goodness of Africans, especially that of Zilia and her little sister, Zoé, who have hidden and fed them for the six months they have been on the island (scene 1). Zilia describes her people as faithful and truthful; but, seeing that her friends are apprehensive, she asks Dorval to play his flute to put them at ease. They listen "with great pleasure," and then Zoé and her friends surround Frontin while dancing a local dance, the *calenda* (scene 5). The composer's perception of the *calenda* is really a typical French dance piece (see figure 2). The duple meter, dotted rhythms, and binary forms (ABB in this instance) had been basic elements of French opera since the *tragédies lyriques* of Lully. Further, the only instrument mentioned in the libretto and the score is a flute played by the main character. According to seventeenth- and eighteenth-century usage, the absence of notation for specific instruments in a reduced score indicates that full strings—the nucleus of opera and concert orchestras—were employed. Thus, again, even in the late 1780s, the implication is clear that composers were still lauding the superiority of French music (in this case, orchestration and dance music) while diminishing that of the sub-Saharan African Other (the absence of any mention of sub-Saharan African music or instruments).

A loud commotion interrupts the *calenda*. The African king is being chased by a tiger; Dorval runs out and slays the tiger, saving the king. More dancing of joy follows. Then they hear more loud noises; a ship approaches. Dorval Senior has arrived; father and son greet each other. Young Dorval tells his father about the extremely hospitable treatment he has received while in Africa and speaks of the goodness of Zilia. Zoé then approaches and, with sadness, tells them of Zilia's punishment for helping Dorval: she is to be sold to white slave traders. Dorval's father says he will solve the problem by buying her himself.

In the meantime, Frontin attempts to play a joke on the sailors by disguising himself as "a Negro." To his surprise, however, they treat him as such, despite his pleas to the opposite. Here, the authors dramatize a major problem rampant in French society—the invisibility and, thus, the inferiority of the black man.

> *Frontin*:
> Not one Frenchman in this place
> Wants to acknowledge me.
> And my best friends
> Treat me like a Negro. (Scenes 10 and 11)[48]

The scene then shifts back to Dorval Senior as he again thanks Zilia and, since she and her sister are orphans, he offers to buy both of them. Further, they will not be his slaves; since he is rich, he will share his wealth with them for taking care of his son. Zilia thanks him,

PARIS, CHEZ BRUNET, 1787

FIGURE 2. *"Calenda,"* **La Négresse, ou le pouvoir de la reconnaissance (1787)**

but says she cannot go with him, because Frontin told her Dorval would take a wife soon. The father realizes there is more at stake here than a simple friendship between Zilia and his son. Dorval wants to marry Zilia, but his father, reflecting contemporary ethnocentrism, warns that such a union would not be feasible (scene 14). The son, however, remains adamant, and finally convinces his father to consent to the marriage. The opera then concludes with a *divertissement-pantomime* in which gifts are exchanged, followed by lots of dancing, drinking, and singing to "instruments of the country." Again, unfortunately, the libretto and the score make no reference as to what constitutes such instruments.

Despite attempts and good intentions of the authors to defend individual rights and equality and to highlight the camaraderie and fairness of the French, they do, in fact, underscore that old *presumed* inferiority of the sub-Saharan African Other at the end of the work. Zilia delivers the last words of the opera. She moves forward, slowly, to center stage and, reflecting her meager knowledge of the French language, addresses the audience:

Mois suis noire en ces instans,	[I am black now,
Mais demain serai blanche,	But tomorrow I will be white,

TABLE 2. *Performances by Public Theatres**†

TITLE/PREMIERE/LENGTH/ COMPOSER/LIBRETTIST	SOURCE OF PLOT AND MAIN CHARACTERS	REMARKS (PURPOSE, SECONDARY ROLES, AND ELEMENTS OF THE OTHER)
L'Amitié à l'épreuve, comédie mêlée d'ariettes Fontainebleau, November 13, 1770 2 acts André-Ernest-Modeste Grétry (1741–1813) Charles-Simon Favart (1710–1792) and Claude-Henri Fusée de Voisenon (1708–1775)	Moral tale of the same name by Jean-François Marmontel (1723–1799) Nelson (member of British Parliament) Corali (Indian maiden) Lady Juliette (Nelson's sister) Blandfort (ship captain)	Reflects contemporary views: city versus nature lifestyles and the civilizing mission of Europeans. Chambermaid of Juliette, an Italian vocal teacher, a notary; choruses: British sailors, Indians, and blacks dancing the *calenda.*
Zémire et Azor, comédie-ballet; mêlée de chants & de danses Fontainebleau, November 9, 1771 4 acts André-Ernest-Modeste Grétry (1741–1813) Jean-François Marmontel (1723–1799)	Adaptation of *La Belle et le bête*, fairy tale by Jean-Marie Le Prince de Beaumont Azor (Persian prince) Sander (Persian merchant) Zémire (daughter of Sander)	Dramatization of contemporary views: repeatedly underscores the fears and weaknesses of slaves in contrast with the bravery and strength of their masters; reflects the power of true and constant love. Ali (slave of Sander) and Fatmé and Lisbé (daughters of Sander).
Le Corsaire, comédie mêlée d'ariettes Comédie-Italienne, Versailles, March 7, 1783 3 acts Revised and performed on July 1, 1793, under new title, *Le Corsaire algérien* Nicolas-Marie Dalayrac (1753–1809) Auguste-Étienne-Xavier de la Chabeaussière (1752–1820)	Contemporary event: struggles between France and the Barbary pirates on the northern coast of Africa Mahamet (rich Algerian corsair) Florville (young French slave and rival of Mahamet) Julie (French maiden, loved by Florville and Mahamet)	Focuses on the *notion* of French superiority versus African inferiority. Nasit (Asian valet and guard of the Serail) and Zima (Circassian and lover of Mahamet). Set in Algeria (acts 1 and 2) and "on the coast of an isolated place outside Algeria" (act 3).

Azemia, ou les sauvages, comédie mêlée d'ariettes Comédie-Italienne, Fontainebleau, October 17, 1786 3 acts Nicolas-Marie Dalayrac (1753–1809) Auguste-Étienne-Xavier de La Chabeaussière (1752–1820)	Contemporary thought: superiority of French over Spaniards and nature dwellers ("savages") Edoin (Englishman, inhabitant of "a rather savage island") Prosper (young Englishman raised on the island) Azemia (daughter of Edoin)	Glorification of the conquering power of virtuous love. Akinson (English lord), Alvar (Spanish ship captain), sailors, "savages," and servants of main characters. Paints "savages" as vicious and carnivorous.
La Negresse, ou le pouvoir de la reconnoissance, comédie, en vaudevilles, mêlée de divertissements Comédie-Italienne, June 15, 1787 1 act Jean-Baptiste Radet (1752–1809) P. Y. Barré (1749–1832)	Contemporary event: the increasing sentiment against enslavement of Africans and their descendants Zilia (young *négresse*) Zoé (Zilia's sister) Dorval (young Frenchman) Dorval (the father)	Plot reflects contemporary trends—goodness and hospitality of Africans, prejudice against or acceptance of mixed marriage (Zilia, African female, and Dorval the son, French male), and the "good effect of these two colors together." Frontin (valet of Dorval the son), Pasquin (valet of Dorval the father). Troupes: sailors, *nègres*, and *négresses*.
La Belle esclave, ou Valcour et Zéila, comédie, en prose, mêlée d'ariettes Théâtre du Compte de Beaujolais, September 18, 1787 1 act François-André-Danican Philidor (1726–1795) Antoine-Jean Dumaniant (1752–1828)	Contemporary views: the ever-recurring friction between France and North Africa and the heroic character of Frenchmen Sélim (slave merchant) Zéila (Indian maid) Valcour (lover of Zéila)	Plot contrasts the greed of slave merchants with the power of virtuous love. Ali (slave and factotum of Sélim), Fatmé and Zisine (slaves of Sélim), and Moroccan corsair and slaves. Set in Morocco.

*All works performed in Paris unless indicated otherwise.

†Numerous libretti, scores, and a variety of sources were consulted for this table, including, but not limited to, Clarence D. Brenner, *The Theatre Italien: Its Repertory, 1716–1793* (Berkeley: University of California Press, 1961); Alain René Le Sage, *Le Theâtre de la foire, ou l'opéra-comique: contenant les meilleurs pièces qui ont été représentées aux foires de S. Germain & de S. Laurent*, 10 vols. (Paris: P. Gandouin, 1724–37); *Le Nouveau théâtre italien ou recueil général des comedies représentées par les comédiens italiens ordinaires du Roi*, 10 vols. (Paris: Chez Briasson, 1743); M. D'Origny, *Annales du Theâtre Italien, depuis son origine jusqu'a ce jour* (Paris, 1788); and Robert M. Isherwood, *Farce and Fantasy: Popular Entertainment in Eighteenth-Century Paris* (New York: Oxford University Press, 1986).

Et tâcher être en tout tems,	And try to be at all times
Simple, naïve & franche.	Simple, naïve, and sincere.
Aujourd'hui si daignez avoir	Today if you deign to have
Indulgence ordinaire,	Ordinary indulgence,
Du noir au blanc, du blanc au noir,	From black to white, from white to black,
Passerai pour vous plaire.	I will die [trying] to please you.]

Zilia's words, her timid presence, and her awkward delivery on center stage reflect crucial aspects of the tug of war enveloping French society: anti-slavery sentiment versus the *presumed* inferiority of the sub-Saharan African Other. The authors illustrate these events through characterizations, costumes, choice of instruments, and the text. The character Zilia was performed by a white person. In fact, no blacks, colored people, or Indians appeared on the French stage; all performers were white. Costumes of these personages also pose a very

FIGURE 3. *"Nègre et Négresse Ballet"*

FIGURE 4. *"Femme sauvage"*

interesting point. In no way does this production provide an accurate representation of clothes worn by France's colonial subjects. Rather, the cloth is the same as that of leading white characters in all types of French opera—silk, velvet, or other fine materials, frequently brocaded with gold designs and adorned with exquisite jewelry, examples of which are shown in figures 3 and 4. According to eyewitness accounts, singers in colonial productions mirrored this custom.[49]

Zilia's final words can be interpreted in different ways. First, some persons might see this text as a corrupted version of the French language. On the other hand, it can be interpreted as the librettist's perception of African creole. Such a view is certainly plausible, particularly in light of current-day research regarding the use of creole and the cultural character of postcolonial French Antilles. Bernabé, Chamoiseau, and Confiant, three of the most important literary talents in the French Antilles, presented several types of *créolité* (creoleness), one of which was "African creoleness."[50] Primarily focusing on their homeland, Martinique, in *Éloge de la Créolité*, they explored the island's creole identity (*créolité/* creoleness), with special attention on the use (conversational, educational, and literary), or lack of use, of the creole language. As founders of the *créolité* movement, Bernabé, Chamoiseau, and Confiant promote a creole culture that embodies a wide diversity of ancestry and cultural heritage (not just that stemming from sub-Saharan Africa or France, but also from Asia, China, India, and other parts of Europe) distinctive to the Caribbean. They maintain that "the process of creolization . . . is not a geographic concept, [but] the cultural confrontation of [Europeans, Africans, Asians, etc.] within the same space, resulting in a mixed culture called Creole."

As indicated above, the score mentions "instruments of the country" and an "African dance," the *calenda*. However, the libretto and the score do not indicate what constitutes "instruments of the country," and the music of the *calenda* is only the white authors' perception of this dance: a typical French dance piece. On the other hand, it is possible that some percussive instruments were used in these two instances, because the fascination of the French for sub-Saharan African dances is amply described in several travel narratives,[51] and in sketches of costumes and décors of opera productions. For example, in one of the above-mentioned sketches (figure 3), cymbals and a tambourine in the hands of the dancers underscore the perception of non-European instruments *supposedly* used by sub-Saharan Africans in their dances. It is important to note, however, that cymbals were not in use as orchestral instruments until the nineteenth century—notably in the pioneering work of Hector Berlioz (1803–69),[52] and the tambourine was generally used to reflect a gypsy or Spanish character.[53] Thus, in early French opera and ballet, cymbals were used to portray a mood of non-European exoticism. Since these prolific producers of musical dramas had little, if any, first-hand knowledge of sub-Saharan African instruments, the use of a tambourine and cymbals is a rather weak attempt to illustrate the polyrhythmic intricacies of sub-Saharan African drums, the various types used, and their importance in African culture.

Thus, I have focused primarily on non-musical components, for rarely did the musical style in works dramatizing various aspects of the concept of the sub-Saharan African Other differ from those operas devoid of such references. Instruments are the Western European orchestral variety with strings as the nucleus; and all vocal airs, *récitatifs*, ensembles, and dances receive the same types of musical settings used in other types of French operas. In the seventeenth century, only occasionally do we see references to "other" or "exotic" instruments, such as Africans playing castanets (*danses de castagnettes*) while performing a short *sarabande* in *Ballet Royal de Flore*; or in *Cadmus*, where Africans play guitars while they join other characters in a huge *chaconne*. By the middle of the eighteenth century, composers were presenting their perceptions of African-based dances (usually in *divertissements*) such as the *calenda* (in several works), which colonial authorities had actually banned in the previous century (see tables 1 and 2).

In sum, *La Négresse* illustrates several ways in which—by the onset of the French Revolution—musical theatre had become a major vehicle for the monarchy's *cultural* political campaign.

CHAPTER 1

ESTABLISHMENT OF COLONIAL HIERARCHY

The history of music in European colonial systems provides us with much valuable information about peoples of these territories. However, we know very little to date about how European colonial powers used their own performing-art forms (opera, court ballet, theatre, and symphony) within the colonies to glorify colonialism and to depict the presence of the sub-Saharan African Other. In order to comprehend how such phenomena occurred during an extremely volatile period in history, and to put these developments in the proper perspective, it is important that the reader have a general understanding of culture and politics in the colonies and, thus, a grasp of conditions under which nonwhite artists emerged. These first two chapters will illustrate various ways in which such issues were directly connected to the participation of nonwhites in colonial opera.

The System

From the early years of French colonization in the Americas (1630s) up until the dawn of the eighteenth century, "the most important, the most heavily populated, and the richest territory in the French Antilles" was the colony of Martinique; and Saint-Pierre, the island's artistic and commercial center, was hailed as "Paris of the Lesser Antilles."[1] While each island generally had its own governing body, all colonies were under the control of one governor (*gouverneur-lieutenant-général des isles*) appointed by the king of France and headquartered in

Fort-Royal (now Fort-de-France), Martinique. The governor was the main representative of the king, a member of the nobility, and a high-ranking officer of the military. He commanded the armed forces, ruled over all inhabitants, and was responsible for administrative, judicial, and financial matters affecting the islands. The governor was also president of the Conseil Supérieur (also referred to as the Conseil Souverain), the highest ranking court, and appointed members for this judicial body.

Inevitably, such a wide range of power in the hands of one individual was bound to cause many problems. From the 1650s through the 1670s, planters and other citizens lodged several complaints of tyranny, exploitation, greed, and embezzlement against a string of governors. Louis XIV attempted to resolve these issues in 1679 by appointing an *Intendant de la Justice, Police et Finances des Isles Françoises de l'Amérique*. The intendant, a man of considerable judicial and administrative experience, handled all administrative, financial, and judicial matters. He was responsible for enforcing all ordinances in these three areas, presiding over assessment and collection of taxes and supervision of bureaucrats, particularly those in justice and finance. The intendant presided over the Conseil Supérieur and selected its members. All branches of the military remained under the direct command of the governor, for his primary responsibilities were to defend and protect citizens and subjects from riots, slave revolts, foreign aggression, and any other events that might threaten the welfare of the public. While it was the responsibility of the governor to quash slave revolts and other uprisings, the intendant controlled investigations of such incidents. Empowered with judicial privileges, the intendant could also preside over these cases.

Such an arrangement of shared power certainly was not new, for the structure as well as duties and responsibilities of the two officials closely modeled those of provincial governments in France. Nevertheless, having two heads of state in one jurisdiction seems to have been a source of constant friction between governors and intendants. Up until the eve of the French Revolution, the two officials lodged a barrage of complaints against each other, and rich plantation owners and other businessmen displayed utter displeasure with the abuse of power exercised by both heads of state. French historians have examined these issues in great detail, particularly the relationship between the two heads of state. It appears that while conflicts certainly did occur between the two men, the judicial, administrative, and financial powers of the intendant actually complemented those of the governor, defender and protector of the public.[2]

In the early 1670s, the Jesuits established the first mission in a small village on the northwestern coastal area of the island of Hispaniola that later, in 1685, officially became the city of Cap Français (now Cap-Haïtien). A glance at the history of Cap Français reveals a hard-working citizenry determined to erect houses, businesses, churches, public buildings and utilities, theatres, and other facilities comparable to those in France—aided tremendously, of course, by a constantly increasing slave-labor force. In the early 1670s, the population consisted of 223 whites and thirty-four slaves, most of which, undoubtedly, were owned by the Jesuits, who steadily increased their economic interests and power in the colony over the next several decades. Concurrently, the city experienced several problems—Spanish invasions in 1691 and 1695, earthquakes, and numerous fires, particularly the one in 1734 that almost demolished the city. Out of 587 houses, 300 burned down. Despite such catastrophic setbacks, the city experienced tremendous growth as citizens kept rebuilding new homes, hospitals, government buildings, theatres, etc. By the middle of the eighteenth century, Cap Français had grown by leaps and bounds—not only in population, but also militarily, financially, and socially. That small village of the 1670s had become the richest and most populous city in the French Antilles and was hailed as "Paris of the Antilles." In 1749, the population totaled 3,400 (1,415 whites, 143 free colored persons, and 1,842 slaves). By the mid 1780s, the number of houses had almost tripled, and the population numbered about 18,500 (7,100 whites, 1,400 free colored people, and 10,000 slaves). The city had seventy-nine public buildings (including the previous mansion and other properties of the Jesuits), two aqueducts providing drinking water, paved streets, and several public markets and monumental fountains.[3]

The French crown officially took control of Saint-Domingue in 1697 and set up the shared power of governing with headquarters in Cap Français. Geographically, Cap Français had several advantages. It was the port nearest to France, and the main point of departure and entry for all trade, naval vessels, munitions, and other government materials and information. The city also developed a great sugar industry, the economic key to the Antilles. In sum, Cap Français was now the primary commercial center—having replaced Fort-Royal, Martinique, as the main seaport—and the military headquarters of the French Antilles colonial empire.

Due to the rapid growth and development of Saint-Domingue and the continuing acquisition of territories by France, the monarchy soon realized that the current division of power had to be revised, for the same problems that had occurred in Martinique also plagued the new colony. On January 1, 1714, Louis XIV officially divided the French Antilles colonies into two seats of government: one in Saint-Domingue (originally in Cap Français, and permanently established in Port-au-Prince in 1750), and the second division in Fort-Royal, Martinique.[4] All French colonies in the Windward Islands came under the jurisdiction of the seat in Martinique, and the Saint-Domingue division governed the remaining colonies in the islands and in mainland America. At the head of each division were a *gouverneur-général* and an *intendant*, with each officer retaining the duties and responsibilities of shared power discussed above.

Of major significance for the present study, however, are the kinds of systems put in place by the monarchy and enforced by governors, intendants, and their subordinates to ensure that everyone adhered to the goals of the *cultural* political campaign. To realize its primary objective of total control, the monarchy instituted a chain of regulations that extended over several decades. In March 1685, France enacted the *Code Noir* (Black Code), one of the most stringent, wide-ranging regulatory documents in that country's history.[5] With the promulgation of the Code, France put an official stamp of approval on the institution of human bondage—an extremely dehumanizing system whose commencement coincided with the dawn of the *siècle des lumières*, the Age of Reason. As we can see in the preamble, the *Code Noir* was instituted primarily for the purpose of regulating slavery in the colonies.

> Louis, by the grace of God, king of France and of Navarre: to all, present and to come, greetings. As we owe our attention equally to all people that divine providence has placed under our submission, we indeed want to have examined in our presence memoirs that have been sent to us by officers in our American islands, by which having been informed of their need for our authority and our justice in order to maintain the discipline of the Apostolic Roman Catholic Church, in order to regulate that which concerns the state and the quality of slaves in our said islands, and desiring to be able to make known to them that although they live in climates infinitely far away from our usual residence, we are always present with them, not only by the extension of our power, but also by the promptitude of our diligence to aid them in their needs."[6]

The monarchy strongly supported the need "to maintain the discipline of the Catholic Church" (Articles 2–11) that, as we shall see in chapter 2, translated into total control of mind and body of the enslaved. Moreover, the crown deemed that only through conversion to Catholicism could slaves be delivered from their deplorable "state of nothingness."[7] The Catholic Church based its support of such regulations on the doctrine that "for those people, no matter who they are, that are fatally doomed to barbarism, . . . it is the duty of the Catholic faith to draw these primitive peoples from their degradation, . . . to instill upon their countenance the confirmation of salvation, [and] to lead them to the future life."[8]

The question of religious observation had posed problems in the colonies for several decades prior to the Code. In the *Lettres-patentes* of 1615, the Parlement de Paris charged all Jews with blasphemy for not adhering to the pieties of the "Christian nation of France"; and, for several years, "against the *Edits* and *Ordonnances* of our predecessors, [they] have disguised themselves to avoid detection."[9] The Parlement ordered all Jews out of France and its territories, effective one month after the publication of said order. Ship captains in the colonies professed their "so-called Protestant religion" publicly on ship and after docking.[10] Moreover, the monarchy charged, they did not bother "to send their slaves to Mass, to catechism, or to take their Sacraments." In this same *Ordonnance*, officials also condemned Jews residing in Martinique who "used Saturday for their ceremonies and compelled their slaves and indentured servants to observe [the Jewish] Sabbath, to work on Sunday, and to show themselves in public during the mourning of the Church, which lasts from Holy Thursday to Easter Sunday, against that which is observed in all the places of Europe."[11] The governor, Jean-Charles de

Baas, ordered that all such activities must cease. One can assume that Jews did adhere to this directive, for, two years later, de Baas appealed to the king to extend to Jews in Martinique "the same privileges that other residents enjoyed," provided, of course, authorities "take the necessary precautions to ensure that the exercise of [the Jewish] religion can not cause any scandal to the Catholics."[12] The *Lettres-patentes* (1615) cited above was reaffirmed in the *Code Noir*. In order to stifle any religious opposition, the monarchy anointed the Catholic Church as the dominant faith, and directed that all Jews ("the declared enemies of the Christian name") were to be forced out of the colonies, with such expulsion to be completed within three months from the date of the Code (Articles 1 and 3).

In order to maintain complete control over the nonwhite sector, the Code enabled authorities to dictate every aspect of daily life of the enslaved, even the amount of food and clothing. Weekly rations for slaves ten years old and above amounted to two and one-half pots of flour, two pounds of salted beef, or three pounds of fish ("or equivalent things"). Younger children were to receive one-half of these amounts, "since they were weaned until the age of ten years." Once per year ("or at the convenience of the master") each slave would receive two pieces of clothing or four ells[13] of cloth (Articles 22–25, 27). At first glance, however, it might seem that the Code legally provided some relief for the enslaved, for Article 26 stipulates that if slaves have not been "nourished, clothed, and maintained by their masters," they could make a formal complaint. However, Articles 30 and 31 seem to nullify such rights by declaring any testimony given by slaves to be worthless, and they could not be part of any legal or court action except to defend their master.

Reflecting the pulse of the nation, the Code clearly emphasized the Western European notion that Africans were inferior, for it stated distinctly that slaves had no rights as human beings, but were merchandise purchased and owned by whites (*Déclarons les esclaves être meubles . . .*) and thus considered as community property "to be divided equally between co-heirs" (Article 44). The article seems to have been misinterpreted by some family members, which caused disputes regarding distribution of property. Louis XIV attempted to clarify and resolve the issue in another edict two years later.[14] The king affirmed that Article 44 pertained only to property acquired "in or after the month of March 1685," the date of the Code. Further, the article was not intended to have "the retroactive effect" of including property acquired and divided prior to enactment of the Code.

The Code also provided ways in which a slave could become a free person (i.e., an *affranchi*). If an unmarried man produced children with his slave, he was obliged to marry the slave "in the forms observed by the Church," and as a result, both mother and child(ren) were to be "rendered free and legitimate" (Article 9). Children born from a union between a male slave and a free woman were *affranchis* (Article 12). A young master, twenty years old, could free his slaves without the consent of his parents, and slaves named as legatees by their masters or as guardians of their children subsequently gained their freedom (Articles 55 and 56).

At the conclusion of the Code, the crown granted to the *affranchis* "the same rights, privileges and immunities that persons born free enjoy" (Article 59). This article and similar regulations pertaining to the status of *affranchis* reflected the myriad of problems with which colonial officials were confronted. Twelve years after enactment of the Code, the governor of Saint-Domingue proposed enactment of a law declaring all mulattos free when they became twenty-one years old.[15] However, according to Moreau de Saint-Méry, one of the most quoted contemporary historians on culture and politics of French colonial society, this practice was already commonly observed in Saint-Domingue and in other colonies.[16] The number of *affranchis* steadily increased during this period, and Louis XIV attempted "to cease the very dangerous abuse" of freeing too many slaves. Referring specifically to Article 55 of the Code, the king noted that several slave owners were motivated by greed, for they did not freely grant liberty to their slaves, but instead sold the privilege to them. As a result, slaves would use "some of the most illicit ways to procure the money necessary to obtain their freedom."[17] The king forbade "these mercenary masters" to free their slaves without the written consent of the governor and the intendant. Anyone failing to obtain such permission would have the freed slaves confiscated and "sold for the profit of His Majesty." Nevertheless, the same problem persisted for several years, and Louis XV (1710–1774, reigned 1715–1774) reissued the *Ordonnance* in 1736 with the addition of stiff monetary penalties for failure to comply.[18]

While attempting to resolve the problems discussed above, the monarchy faced an equally unsettling issue. As indicated above, it had become increasingly evident by the second decade of the eighteenth century that colonial officials were finding it extremely difficult to carry out the mandates of the monarchy as set forth in the *Code Noir*, particularly with regard to converting slaves to Catholicism. Apparently in agreement with the "redeeming" value of the training and discipline of the Catholic Church, whites expressed a desire to send some of their slaves to France for this purpose, and "at the same time, to have them learn some art and skill, by which the colonies would receive much usefulness upon [their] return."[19] The regent of France (1674–1723, r.1715–1723) attempted to resolve these issues in the *Édit* of 1716. He emphasized that since the regency's recent advent to the crown (1715), its main concern had been "to make amends for losses that citizens had incurred due to war and to look for means to make them taste the fruits of peace."[20] The regent granted permission to slave owners to bring to France (or to send with other persons of authority) slaves of each sex, after obtaining the written consent of the governor and the intendant. However, the *Édit* clearly pointed out that the top priority remained that of instruction in Catholicism (Article 1). The *Édit* also stressed that slaves in France had no rights in that country; they were not to think of themselves as free, and must return to their masters as more useful slaves. The regent seems to have considered null and void a previous order of Louis XIV that stipulated, "all [slaves] who are taken from the islands to France by their masters will be free according to the laws and the usage in the kingdom and cannot be forced or constrained to return [to the islands]."[21]

Further, the regent stressed that all goals stated in the preamble to the original Code were to be aggressively pursued; for it was the regent's desire that all slaves learn and then return to their masters to "nourish and entertain them" (Articles 1, 2, 8).

Efforts of the regent seem to have been rather futile, for similar problems continued to plague the monarchy. Slave owners were not returning to the colonies; nor were slaves receiving adequate training in Catholicism or learning "useful arts and skills." Consequently, in 1738, Louis XV issued a *Déclaration* upholding and reinforcing the *Édit* of 1716.[22] Permission to take or to send slaves to France carried more restrictions. Prior to departure, owners had to file several registration forms with the appropriate governor or intendant, containing the name of the slave owner; the name, age, and description of each slave; and name(s) of person(s) charged with taking slaves to France and returning them to the colony. Owners or other persons taking slaves to France also had to file similar forms with the ship commander at the port prior to departure. Such persons were also responsible for the conduct of slaves, for registering the permission granted by the governor (or other appropriate official) with authorities at the port of France, and for registering all papers in the jurisdiction (at the Parlement de Paris or at offices of provincial intendants) where slaves were to reside (Articles 1–3). Again, the monarchy stressed Catholic instruction as a priority for all slaves; "they cannot pretend to have acquired their liberty under the pretext of their arrival in the kingdom," and at the conclusion of training, they must be returned to the colonies (Articles 1, 4, 11, 12). In preparation for return to the colonies, the responsible persons were to adhere to the same procedures of registration with the appropriate authorities.

The status of blacks and colored people in France continued to be a highly problematic issue throughout the eighteenth century. Since slavery was "not admissible" in France, once allowed into the country, "jurisdictionally, slaves became free."[23] Nevertheless, slave owners, with the support of ship captains and other officials, did not hesitate in returning them to the colonies as slaves. While there are ample examples of whites in France employing one or two blacks or colored people in their homes, government officials generally felt their presence in France was the cause of the greatest disturbances in the cities, particularly in Paris. On the other hand, when slaves were returned to the colonies, many whites became increasingly annoyed and suspicious of their behavior, complaining that these slaves now "exhibited a spirit of independence and indocility and became more noxious than useful."[24] Louis XVI (1754–1793, r.1774–1793) attempted to resolve these issues in the *Déclaration* of 1777, thereby prohibiting entry into France of any "black, mulatto or other colored person of either sex . . . after publication and recording of the [*Déclaration*]."[25] The regulation lays out types of fines to be levied against *colons* (plantation owners), ship captains, merchants, and any other person(s) who defy the prohibitions. "All blacks, mulattos, and other colored persons of either sex who are not in service" (i.e., not enslaved, but "freed") at the time of the *Déclaration* must present to the appropriate officials proof of identity (name, surname, age, profession, place of birth, and date of entry in France) and will then receive an official certificate displaying such information that would entitle them to remain in France as *affranchis*. "Any blacks, mulattos, and other colored persons of either sex" failing to submit such information and obtain a certificate would be subject to arrest and taken to the port for embarkation to the colonies.

Added to the myriad of difficulties confronting colonial officials were the constant slave uprisings, and runaway slaves (*marrons*) escaping into the mountains and forests. Equally disturbing, numerous *affranchis* and white sympathizers provided refuge for runaways. The risks taken by *affranchis* were enormous, for they could be "reduced to the condition of slave and, as such, sold to the highest bidder."[26] On the other hand, the white population, finding itself vastly outnumbered by blacks and in a state of constant anxiety, complained that the Code must be modified to include sterner measures. Their fears of the burgeoning black population were supported not only by the enactment of a continuous flow of strict regulations, but also by some rather glaring statistics. In 1678, there were approximately 27,000 slaves in the colonies. Four decades later this figure had jumped considerably, for in Saint-Domingue alone, of its 130,000 inhabitants 100,000 were enslaved; and there were 26,800 slaves in Martinique and 13,300 in Guadeloupe.[27] By the early 1740s these figures had risen to 172,000 inhabitants in Saint-Domingue, of which 154,000 were slaves; 66,000 slaves in Martinique (total population 79,000); and 40,000 slaves in Guadeloupe (total population 53,000). At the outbreak of the French Revolution in 1789, there were about 552,000 slaves in Saint-Domingue (total population 620,000); 84,000 slaves in Martinique (total population 102,000); and 86,000 slaves in Guadeloupe (total population 104,000), amounting to more than 700,000 slaves in the three colonies (see figure 5).[28]

The continuous flow of laws enacted to control the nonwhite population had the support of several whites in France who viewed the Code as "favorable" because, they deemed, not only did it provide ways in which slaves could obtain their freedom, but it also regulated punishment for those remaining in slavery. In reality, abuses continued, and Bernardin de Saint-Pierre[29] brought this out explicitly as he voiced deep frustration, not only with regard to slavery abuses in these locales:

> People say that the Code Noir is made in [the slave's] favor. Granted; but the harshness of masters exceeds the allowed punishments, and their greed withholds nourishment, rest, and compensation that are due. If these unfortunate people wanted to complain, to whom would they do so? Their judges often are the primary tyrants.[30]

He was also troubled about the lack of concern of religious institutions:

> Some theologians assert that for a temporal slavery, they procure for [slaves] a spiritual liberty. But most of them are purchased in an era where they can never learn French, and

FIGURE 5. *Population Growth in the Colonies, 1740–1789*

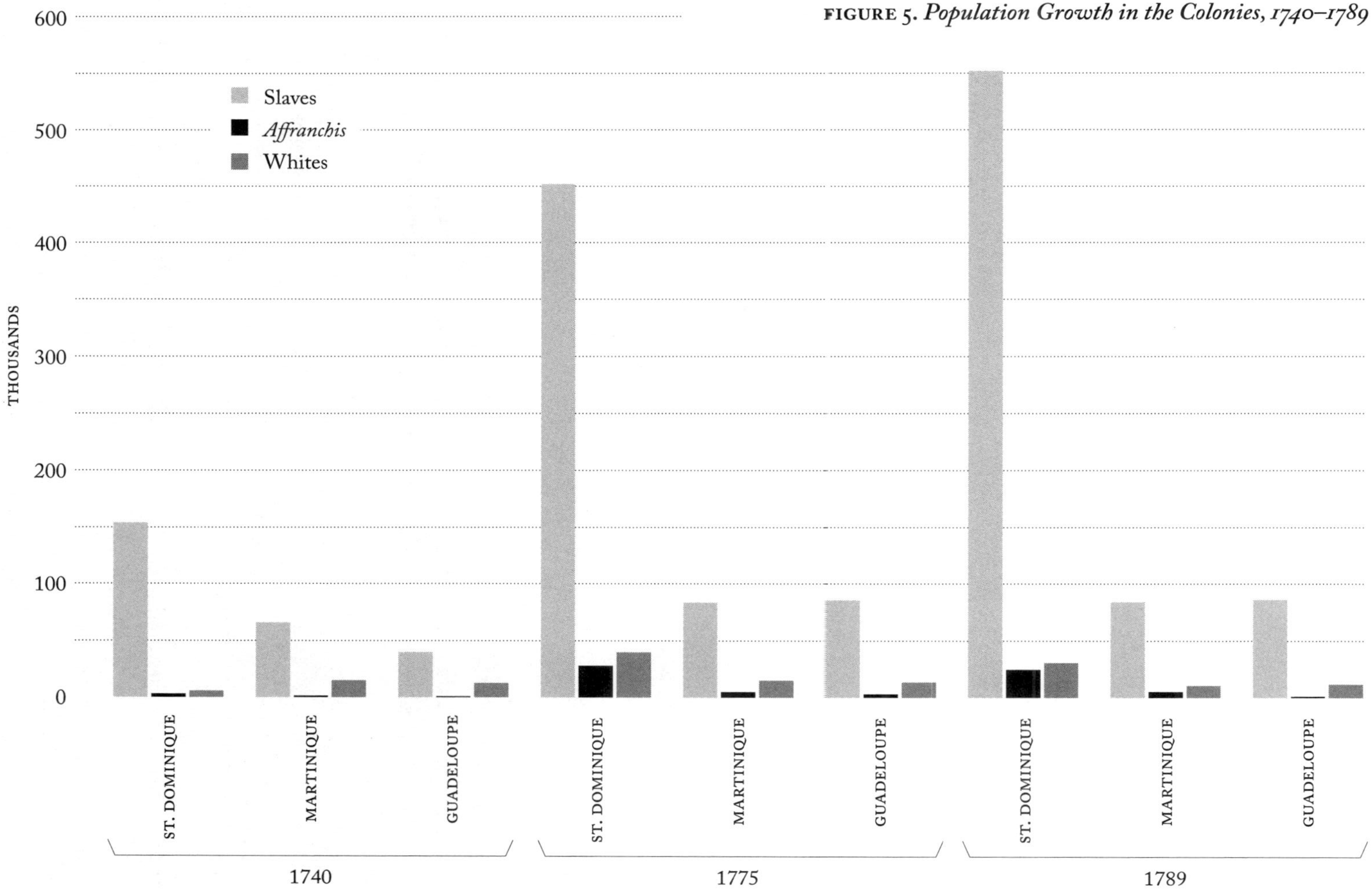

> the missionaries do not learn their language. Besides, those who are baptized are treated like the others.[31]

and the silence of the *philosophes*:

> I am angry that the *philosophes* that fight abuses with so much courage have hardly spoken of the slavery of blacks except in jest. They turn away and talk about Saint-Barthélemy [and] the massacres of Mexicans by Spaniards, as if these crimes are not in our time, but in which half of Europe has taken part.[32]

Unfortunately, for more than a decade the pleas of Bernardin to the *philosophes* seem to have fallen on deaf ears. As indicated above, Rousseau spoke of slavery in terms of voluntary servitude and of "agreements [as] the basis of all legitimate authority among men."[33] It is evident that Rousseau was totally ignoring French colonial policy, for the two terms "voluntary servitude" and "slavery" are contradictory, because there was certainly no "agreement" between European slave owners and Africans forced into slavery. Voltaire frequently couched his criticisms of systems of servitude in blatant accusations against religious institutions that, he deemed, were equally responsible for abuses:

> [It is] justly said that it is not Christian charity that has broken the chains of servitude, since this charity has tightened them repeatedly for more than twelve centuries; and, yet, one can even add that with Christians, even the monks, very charitable that they are, still possess some slaves, reduced to an atrocious condition, under the names of *mortaillables*, *mainmortables*, and *serfs de glèbe*.[34]

One must not, however, be misled into thinking that Voltaire was a great champion of equality for all human beings; for we need only to be reminded of his distaste for persons of African descent:

> Negroes and negresses, when transported to the coldest climates, always continue to produce animals of the same kind, and the mulattoes are only a bastard race from a black man and white woman, or a white man and a black woman.[35]

and for Carib Indians, whom he described as "excrements of society that would do anything to attract attention or to arouse pity."[36] It is important that the reader keep in mind that such disdain and hostility towards these peoples flow from the pen of one who never ventured outside Europe, but, instead, relied primarily on travel narratives to form such opinions.

Montesquieu repudiated abuses of slavery; however, he did not favor abolishment of the system. In his reform process, "freed men" were not truly liberated, for they were still bound to their previous masters ("The civil laws must specify what they owe to their patron, or the contract of emancipation must specify these duties for them").[37] Whether defending the system or condemning slavery abuses, Montesquieu seems to have been thinking more in terms of the good of the state rather than equality for all human beings.

> The trouble is that, if there are too many slaves, they cannot be contained; if there are too many freed men, they cannot survive and they become a burden to the republic; moreover, the republic can be equally endangered by too many freed men and by too many slaves.[38]

Very few *philosophes* really explored the ills of the Code and France's heavy involvement in the slave trade. However, Diderot and Raynal, undoubtedly influenced somewhat by Bernardin de Saint-Pierre's condemnation of the *philosophes*, based their assault on moral and rational grounds, for they opined that it was against the laws of nature that those who toil receive no fruit from their labors.[39] They questioned the policy of taking possession of remote lands and forcing on innocent inhabitants the evils of European customs. The two *philosophes* did not ignore the thorny issues of the Atlantic slave trade and slavery abuses in the French Antilles. In a sweeping condemnation of these evils, Diderot called on his government to abandon "the state of humiliation" to which its cruelty, excessive ambition, and insolence had reduced the nation, and to seek the more advantageous path of moderation.[40] Like the British, Dutch, and Portuguese colonists, France "has sought, without remorse, to increase her fortune through the sweat, blood, and despair of these unfortunate souls. What a frightful system!"[41]

Social Stratification

Irrespective of numerous legal and moral proclamations regarding the status of persons of African descent (free and enslaved), abuses were encouraged and sustained by attitudes of superiority and greed of whites, and continued to occur throughout the period of slavery. Such views also gained momentum from scientists in the latter half of the eighteenth century. Some observers were offended by the personal habits of the Other, which they deemed to be inferior to the "refined" customs of the French. Thibault de Chanvalon, a member of the Académie Royale des Sciences, was appalled at the "strong and disagreeable odor" of the Caribs.[42] In one of his essays, he rated their intelligence as equally distasteful:

> Their rationale is less clear and less prudent than the instinct of beasts. [The reasoning] of people of the most uncivilized country, even that of blacks raised in parts of Africa most

> remote from commerce, occasionally discloses an intelligence that, while still undeveloped, is capable of growth. That of the Caribs does not even seem to be receptive to development.[43]

Here, Chanvalon seems to have been disposed more favorably toward Africans. However, a few pages later, he was equally critical of the enslaved, particularly those imported from Guinea, who, he stated, were extremely superstitious and had the same level of intelligence as the Caribs.[44] In fact, Chanvalon generally painted all slaves with a broad stroke of the brush, branding them "liars" and "thieves."

> It is difficult to decide if this vice [lying] is a concealment of character which is natural to them or one that *their predicament makes them believe it necessary*. . . . They always want to have repeated to them the question that one poses as if they had not understood it, while having time to prepare the response. They are thieves. . . . For example, a Negro who wants to steal, without being perceived, a piece of money he sees on the ground will pick it up with his toes, raise it behind him up to his belt, [and] take it with his hand. Then, due to the lack of clothing, his mouth will receive his larceny. If they are caught in the act, *they do not become disconcerted*; they say it is not them; it is the devil who, in order to do malice toward them, has put in their pockets or in their hands whatever one finds there.[45]

However, it is important to note that Chanvalon observed two essential points: "their predicament makes them believe it necessary" and "they do not become disconcerted." Such actions of the enslaved certainly point to an appreciable degree of intelligence, because they perceived *with logic and reason* how crucial it was to assert their wit for self-preservation.

A wide range of philosophical discussions in France prompted several theories on the nature of man. One of the most heavily debated topics in this area was the question of skin color—discussions that promoted the concept of the inferiority of the Other. Perplexed by the differences in complexions of Africans and Indians, several doctors, naturalists, and other scientists put forth a host of theories. Some regarded bile, blood, and other body secretions as primary causes for blackness of skin color, whereas others supported the theory of an extended hot climate as the overriding factor.[46]

One of the most widely read French naturalists, Georges-Louis Leclerc, Compte de Buffon (1707–1788), wrote extensively on the subject.[47] Buffon presented several medical and scientific theories of his contemporaries; but primarily, he used nonscientific accounts of travelers to explain the differences in skin color and other physical traits of the Other. Nevertheless, he was extremely skeptical of the veracity of travel narratives, with their "exaggerations, fables, and bizarre tales . . . [by] men who take the trouble to go and see things that are far away [and] believe that the hardships they have borne entitle them to render their accounts more marvelous."[48] It is interesting to note that several years before Buffon issued this statement,

Rousseau, his friend, who also relied on travel narratives, had voiced a similar and equally critical opinion of the authors.

> There are hardly more than four types of men who make ocean voyages: sailors, merchants, soldiers and missionaries. Now one could scarcely expect the first three classes would provide good observers; and as for those in the fourth, absorbed by the sublime vocation that calls them, while they are not subject to prejudices of station as are all the others, one has to believe they would not readily engage in inquiries that appear as pure curiosity and would distract them from the more important work to which they are destined. Moreover, to preach the Gospel usefully requires only zeal, and God grants the rest; but to study men requires talents that God does not take upon himself to grant to anyone, and that are not always the lot of Saints.[49]

Nevertheless, Buffon's discussions on the nature of man are a synthesis of such literature.[50] There are, however, some inconsistencies. It seems that whatever the theory, Buffon could find some area of agreement. At one point, he supported the view that a hot climate was the main cause of blackness. On the other hand, Buffon attempted to substantiate the views of several doctors who proposed that "the blood of Negroes is black, and their blackness originates entirely from their blood."[51] He also agreed that an "occasional and not the primary cause of blackness" could be attributed to the presence of "a kind of jaundice [in all newborn black children] that, among white people, soon passes off and leaves no impression; but in Negroes, on the contrary, it gives an indelible color to the skin, which always becomes more and more black."[52] While Buffon repeatedly supports the view of a hot climate as the main contributing factor in skin color, he also gives some weight to genetic factors. In the end, he is emphatic in his belief that "the rudiments of blackness are communicated [to the children of Negroes] by their parents; for regardless of which part of the world a Negro is brought forth, he will be equally black as if he had been born in his own country."[53]

Medical and nonscientific opinions such as these did not go unnoticed by the *philosophes*. Montesquieu favored the theory of climate as a major contributing factor in both physical and mental views of man.

> In cold climates [there is] a certain strength of body and spirit that makes men capable of long, arduous, great, and daring actions. . . . Therefore, one must not be surprised that the cowardice of the peoples of hot climates has almost always made them slaves and that the courage of the peoples of cold climates has kept them free.[54]

Voltaire leaned toward the body-function-secretions theory regarding skin color, and spoke of an experiment by a scientist in which "a Negro was dissected" to reveal the black membrane that is responsible for "this inherent blackness."[55] According to Voltaire, the Negro could lose such blackness "only through sickness or disease, which can break up this tissue and allow the fat that has escaped from his cells to make some white spots beneath the skin."[56]

With scientists, *philosophes*, and other intellectuals absorbed in and proposing such radical views, is it any wonder that an elaborate system of social casting—not seen in any colonies governed by other European nations—emerged and was perpetuated throughout the French system? It was inevitable, for we must remember that the monarchy had waged its *cultural* political campaign since the beginning of the seventeenth century, and such views gave enormous credence to goals of the campaign. In this unique social hierarchy, the king and the royal family were, of course, at the top, followed by heads of state, members of the nobility, and other appointed officials. On the next level were *grand blancs* (owners of large plantations, and other rich and influential businessmen). Missionaries and *petits blancs* ("little whites")[57] formed the next rung of the social ladder. The latter group consisted of carpenters, plantation managers, goldsmiths, masons, merchants, and other small-business entrepreneurs.

Next in line were *engagés* (indentured servants), white people who, generally, could not earn a living in France and were drawn to the island by fantastic stories of opportunities to enrich oneself in a relatively short period. This was particularly true with unemployed domestics and other skilled workers who willingly contracted their services (*engagés volontaires*).[58] On the other hand, the government provided a large work force for *colons* by dispatching to the colonies less fortunate groups of vagabonds, smugglers, troubled youth, and others on the low rungs of French society (*engagés forcés*).[59] Both classes of indentured servants were contracted for three years of service to the plantation owner who paid for their passage. Contract terms were reduced to eighteen months in 1670, and then raised back to three years in 1699. At the end of the contract, an indentured servant received his pay in several pounds of sugar, tobacco, and/or cash and could then return to France. On the other hand, several indentured servants remained in the colonies at the end of their contract, purchased slaves, and eventually became *grand blancs*.[60] However, not all indentured servants who chose to remain in the colonies were successful. Out of the ranks of the *engagés forcés*, several persons resorted to their old vices and other character flaws (debauchery, theft, laziness, etc.) and became part of the continually growing sector of undesirables on the lowest rung of white society. By the second quarter of the eighteenth century, the indentured servant was almost nonexistent in the colonies, due primarily to one overriding factor: purchasing slaves for plantation and domestic work was far less costly for everyone (except, of course, for the enslaved).

The lower half of the social ladder consisted of all nonwhite persons (free and enslaved) in the following order:

1. free colored people (*affranchis*)
2. enslaved colored people

3. free blacks (*affranchis*)
4. enslaved blacks

While the phrase "colored people" has always held very negative connotations for black Americans, this was not the case in French colonial society. The social ordering nurtured an environment in which the terms "*les noirs*" (blacks), "*créoles*," and "les gens de couleur" (colored people) held specific cultural and political significance. Use of these terms served as one of the most effective ways to confine these peoples to the "purely relative category of otherness," thereby promoting the monarchy's cultural political campaign.

In keeping with the French penchant for attaching labels to almost everything—many times inconsistently—colonial authorities and writers adopted a myriad of terminology that underscored and promoted class distinctions within the nonwhite population. The slave sector consisted of two subcategories: plantation slaves and city slaves. The former referred to those who worked on the plantation (in the coffee and sugar-cane fields, refineries, and other factories), whereas the latter worked as domestics or had jobs on the docks or elsewhere in the city. The terms *les noirs* (blacks), *nègres* (Negroes), and *le nommé* (or the feminine, *la nommée*), meaning "called" or "named," applied to all slaves, regardless of whether they were recent imports from Africa or born in the colonies. The term *le nommé* preceded the name of the slave, which was the surname of the slave owner, or a forename given to the slave by the owner (as in *le nommé* Rousseau, *le nommé* Pierre, or *la nommée* Giselle). Slaves not born in the colonies were also referred to as *nègres nouveaux* (new or newly arrived Negroes). To complicate matters further, these terms (with the exception of *nègres nouveaux*) also referred to free blacks, and whites occasionally referred to free coloreds as *les nommés*, not only to reflect their recently acquired free status, but also as a constant reminder of their inferior status within the established hierarchy.

In the first half of the seventeenth century, the term *créole* designated a white person born in the French Antilles. However, by the middle of the century, literary and official documents frequently used the terms "black *créole*," "white *créole*," and "Indian *créole*," not only to make the distinction between the races, but also to identify those blacks born in the French Antilles. By the second half of the eighteenth century, "*créole*" generally applied to all people born in the colonies, regardless of race.

The term "Indian *créole*" appears infrequently in contemporary sources—and, seemingly, only in the second half of the eighteenth century. However, the French, rather than adopt conventions of their European neighbors,[61] simply called all Indians "*sauvages*," a term commonly seen in French scientific literature:

> *Savage* is an epithet which is used in medical material to designate savage animals and to make a distinction between wild animals and those that are tamed. . . . A large part of

> America is populated by savages, . . . barbarous peoples who live without laws, without police, without religion, and with no fixed residence. . . . Natural liberty is the only aim in the police of savages; with this liberty, nature and climate reign almost alone for them. Occupied by the chase or by pastoral life, they do not burden themselves with religious practices, nor do they adopt any religion that regulates them.[62]

French colonists continued to categorize Indians as *sauvages* (savages) throughout the subject period—never as *affranchis*, and very rarely as *les gens de couleur*. These two terms were reserved strictly for descendants of mixed unions between white French men and black African women. Even those descendants of mixed unions between white men and Indian women or between coloreds and Indians were called *sauvages* or subcategories thereof, such as *marabou*, *sacatra*, etc. (see appendix 3). Usage of such a wide variety of terminology underscored Western European opinion that vast distinctions existed between "civilized" peoples (Western Europeans) and "barbarians" or "savages" (Africans, Indians, and other non-Caucasians). The French magnified such prejudicial views with the promulgation of the *Code Noir* and, subsequently, a multitude of regulations aimed at confining the enslaved and *affranchis* to that "purely relative category of otherness."

The term *créole* also applied to the language spoken primarily by blacks (enslaved and free). It seems that most whites viewed *créole* as a "corrupted" version of the French language mingled with African words, and therefore, with such a close association with African culture, they considered *créole* to be an inferior language. On the other hand, Moreau de Saint-Méry recognized its "special qualities:"

> There are a thousand nothings that one would not dare say in French, a thousand voluptuous images that one would be unable to paint in French, and that *Créole* expresses or renders with an infinite grace.[63]

As indicated above, the term "colored people" has always held very negative connotations for black Americans; but this was not the case in any French colony. The French system, as outlined in the *Code Noir* and subsequent revisions, was quite the opposite and very complex. Although blacks—enslaved and free—were on the bottom rungs of the cultural and political ladders, colored people assumed an intermediate status between whites and blacks; and, as descendants of mixed unions, the lighter the skin, the higher one's status. Thus, while attempting to eradicate the "stain of slavery," free colored people found themselves trapped in a unique social order based not only on the color of one's skin, but also on the date of discharge from slavery, education, and value of material belongings. Nevertheless, colored people on all levels of the social order generally suffered indignities from whites. Their place of residence, travel, employment, and many other facets of their daily lives were severely restricted. According to the *Code Noir*, even the legally free coloreds had to "show respect for their old masters, their widows, and their children." Otherwise, they were subject to "severe punishment," even to the point of having their free status revoked and, thus, being returned to slavery (Articles 55–59). Such fear was based on the stark realities forged by the systems in place. An example of this threat can be seen in ordinances pertaining to conditions in Martinique. As the number of free colored people on this tiny island had increased considerably by the middle of the eighteenth century, government officials attempted to check such growth. In a directive dated September 1, 1761, the governor and intendant ordered all *prétendus libres* ("so-called freed persons"—those whom slaveholders had freed without the written consent of the governor and the intendant) to present their papers (entitlement of freedom) to the parliament advocate, who could confirm or deny their free status. Anyone failing to present such papers "were to be confiscated [and sold] as slaves for the profit of the king."[64] The regulation seems to have been widely enforced, for colonial newspapers and other documents are replete with instances of freed persons having their liberties revoked.

It is truly amazing to see the lengths to which the French actually went in order to classify colored people. In fact, the phrase "colored people" encompassed far more intricacies than any other terminology assigned to the nonwhite sector, and by 1700, the term applied to a host of subdivisions as a result of sexual intercourse between white men and their slaves. The crown struggled with this issue throughout its involvement in, and perpetuation of, slavery in the Americas. At the core of the problem was the French male's fascination with black women. Since the early days of French colonization (1630s), it seems that everyone—officials, plantation owners, travelers, musicians, poets, etc.—was extremely impressed by African dances performed by slaves. Travel narratives abound with adjectives such as lively, voluptuous, grave, melancholic, and passionate.[65] Missionaries denounced such performances, describing them as "lascivious" and "degrading," while authorities attempted to rid the Frenchman's mind of erotic thoughts and behavior—but, evidently, to no avail.[66] Instead, the French male's strong attraction to African dancers seems to have marked the beginning of large-scale miscegenation throughout the colonies that, of course, led to a constantly increasing colored population.

The first of several attempts by the crown to control such growth can be found in Article 9 of the *Code Noir*: any married man who fathers a child by his slave would be fined and deprived of the slave and the children, who would be confiscated without ever being freed. If the slave owner was unmarried, he must marry the slave "in the forms prescribed by the Church of the said slave," and she and her child would be rendered free and legitimate. Subsequently, several regulations were enacted to control miscegenation.[67] Although the king specifically forbade sexual contact (marriage or concubinage) between whites and "blacks, mulattoes, or other colored people" residing in France,[68] it seems that interracial marriage was never outlawed in the colonies. Nevertheless, officials made repeated attempts to eliminate it by levying steep fines and by other punitive measures, such as the loss of nobility or other high-ranking positions.[69] Regardless of the severity of penalties given, interracial marriages still occurred, and the practice continued to be a constant source of agitation for officials throughout colonial rule.

Due to the widespread practice of miscegenation, the number of free colored people continued to increase significantly in all colonies. By the end of the third quarter of the eighteenth century, this segment of colonial society numbered approximately 28,000 in Saint-Domingue (40,000 whites and 452,000 slaves); 4,851 in Martinique (15,000 whites and 83,416 slaves); and 3,044 in Guadeloupe (13,466 whites and 85,461 slaves) (see figure 5).[70] Miscegenation occupied the attention not only of government officials; several missionaries, explorers, and other visitors to the islands devoted several pages to this issue in their travel narratives, *mémoires*, etc. This was particularly true with Moreau de Saint-Méry, as reflected in his monumental *Description . . . de la partie française*. However, when discussing Moreau's views on lifestyles in Saint-Domingue, and particularly in Cap Français, his adopted home during the 1770s and 1780s, one must keep in mind a few basic facts. When the voluminous work was published (1797–1798), Moreau had been living in Philadelphia, Pennsylvania, for seven years, far away from the turmoil of his beloved island. Although Moreau speaks in the present tense, he is actually describing what used to be—a phenomenon of the past. By this time, in the late 1790s, Cap Français was no longer the bustling, charming city he consistently glorified in the work. Both volumes were published after the onset of bloody slave revolts that resulted from decades of unbridled exploitation and brutality suffered by persons of African descent. The colony was in a state of devastation resulting from mass slayings of thousands of plantation owners and other whites, as well as the destruction of hundreds of houses, plantations, stores, and other businesses as they went up in flames. The major show places of the island, the Cap Français and Port-au-Prince theatres, had burned to the ground two years before Moreau was forced to flee Paris in 1793, and six years prior to publication of *Description . . . de la partie française*. The Saint-Domingue that Moreau describes is the colony of the 1780s—the last decade of French control—and nowhere in the voluminous work does he reflect the realities of the 1790s. For the purposes of the present study, however, as well as for anyone searching for information on pre-revolutionary Haïti, Moreau's work is a must.

Moreau went to great lengths not only to praise miscegenation but also to illustrate its effects after seven generations.[71] He devised an elaborate mathematical hypothesis to illustrate the extent to which seven generations of miscegenation affected skin color. He proposed that by the eighth generation, there exist in descendants of mixed unions 128 genealogical parts of white and black blood in varying degrees. For example, one particular descendant, the *sang-mêlé*, would be "1/8191th black," which would really produce pigmentation "only infinitesimally different from that of a white person."[72] A few examples of Moreau's listing are provided in appendix 3.

In going to such lengths to classify colored people, Moreau also reveals his preoccupation with the women in this category, to which he devotes several pages. Simultaneously, however, he also betrays certain facets of his own character. Moreau favored miscegenation, a practice that nurtured the white man's sexual fantasies, greed, and need for control over the nonwhite sector. Besides, according to Moreau, no colored person could ever equal the intelligence, "bodily grace," and fortitude of a white person, regardless of the level of white blood flowing through his or her veins. In sum, his views actually support the policy of confining these persons to the "purely relative category of otherness," while at the same time, they underscore his own fascination with colored women.

Conclusions

To the modern psyche, empowered with incredible medical, scientific, and technological advances of the last two centuries, opinions of scientists and *philosophes* cited above may seem to be grounded in baseless theories rather than in scientific facts. However, we must remember that these ideas were formulated in a period absorbed with rationalism, empiricism, and natural laws of nature. This induced a climate of enduring skepticism. Intellectuals reinterpreted and, in some cases, rejected traditional Christian values and searched for a rational, or natural, religion. They were proponents of a higher form of social organization in which natural rights and democratic ideals were of paramount importance, and the most important vehicle to use in order to achieve these goals was the power of the mind. On the other hand, we must also remember a certain reality: For the monarchy, it is established fact and certainty that the most important entity in the colonies was forced labor, the backbone of the immense accumulation of wealth for the sole benefit of France.

As indicated above, slaves greatly outnumbered whites. Not only did the continued growth of the colonies depend on slave labor, but skilled workers were also in demand because, by the second quarter of the eighteenth century, very few indentured servants and other whites remained in the colonies. Large numbers of slaves were able to replace indentured servants because, over the decades, many slaves had been able to upgrade their value by learning trades very useful to the colony: sugar refining, wig making, hairdressing, sewing, cooking, etc. Concurrently, a number of *affranchis*—with the support of former masters—eagerly attempted to fill the need for artisans. Primarily, these were small shopkeepers, teachers, carpenters, masons, blacksmiths, butchers, innkeepers, and cabaret owners.[73] As a result, many free colored people were very successful and wealthy, and also became *colons* and slave owners. Unfortunately, we do not have a well-rounded picture of their successes, character, or feelings regarding their lifestyles, for, as indicated above, contemporary information on these subjects was authored by whites and reflects their own opinions rather than those of *affranchis*.

Despite endless efforts and contributions of *affranchis* to French colonial society—and particularly to the theatre—it seems that these persons could not erase that deplorable "stain of slavery," which was reinforced by several revisions of the *Code Noir* and enactment of new regulations. First and foremost, the French government fully sanctioned all such measures. Official mandates sent to governors of the colonies emphasized the subordinate role of all colored people, pointing out that "they still maintain the stain of slavery and are incapable of all public functions. Such men, who descend to whatever degree from a colored woman, cannot enjoy the prerogative of nobility."[74] Regardless of their so-called "free" status, it seems that officials, attempting to underscore the inferiority of all coloreds, deemed it necessary to forbid all *affranchis* to take the titles of "Monsieur" and "Madame."[75] Thus, all "blacks, mulattos, and other colored people of either sex," regardless of the degree of white blood flowing through their veins, were trapped in a system that flourished on their labors, rigidly controlled by the greed and notions of superiority of *colons* and other whites. This created a racial hierarchy based primarily on the gradation of hues. Value of material belongings, date of discharge from slavery, and education were also used to determine one's status. In France, blacks and coloreds also came under attack because the nation did not want slaves and free colored people on the precious soil of their cities and blamed them for most disorders occurring there. On the other hand, upon being returned to the colonies, slaves were also blamed for turmoil among their counterparts with their ideas of independence and freedom.

From the beginning of French colonialism in the Americas in the early part of the seventeenth century up to the abolition of slavery in these territories in 1848, the primary objective of the French crown remained intact: to maintain absolute control over colonies solely for the maximum benefit of France and her citizens. In order to achieve this goal, it was, of course, necessary to entice a portion of the French citizenry to relocate to the islands in the early stages of colonization to build houses, public buildings, and utilities, and to oversee the nonwhite population. This required a policy and practice of absolute control over both enslaved and free persons, directed not only at the physical body, but also at the spiritual body, the mind and soul of all persons of sub-Saharan African descent. Concurrently, as indicated above, the French population had become fascinated with a new literary phenomenon—travel narratives of explorers, missionaries, and other visitors to the colonies. Their tales of the beauty and splendor of these "exotic" islands fueled Frenchmen's illusions of enriching themselves within a few months after arrival on the island. However, once they were settled in the colonies, more than a fantasy was needed to retain these new arrivals. As in any country or culture, relaxation and social activities are basic necessities. The monarchy strove to build several miniatures of Paris in the colonies in order that their subjects could enjoy the same pleasures and privileges as those residing in France. The musical theatre played a major part in the social fabric of the colonies—very similar to that seen in France.

Official approval of slavery, a vast system of social casting, and the problems associated therewith make it even more remarkable that black and colored entrepreneurs, musicians, singers, and other artists emerged and attained such high esteem in colonial theatres. In the following chapter, I shall delve much deeper into the various ways in which colonial politics and power nurtured an environment of inequality, injustice, and racism while, at the same time, persons of sub-Saharan African descent used their energies and intellect to achieve success in various entrepreneurial ventures. In their quest for equality and independence, a few slaves and free coloreds were aided, sometimes unwittingly, by officials, *grand blancs*, and missionaries who provided them with opportunities to perform on the hallowed concert and opera stages.

CHAPTER 2

POLITICS AND POWER

The power of the French colonial empire can be broken down into three categories—religious, military, and political. Each category had its own musical repertoire that, in turn, reflected the three goals of the cultural political campaign—to maintain the peace, to ensure absolute respect for the social hierarchy, and to promote French culture. This chapter will illustrate that within these categories of power, three very distinct paths of socialization emerged in the colonial hierarchy. Although these powers affected everyone in the colonies, each category was geared primarily to a particular section of the nonwhite population. Religious power focused on plantation slaves, military power on city slaves and free blacks, and political power on free colored people. Against a backdrop of the monarchy's continuous attempts of mind control of nonwhites, the long road from a plantation mentality to one filled with hope and successful theatre opportunities began in the early days of the cultural political campaign, when the monarchy planted the seeds of a very important tradition: training the enslaved in musical techniques. The first institution that excelled in this area was the Catholic Church.

Religious Power

In the second quarter of the seventeenth century, the Catholic Church began to dispatch numerous missionaries to the colonies to establish several churches and to convert the enslaved to Catholicism. By the late 1680s, the three island colonies were home to over forty churches that were served by clergy of four orders: Jesuits, Dominicans, Capuchins, and Carmelites.[1] In 1704, however, the Capuchins surrendered their mission in Saint-Domingue due to the inability to provide a sufficient number of priests; they were replaced by the Jesuits.[2]

The monarchy paid missionaries extremely well for their services: free passage to the colonies and, when appropriate, similar arrangements for their return to France; free lodging; and land for building churches and for cultivation of crops to sustain themselves. In addition, priests received approximately 12,000 pounds of raw sugar for each district they served. For the cultivation of sugar cane (the primary crop of the islands), refinement of raw sugar, and for personal domestic services, the government provided priests with funds to buy slaves for these tasks.[3]

As the colonies grew, so did revenues of the missionaries. By the second decade of the eighteenth century, several *colons* began to grow impatient with the missionaries, who, they claimed, were more concerned with expanding their own revenues than with religious duties and responsibilities. Moreover, according to the governor and the intendant of Martinique, revenues amassed by the four orders in Guadeloupe and Martinique could fully support twenty times the number of missionaries presently residing in the entire French Antilles.[4] They owned numerous slaves, plantations and other real estate, personal property, sugar refineries, and cattle. Even the mendicant friars (Capuchins, Carmelites, and Dominicans)—noted for their vows of abstinence, austerity, and lack of personal and community property—possessed substantial economic interests. By the middle of the eighteenth century, it seems that while the Capuchins possessed no plantations, they did own at least 30 slaves; the Carmelites owned one plantation and 80 slaves; and the Dominicans had at least four plantations, over 600 slaves, several herds of cattle, and personal property. The possessions of the Jesuits outnumbered by far those of the other orders combined. In Martinique alone, they owned several houses and over 500 slaves; in Guadeloupe more than 300 slaves; and in Saint-Domingue, Jesuits owned several plantations, somewhere between 900 and 1,000 slaves, several plantations, sugar refineries, and numerous herds of cattle.[5]

It seems, however, that the clergy posed a far more alarming problem for the *colons*. The latter claimed that missionaries, with their teachings of dignity of the human spirit acquired through Christianity, awakened in the slave dangerous thoughts such as freedom and revolt. In fact, so powerful did the clergy in Saint-Domingue become—especially the Jesuits—it was forbidden in some districts to open a school without acquiring a "favorable position" from the parish priest.[6]

Similar incidents also occurred in the other two colonies. Extremely troubled by humanitarian activities of the Jesuits, the *colons* accused them of being "the cause of all misdeeds committed by blacks."[7] One such "misdeed" occurred in Basse Terre, Guadeloupe, and was the subject of a letter, dated May 8, 1733, from a prosecutor in Guadeloupe to the magistrate of that colony.[8] According to the prosecutor, on the previous Sunday, Father Marée, the Jesuit parish priest, mounted the pulpit and preached as usual. However, upon having completed his sermon, Father Marée told his flock (the enslaved): "Men revolt against God; blacks revolt against whites and, in this way, avenge God; and the time is not far." An equally disturbing "misdeed, . . . so ridiculously bizarre," occurred in 1753 in Saint-Pierre, Martinique.[9] Citizens had complained to the governor that the two parish priests (one Jesuit and one Dominican) constantly competed with each other by showcasing their slaves in extremely lavish costumes on holidays and other special occasions. The governor decided to go to Saint-Pierre during the celebration of Corpus Christi[10] to follow up on the complaint. What he witnessed was very troubling to him. In a very long and solemn procession, several blacks represented "great officers of the crown . . . with as much order as any of the troops of the king," while others, "dressed in very rich habits," represented the entire royal family. In one of the parishes, the priest brought into the sanctuary a monkey and an ape, which imitated the king and the queen, and placed each in a chair! These spectacles made the governor shudder because, in addition to witnessing such disrespect for the monarchy, he reflected that at this very moment, he was surrounded by 15,000 to 18,000 blacks "all aroused and excited." A few days later, back in the secure confines of the governor's mansion in Fort-Royal, the governor forbade all such processions and similar displays in the future.

The tug of war between government officials, *colons*, and Jesuits continued for several years and came to a head in 1763, at which time the monarchy confiscated all properties and other goods of the Jesuits and expelled them from the colonies.[11]

Despite such problematic issues, however, missionaries were very instrumental in promoting the cultural political campaign and, thus, were of immense help to colonial authorities in maintaining control over the enslaved. Concurrent with their "teachings of dignity of the human spirit acquired through Christianity," priests also administered to slaves a "special catechism." Jean Fouchard, the distinguished Haitian historian, strongly suggests that such training was designed to transform the enslaved into broken and extremely submissive servants, and to keep them in an abyss of ignorance—a state in which learning to read and to write was strictly forbidden. Such colonial ritual preached punishments of hell and eternal damnation for failure to convert to Christianity, because disobedience of the laws of Christianity would surely incur the wrath of God.[12]

On the other hand, however, it is certain that within the boundaries of colonial catechism, missionaries continued their traditions of educational and charitable works. For the Jesuits, historically men of great missionary, cultural, and educational works, music was an essential part of the transmission of Western European culture. Since the early medieval period, bishops and monks, conscious of the power of knowledge of the arts, were almost the "exclusive depositories" of such knowledge.[13] Embodied with such rich cultural heritage, several missionaries expended considerable effort in supporting the goals of the monarchy's cultural political campaign in the colonies. Priests put to the test their spirit of enterprise and their pedagogical talents, using as their models the parishes of Paris. Performances of the most elaborate portions of the Mass utilized the same musical structures and Latin texts as did churches in France.[14] The Jesuits had at their disposal excellent choruses because they had an abundance of slaves from which to choose the most gifted of their young flock. Taking great pride in their work, priests would administer the catechism to the enslaved in patois every Sunday and on holidays; then they would sing a grand Mass, commencing with the Kyrie. Priests also stressed the singing of canticles because of their "melodious, descriptive, and narrative" character, and although the enslaved did not know how to read French or Latin, the Church fathers tell us that "they sang very well and with very good technique."[15] Not being content with just a phonetic experiment, however, priests taught the young and the more gifted how to read and to write music, other musical techniques such as *solfège*,[16] and how to play the violin, violoncello, contrabass, and flute. These activities permitted a more extended repertoire and facilitated the comprehension of texts that, according to the Church fathers, "the slaves sang with much fervor and emotion."[17] So moved by the beauty of devotional songs performed by slaves, one priest found it "difficult to hold back tears on these occasions."[18]

According to Church doctrine, it was the duty of the clergy "to draw primitive peoples from their degradation." One of the most troubling types of "degradation" from which the priests strove to deliver the enslaved was African dance. It seems that if slave owners refused to allow slaves to dance on the plantation, slaves would slip away after midnight and walk as far as six to eight miles to some place where they knew there would be dancing.[19] This marked the creation of secret societies—or assemblies, as they were generally called. The primary dance in assemblies was the *calenda*.[20] Although the *calenda* held special significance for the enslaved, the Catholic Church condemned it. To give you some idea as to why the Church objected so strenuously to the *calenda*, here is a description of that dance by Moreau de Saint-Méry.

> For the female dancer, who holds the corners of a handkerchief or the two ends of her apron, the art of this dance consists mainly in moving the lower part of the torso, while keeping the rest of the body almost motionless. To speed up the movement [of the *calenda*], a dancer will approach [his partner], throwing himself forward, almost touching her, withdrawing, then advancing again, while seeming to implore her to yield to the desires that invade them.
>
> There is nothing lascivious or voluptuous that this tableau does not depict. It offers a kind of contest in which every trick of love and every means of triumph are displayed: fear, hope, disdain, tenderness, caprice, pleasure, denial, delirium, flight, intoxication [and] despair. . . .
>
> I find it difficult to note the impressions this dance produces when it is precisely performed. It affects each look, it moves our sensibilities, fires our imagination; it even incites older people.[21]

We can certainly understand why the Church strove to banish such "lascivious" and "voluptuous" activity, for it seemed to them that everyone was obsessed with the *calenda*—the old, and even children so young they could hardly stand up by themselves. As one priest opined, "It seems as if they had danced in the womb of their mothers."[22] Further, according to eyewitness accounts, French men, so fascinated by African dancers, seemed to be transported to another world wherein the bewitching allure of the black female reigned, a trend that continued throughout the eighteenth century.[23] Hence, the *calenda* and all assemblies were strictly forbidden. Articles 16 and 17 of the *Code Noir* stipulated that any slave owner who permitted these activities would be fined severely; frequent violations by slaves were punishable by death.

Missionaries wrote extensively in journals, letters, and other documents about their efforts to banish the *calenda* and similar dances. Fathers Du Tertre and Labat, Dominican missionaries and two of the most quoted contemporary sources of French Antilles history,[24] brought some rather curious aspects to these issues. Although both were mendicant monks, they seemed to have put on the back burner their vows of extreme simplicity, poverty, and non-ownership of personal or community property, for both served as directors of several properties owned by the order. In addition, both were slave owners and, as such, seem to have observed African dancers quite frequently. Du Tertre vividly described the "vigor and excitement" of such performances that were allowed, and sometimes encouraged, by *colons*:

> They make such constrained postures and excessive body contortions while dancing that I am often astonished as to how they can even move after having ceased this laborious exercise. Yet, upon their departure, they are so fresh and appear tired so little that one could not tell upon seeing them that they had danced. Not only do they spend the entire Sunday afternoon at these diversions, frequently they also continue [dancing] all night, breaking up only in time to return to their respective plantations to rejoin the others at the hour they are taken to work.[25]

Our other mendicant friar, Father Labat, left an indelible mark on Martinique culture, which one can still observe today at Fonds Saint-Jacques, an old *habitation sucrerie* (sugar plantation) on the northeastern coast (see figures 6 and 7).[26] Nevertheless, Labat, like his predecessor, Father Du Tertre, faced similar obstacles. Reflecting on the inherent dangers of allowing slaves to join their counterparts on other plantations, Labat underscored the difficulties he and other missionaries encountered in their efforts to carry out the doctrine of the Church:

> It is always best to have all one's slaves at home on holidays and on Sundays, not only to remedy any fire accidents that may burn in the sugar cane fields, or for other needs, but also to prevent them from running to neighbors' houses and committing some disorder. I would rather permit our slaves to dance all types of dances, *except the calenda* [emphasis

FIGURE 6. *The Old Chapel, l'Habitation sucrerie du Père Labat, Fonds Saint-Jacques, Martinique*

> added], than to allow them to go out. Occasionally, I would assume full responsibility and give them a few jugs of brandy to entertain themselves together. I really believe that in spite of all my precautions, they dance the *calenda* with all their might when they do not fear being discovered.[27]

French travelers were so impressed with the gestures and movements of African dancers that they began to critique dance performances within their own country. A member of the Académie Royale des Sciences visiting Martinique around 1750 made the following comparison between dance movements of the enslaved and those of professional dancers in Paris:

PHOTOGRAPH BY THE AUTHOR

FIGURE 7. *Interior of the Chapel, l'Habitation sucrerie du Père Labat, Fonds Saint-Jacques, Martinique*

> In our theatres we see that movements of dancers are almost always disjoined. Some who form the same steps do not rise together and almost never descend at the same time. Some are still in the air when the bodies of the others are already at rest; it is a succession of leaps that, added to the unevenness of their height, forms a type of ladder as disagreeable to the eyes as to the ear. I have seen between seven and eight hundred blacks accompanying a wedding to the sound of a song. They would rise in the air and fall again all at the same time; this movement was so precise that the noise of their fall made only one single sound.[28]

Despite their fascination with African dances, the French were blind to—or simply ignored—the importance of dance to the enslaved. The colonial gaze of the French viewed African dances as erotic, lascivious, and decadent. Colonizers failed to understand that for the enslaved, dance was crucial: it was a vital part of their cultural heritage; it was a refuge and a means of resistance and escape from the dehumanizing rigors of slavery. From the very beginning of their enslavement, blacks were not allowed to leave the plantation and were forced to toil in sugar-cane fields and factories from sunrise until late into the night. Thus, their primary vehicle of refuge, resistance, and escape was religion—*not* Catholicism, but religious traditions of their homeland. They believed in a unique and supreme deity around which all religious themes revolved. Thus, a ceremony always included sacred dances such as those devoted to war, to man, to death, and to the fertility of the earth. The dance of war was a manifestation of their resistance to being enslaved, and the dance of man represented survival. Plantation slaves invoked the god of death because it was a primary avenue through which they could escape their deplorable state, underscoring the belief that after death they would be transported back to their native land.[29]

In sum, colonial authorities struggled constantly to obliterate all traces of African cultural traditions, particularly dances and instruments. One of the most interesting measures to control the types of dances slaves performed was undertaken by governors, priests, and other persons of authority who instructed dance masters to teach slaves the art of *galant* dances, such as the *menuet*, the *courante*, and the *bourée*—that is, those dances that were performed in the French court and, later, would become extremely important in French opera.[30] In addition, priests continued with more urgency the practice of training slaves to play European instruments, especially the violin and other strings, the nucleus of concert and opera orchestras. The emphasis on such early training established an important tradition and became an integral part of colonial culture. It prepared the enslaved very well for performances in national fêtes and operatic *divertissements*. Nevertheless, the participation of slaves in these productions was a subject of constant disagreement between theatre directors and *colons* (plantation owners) because the latter felt that these productions required too much slave time and energy that could be better spent in the sugar-cane fields or performing other servile tasks. In spite of the constant bickering between the two groups, however, theatres in the colonies flourished—as we shall see in the succeeding chapters—with opera and dance being the preferred types of entertainment; and several *affranchis* and enslaved blacks occupied substantial positions in those works.

Military Power

The remainder of this chapter refers to all sectors of the three colonies—with one notable exception, in some instances: the southern peninsula of Saint-Domingue (South Province). Located far from the bustling port city of Cap Français and isolated by the island's mountainous terrain, the peninsula was settled by buccaneers, French immigrants, and enslaved Africans, all of whom regularly married across racial lines. The formation of mixed-race families owning slave plantations created a planter elite society that was based primarily on social class rather than ancestry, a trend that endured throughout the first two-thirds of the eighteenth century. The planter elites were "deeply interconnected" and thus "created a free population of color; though when these men and women were wealthy, their neighbors rarely used racial labels to describe them.[31] At the bottom half of this social hierarchy were the less fortunate free coloreds who owned less (or no) slaves or other property. Relevant events in this society that differ from those in Cap Français, Port-au-Prince, and surrounding areas (North and West Provinces) will be indicated as the discussion evolves.

The repertoire of this category focused primarily on city slaves and free blacks. By the first quarter of the eighteenth century, it was common for free blacks to gather near the market, on the quays or in other public places, and to frequent small, crowded cabarets in the evenings. Runaway slaves, soldiers, marines, pirates, indentured servants, shopkeepers, and other lower-echelon whites also attended these nightclubs regularly.[32] Everyone went there to be "in the know," to mingle with "the witty people," and to relax.[33] They would sing, dance, play games, and indulge in bantering and drinking. It is in this setting—in the midst of an extremely affluent colonial society, forced free labor, slave revolts, and other unsettling events—that African and European cultures existed harmoniously side by side, albeit quite fleetingly, giving birth to French Antilles creole music and dance. Their songs were about love, anger, discontent, battles, voyages, and other memories of past adventures. Frequently, they would accompany their songs with dances of their own culture, with African rhythms tending to dominate. Such meeting places and associations provided many runaway slaves and free blacks with a refuge and momentary escape from the rigors of colonial rule. Cabarets were also venues in which were cultivated the deep seeds of discontent with the dehumanizing conditions under which these unfortunate people were forced to live. These blacks resisted absorption of French culture; they clung to traditional music, dances, songs, and other cultures of particular areas of Africa, *their* mother country.

As the "seeds of discontent" became more pronounced (numerous runaways, revolts, and rebellions), the French throne exercised its overpowering force through the military. Always conscious of the goals of the *cultural* political campaign, the military dutifully exercised its primary responsibility: to maintain the peace. One of the largest obstacles to this task was the growing popularity of cabarets in all colonies. As the number of cabarets increased, so did the brawls, noisy crowds, and other disturbances. Authorities responded by enacting laws geared to maintaining more control of such establishments, for in no way did such behavior promote the goals of the cultural political campaign. By the middle of the eighteenth century, the situation in Saint-Domingue had degenerated considerably with the increasing number of "errant people and vagabonds" frequenting these establishments.[34] To eliminate the resultant abusive behavior of this sector of the clientele, the king forbade all cabaret owners (as well as all residents of Saint-Domingue) to lodge or entertain any person, foreigner or French, "without immediately informing commanders, prosecutors of the king, or other police officers with the name and circumstances of that person."[35] Anyone failing to adhere to this *ordonnance* would be fined, "one-half applicable to the hospital and one-half to repairs of public works, [as well as] eight days in prison." Several laws enacted during the second half of the eighteenth century included orders to close all cabarets at 8:00 P.M. and to prohibit any firing of guns or pistols after sunset.[36] With such measures, authorities deemed they could control activities within the walls of cabarets, as well as duels and other dangerous actions that might occur after they had closed.

The units most responsible for policing cabarets were the *maréchaussée* (rural police), and the militia, the local branch of the military. Although it was common practice to disallow mixing of races in these units, the governor of Saint-Domingue made it quite clear that the established social ordering was to be strictly enforced:

> Nature having established three different classes of men, that is, whites, *sang-mêlés* and free mulattos, and free blacks, this difference will always be observed in the composition of the militia, . . . [and] one can never have any companies mixed with two different species.[37]

Units of free colored men, ages fifteen to sixty, were commanded by white officers. Their duties, for the most part, consisted of taking part in chases of runaway slaves and militia deserters, guarding slaves on plantations, and policing all areas populated and/or frequented by free blacks and free colored people. Any "free mulattoes, *griffes*, and blacks" attempting to evade service in the militia could be returned to slavery.[38] Conscious of the constantly growing population of free colored people, the establishment of a militia of free colored men was fully supported by whites because they viewed it as a guarantee against revolts, runaways, and other disturbances posed by slaves. Such reasoning is easy to understand, for colored men were their own sons, grandsons, nephews, etc.

For the free colored man in the North and West Provinces, acceptance in the militia represented one of the primary means of distancing himself further from the "stain of slavery." To be in the military—or associated with it on a lower scale, i.e., the militia—carried a high level of social prestige within the hierarchy of free colored people. The military was the protector of citizens, property, and subjects, and thus wielded a considerable amount of power. Membership in this elite institution was looked upon not just as a duty, but as a privilege. One Saint-Domingue white creole even suggested that it enabled the soldier, marine, etc., to be in contact with "the most worthy and civilizing elements of the colony, as well as with gentlemen emigrating from France, and to be faithful servants of the law and of the King."[39] Free colored men in the South Province did not, however, share the sentiments of those in the North and West. As detailed in the previous chapter, colonial authorities passed several laws restricting freedoms previously enjoyed by free coloreds, regardless of their material possessions. In addition, their incessant appeals for equality, clearly granted to *affranchis* almost a century before in the *Code Noir*, were rejected repeatedly. Subsequently, in the 1770s and 1780s, this frontier society was transformed into a social hierarchy based on race, like the other colonies. Service in the free colored militia was mandatory, an act that wealthy colored plantation owners seem to have resented, and that some even viewed as "a kind of slavery."[40]

While the militia was relegated primarily to maintaining order in those areas described above, it was white members of the military who were selected to produce music for, and to assume the most prominent roles in, national festivals, official balls, and military-related events such as war victories, peace treaties, and military reviews. Such events were celebrated in France with much grandeur and pomp, and were always observed in the colonies in similar fashion. Music for these activities primarily consisted of marches, *symphonies*, and variations on popular French songs. An elaborate version of the ancient Christian hymn *Te Deum laudamus* (We praise thee, O God) generally closed the ceremonies.

By the middle of the eighteenth century, each branch of the military had its own corps of musicians, dancers, and singers. In order to strengthen the military power of the throne through the arts, on board each ship of marines there was at least one dance master who taught the men various types of French dances. Sailors performed court dances at official balls, after which city slaves executed a mixture of French and "non-offensive" African dances.[41]

The power of the French crown was omnipresent in the colonies. Events in the royal family were scrupulously observed, with all three categories of power adhering to the goals of the cultural political campaign. Take, for example, the death of the Dauphin (son of Louis XV) on December 20, 1765. Ceremonies began with the military firing a 21-cannon salute, followed by the same number of strokes on the parish clock. The military repeated this exercise several times a day during the following week. On the first day of observance, everyone attended a Mass for the prince while a segment of the military circled the church.[42] In an effort to thwart any plans for revolt or escape by slaves, the infantry guarded all exits of the plantations, as was the custom for all national ceremonies and other large social events.

Military reviews were common, and each colony subscribed to the same format.[43] At 9:00 A.M., the governor, intendant, and their cortège (military and civil officials) would assemble in front of City Hall or some other government building. They boarded stagecoaches, and the cavalry, with their trumpets blaring in a triumphant march, led the cortège to the town square or some other appropriate site where the review would take place.

The review began at 10:00 A.M. Musicians from each branch of the military played a variety of *symphonies* as their contingent filed by the reviewing stand. First in line were the cavalry on horseback, who engaged in a tilt match. Next were the marines, then the infantry. The last group was the militia, comprised of free colored men on foot, preceded by two or three slaves beating drums. The placement of the militia at the rear of the cortège clearly illustrates that inescapable bond between free colored men and the "stains of slavery," a bond reinforced by the accompaniment of that unmistakable voice and heartbeat of African culture—the drum.

At 11:00 A.M. the Mass commenced, with music (short *symphonies*) supplied by marine musicians.

At 12:00 noon the governor hosted a banquet at his mansion. Everyone paid homage to the king by singing a royal hymn, accompanied by all musicians.

In the afternoon, all musicians—including the militia—participated in a concert. Dancing, dinner, and more dancing followed until the early evening hours.

By the latter half of the eighteenth century, the evening entertainment had expanded considerably. It now consisted of a light opera (usually one act), a fireworks display in front of the theatre, an elaborate banquet, and a grand ball that lasted until the next morning. The governor and intendant always attended military reviews, the concert, opera, and occasionally, the grand ball. While *affranchis* were allowed to view the military parade and to attend the concert and the opera, taking their places in areas specifically designed for them, none were permitted to attend the grand ball, for that would entail mixing of the races. In fact, it was quite common for the military to draw a line of distinction between their units (all white men) and colored people; this can be seen clearly in announcements of their performances such as the following:

> Musicians of the Regiment of Port-au-Prince gave on last Sunday, 16 January, and will give on next Sunday, 23 January, a grand vocal and instrumental concert that the [Governor-] General has honored and will honor with his presence. It begins at 5:30 P.M. and finishes at 8:00 P.M. There will be a grand ball at 10:00 P.M. where people will pay an admission charge at the same price as the concert. *Colored people will not be admitted, even by paying.*[44]

As testimony of the high esteem colonial officials and the public bestowed upon the military, weekly newspapers generally announced and commented on their performances.[45] In the second half of the eighteenth century, military regiments in each colony produced a series of concerts on a regular basis.[46] These were usually held on Sundays, starting at 5:30 P.M. and lasting two-and-one-half to three hours. Concerts included both instrumental and vocal music, some of which were variations on popular French songs. However, the most prominent types of concert music were *ouvertures*, dramatic *symphonies*, ensembles, *airs*, and *ariettes* from some of the most successful operas.

Military musicians supplied much of the music for opera productions that featured military events. One of the best examples that illustrate the importance of their participation in the musical theatre occurred in 1783. On November 25 of that year, *Aucassin et Nicolette, ou les moeurs du bon vieux temps* was performed in Port-au-Prince, Saint-Domingue.[47] The orchestra consisted of musicians from the ranks of the military. The *ouverture*, with its prominence of horns, trumpets, and drums, foretells the pending battle between Aucassin and enemies of his father. The plot illustrates the struggle between the traditional themes of glory and love. The Count (father of Aucassin) urges his son to battle because it is his duty (glory) to defend the father's honor. On the other hand, Aucassin is preoccupied with thoughts of Nicolette, whom his father has forbidden him to marry. Finally Aucassin agrees to fight provided that he can see Nicolette "for one instant only" to bid her a final farewell. As the story unfolds, the scoring mentioned above occurs several times throughout the work, emphasizing the glorious military stature of the hero (Aucassin's departure for battle, several allusions to his heroic stature and deeds, and his triumphant return home).

Military musicians frequently provided the music for the spoken theatre as well. For performances of *Tartuffe*[48] and *Tancrède*[49]—plays by Molière and Voltaire, two of France's most gifted writers—the military performed several pieces between acts (*ouvertures*, *ariettes*, and clarinet duos). There were also many instances in which soloists and ensembles from the military performed instrumental ensembles arranged for clarinet, bassoon, oboe, horns, and trumpets prior to the curtain rising and after the last act of an opera (or play). While such instruments were primarily the heart of military reviews and official ceremonies, it is interesting to note that nowhere in the research did I find an example of solo violinists or other string players in the ranks of the military—even though strings, the nucleus of symphonic and operatic productions, were used in operas in which military musicians performed. Rather, as illustrated in chapter 4, it appears that some of the most accomplished solo violinists emerged from the ranks of the enslaved and *affranchis*.

As further testimony to the high esteem that military musicians enjoyed, the theatre occasionally devoted a work to a specific unit of the military. Dancers paid tribute to the infantry in a production of *Les Grenadiers, ballet-pantomime*.[50] The Cap Français opera company honored the musicians by hosting an elaborate benefit for them with a lavish production of *Aucassin et Nicolette, ou les moeurs du bon vieux temps*.[51] Stage décor also reflected the status of the military. A statue of the king, placed between a cluster of military arms and a genealogical tree of the Bourbon monarchy, became part of the setting in several works related to the military.

Political Power

In this category we will continue to observe the struggle by nonwhites for equality and independence, as well as how the tradition of training slaves in European musical techniques and orchestral instruments helped to prepare the way for their descendants to perform in grandiose productions of operas. *Affranchis* on the upper levels of the colored hierarchy were part of that "intermediate class"; but they were further divided into two distinct subcategories: aristocracy and middle class. The primary element that set them apart was the value of material belongings, for their growth was remarkable, not only in numbers but also in various types of business ventures. The most successful and wealthiest *affranchis* were engaged in the cultivation of sugar, the most lucrative business in the French Antilles. In the early 1720s, some planters (particularly in Martinique and Guadeloupe) also began to focus on coffee, for the crop required less land and fewer slaves than sugar-cane production. *Affranchis* were also very successful as cabaret managers or owners, tailors, shoemakers, goldsmiths, and carpenters.

As sons and daughters of rich white planters, many *affranchis* managed their parents' plantations and were legitimate heirs of the father's estate, for the *Code Noir* placed no restrictions on inheritance of property. As owners of the estate, they became part of the powerful and rich planter elite (the colonial aristocracy). They were the wealthiest group of *affranchis*, which aroused much envy and hatred from whites, particularly the *petits blancs* on the lowest rung of the white social ladder. However, these free coloreds maintained close ties with their white relatives and acquaintances, and, in turn, cherished their support—all of which functioned as important buffers from hostilities and insults hurled at them by detractors. The free colored planter elite associated primarily with other members of the colonial aristocracy and, unlike the coloreds in other business enterprises, had very little contact with other coloreds.[52] Primarily, it is this sector of *affranchis*, the colored planter elite, who frequented the opera and dutifully claimed the seats assigned to them in an upper section of the theatre, the *Paradis pour les gens de couleur* (Paradise for Colored People).[53]

While many *affranchis* purchased slaves and started their own plantations or other business enterprises, others made a career out of military service—the second most successful arena for free coloreds in the colonies. Thus, next in the line of economic accomplishments was what Stewart King calls the "military leadership group [with] many of the characteristics of a rising middle class."[54] This group maintained close ties to other coloreds, not only to those in their own group, but also to persons on the lower rungs of the colored hierarchy. Ties of kinship were "recorded and strengthened through 'family' notarial and parish register acts: marriages and marriage contracts, wills, wardship of orphaned children, godparenthood, serving as official mourner at funerals, and the like."[55] Unlike the colored planter elite, they had little or no social, personal, or economic ties with whites.

The status of *affranchis* as an intermediate class was, indeed, very evident in social functions. The colored planter elite strove to shed the shackles-of-enslavement status by imitating the white planter elite and thoroughly absorbing themselves in the musical repertoire of political power. In this area, which was under the control of the governor, the focus was on national festivals and official ceremonies that were held to commemorate births, marriages, weddings, and other events and accomplishments of the king and the royal family. The music was very elaborate and generally included performance of one or more operas. Such events were very important because, as demonstrated above, it was the desire of the French crown that all citizens enjoy the pleasures of musical theatre and other types of French culture. In fact, it was crucial because conditions in the colonies—slave revolts, hot and humid weather, hurricanes, etc.—made it increasingly difficult to attract large numbers of the French populace to relocate to the islands. As a result of the heavy emphasis on promoting French culture, small private theatre productions emerged in the early eighteenth century, and larger theatres were built in the latter half of the century.[56] Artistic centers sprang up; singers, actors, and dance masters were imported from France for lavish productions of operas and plays that were modeled on those performed in Paris.[57] Attendance at, or participation in, concerts, operas, spoken theatre, and grand balls played an important social role, as such activities indicated a certain level of social distinction and prestige. On a smaller, more intimate level, *colons* and other rich and powerful white businessmen imitated Parisians' fondness for entertaining guests in their homes with concerts or excerpts from operas and plays.

Conscious of the importance of stature in colonial society and, thus, motivated by a desire to distance themselves from the status of enslavement, many free colored people closely followed social patterns of the *colons*. This group, primarily at the top of the *affranchi* hierarchy, transmitted French music by organizing dinner parties where court songs and excerpts from operas were performed. Nevertheless, they, like other coloreds and the enslaved, were still considered to be qualitatively different, i.e., inferior, *the Other*. As further proof of exploitation of free colored people, a Martinique businessman, requesting official permission to build a new theatre in Saint-Pierre, argued that by adopting French cultural ideals, free colored people could lose much of the "barbarity" of their origin and, thus, become "civilized" in their manners and customs.[58] Further, to bolster their racist views, white creoles utilized dance and opera not only to promote and encourage division between the enslaved and free colored people, but also to create numerous subdivisions among free colored people. Whites encouraged such stratification, for they regarded *affranchis*, many of whom were their own sons and daughters, as allies against threats of slave revolt. They played on any jealousy, resentment, or other negative feelings or incidents that might periodically arise between free colored people and the enslaved—actions that were sorely provoked by the social hierarchy. French authorities relied on the age-old theme of divide and conquer, viewing a divided nonwhite population as a necessity in order to maintain the peace, to ensure absolute respect for the social hierarchy, and to promote French culture.

As previously indicated, dance was an integral part of French opera of the seventeenth and eighteenth centuries. The fascination with dance, so prevalent in the court of Louis XIV, garnered similar attention and status in the colonies. With increasing fervor, dancing after the conclusion of an opera performance became as important as the opera itself. The *bals de nuit* (night balls) were held in the theatre, commencing about 9:00 P.M. and lasting until the wee hours of the morning. However, due to the excessively hot climate, *bals de nuit* were soon replaced by *bals parés* (full-dress balls of a shorter duration, also called *redoutes*) that were held from 5:00 to 9:00 P.M. This arrangement seemed to be more convenient and pleasing for everyone.

> This choice of hours was good; when the *redoute* begins, businesses have closed; when one leaves [the ball] it is supper time; one has all night to rest, and old parents have less excuses for attending because the *redoute* costs only half as much as the *bals de nuit*.[59]

> [The *redoute*] is the most delicious spectacle. . . . The prettiest figures, the most seductive graces, the most elegant adjustments, all are ravishing, and at the departure from these charming fêtes, the spirit is in a type of delirium.[60]

These grand balls were private events, and although they were generally held in the theatre, *affranchis* were not allowed to attend; they could only watch the white attendees from their restricted space (*Paradis pour le gens de couleur*) located far above the dance floor. Such demonstrations of disdain for colored people at the theatre were very common, for we only have to remember that even military musicians refused to admit colored people to their grand balls held for "all concert attendees."

According to Fouchard and Moreau de Saint-Méry, two of the most quoted authorities on French Antillean lifestyles in the eighteenth century, everyone—blacks, colored people, and whites—was extremely enthusiastic about dancing.[61] The dance palace (*Vaux-Hall*), a new fashion that had seduced Paris in the early 1760s, became a tremendously successful business enterprise in the colonies a few years later. The design of the dance hall in Cap Français seemed to set the stage for others to follow. Built in 1776, it consisted of several rooms, with the two most expansive areas being reserved for public balls and large parties. *Affranchis* were allowed to attend public balls at the Vaux-Hall or to hold private balls in their homes, for love of the dance ran just as deep for them as it did for the enslaved and other sectors of the population.[62] The setting as well as the types of dances differed greatly from those of the enslaved who viewed dance as an integral part of their religious traditions, whereas *affranchis* on the upper level of the colored hierarchy regarded dance as a social function and closely followed French traditions. Nevertheless, *affranchis* were confronted with certain restrictions. They could only have "day dances" that must end before 9:00 P.M., and all "assemblies for night dances or *calendas*" were strictly forbidden.[63]

The composition and function of balls reflected the different levels of society. In addition to the amount of one's accumulated wealth, the different shades of skin color also separated the classes; and those at the bottom of the social order, perturbed by this "psychosis of color," attempted to climb the social ladder in various ways.[64] However, their actions, for the most part, helped to perpetuate social distinctions. Following what they conceived to be proper (French) customs and manners, *affranchis* put forth extra effort to learn the "proper" dances by enrolling in classes taught by dance teachers imported from France. They also focused their attention on the "proper" clothes to wear and on the "proper" way to conduct oneself.

The public ball also became a prime place for matchmaking. Adhering to customs of white creoles, each social group of *affranchis* was characterized by its dances, its guests, and above all, the amount of money spent on gowns and other items of finery. In fact, it seems as though some colored families, imitating white creoles, would spend inordinate sums of money on dresses and other attire in order to increase a daughter's prospects for a husband or, unlike white creoles, for a well-to-do white sponsor.[65]

The most sensational balls were undoubtedly those hosted by *mulâtresses*. Generally, guests were white men and colored women, and French music and dances of the French court (*menuet*, *gavotte*, *bourée*, etc.) were the featured entertainment. The "mulatto ball" was hailed as "the event of the season." Everyone talked about it for a long time (before and after it occurred) and also complained about the long, empty space between the previous ball and the next one.[66] This seems to have been especially true in small towns where there was no Vaux-Hall. On the other hand, there was another very logical reason for the huge success of these balls: the appeal of mulatto women. Contemporaries and modern Antillean scholars describe them as "queens of the colonies" and "priestesses of Venus" who seduced all European men "at first sight"; and there were those women who, supported by the richest merchants, further enhanced their "intoxicating and natural beauty" with "Asiatic luxury."[67]

In sum, this is the Saint-Domingue lifestyle that Moreau de Saint-Méry describes with so much enthusiasm in his monumental *Description . . . partie française*: the golden days of French rule and, truly, a phenomenon of the past, wherein we have observed three very distinct paths of socialization emerge in the colonial hierarchy. Although the enslaved were exposed on a daily basis to French music on the plantation, on the docks, in their masters' homes, or on other city jobs, many chose to cling to their African cultural traditions as much as possible. They strongly resisted French culture. For many of them, creole music and the cabarets represented an escape, albeit rather fleeting, from the rigors and status of enslavement. The second group, the rich colored planter elite, imitated their white parents and friends and seems to have thoroughly absorbed French culture. On the other hand, the third group, the "middle class," was further divided. Some resisted French culture while others, perturbed at the "psychosis of color," actually, but perhaps unwittingly, also imitated social patterns of white aristocrats. Regardless of which path a particular group followed, members on each level of the hierarchy were affected by, and contributed in some manner to, the development of colonial opera productions. The colored planter-elite sector, imitators of white colonial aristocracy, frequently attended the theatre and dutifully claimed their seats in the *Paradis pour les gens de couleur*. In striking contrast, however, we shall see the talented artists of the musical theatre—instrumentalists, singers, and dancers—emerge from the three lowest rungs of the social ladder.

CHAPTER 3

COLONIAL SOCIETY AT THE THEATRE

French composers, writers, and patrons of the arts frequently discussed and wrote numerous essays and treatises on the calming influence of music on the soul. They defined their music as delicate, refined, and culturally uplifting—attributes that, they deemed, had an extremely positive influence on the listener. Official communications between France and colonial authorities underscored this view. As indicated above, administrators in Martinique, addressing the need for a new theatre, opined that through constant exposure to French music and theatre, "free colored men could lose much of the barbarity of their origin and, thus, become civilized in their manners and customs."[1] For patrons in Saint-Domingue, the theatre was "indispensable," for this was the place where the youth would find "lessons of good sense, good language, good taste, and decency."[2] Like their counterparts in the other two colonies, they also deemed it necessary that a theatre "provide a passageway that would allow *affranchis* to enter and to leave without mixing with white people." Thus, the musical theatre became a major force in French Antilles colonial society, supporting and strengthening the cultural political campaign. It helped to maintain the peace by providing elaborate musical entertainment designed to divert the attention of the nonwhite population away from "unruly" thoughts such as equality and independence. The exposure of *affranchis* to the best traditions of French music and theatre, performed by some of the most acclaimed French and local artists, certainly promoted French culture. Equally important, colonial authorities strictly controlled participation, seating arrangements, and attendance at all theatres in attempts to ensure absolute respect for the social hierarchy.

By the latter half of the eighteenth century, the theatre had become a thriving enterprise in the French Antilles, with at least eleven theatres offering the best traditions of French music and drama—eight in Saint-Domingue, two in Guadeloupe, and one in Martinique. Of the eleven, the largest and most successful theatres were established in thriving seaport cities: Cap Français and Port-au-Prince, Saint-Domingue, and Saint-Pierre, Martinique (see table 3). The main attraction in each city was the theatre. Architecture, décor, and costumes were just as elaborate as those displayed in Paris and in other European cities. Plays and operas at their height of popularity in France were performed in the colonies soon thereafter with all the pomp and lavishness of Parisian productions.

Cap Français

The birthplace of French colonial theatre was Cap Français, that bustling city on the northern coast of Saint-Domingue and the main seaport in the French Antilles. Two extremely important business enterprises were undertaken in Cap Français: the establishment of the first printing press in the colonies and, shortly thereafter, a newspaper. The intendant outlined the proposed format of a weekly newspaper and plan of distribution throughout the island in an eight-page *Prospectus de la Gazette de S. Domingue*, dated January 10, 1764. He began by underscoring the necessity for such an enterprise:

> The little communication that exists between the various districts that compose the French colony of S. Domingue is one of the main obstacles that, until now, has stopped the progress of its establishment, the perfection of its cultures, and the degree of interior commerce and population of which it is capable. The neighboring districts are in some respects strangers and even unknown to each other; this reciprocal ignorance increases in proportion to the distance [between them]. . . . To render the work of citizens more fruitful . . . and to sweeten the weariness of their solitude by satisfying their curiosity for all things that, by nature, stimulate it, are the two objectives that we propose in the work that we announce here under the title of *Gazette de S. Domingue.*

For the theatre, the publication of a weekly newspaper was very significant, for it marked the beginning of regular documentation of concert and theatre (musical and spoken) productions throughout the colony. Although there was no freedom of the press in French colonies (newspapers were subject to censorship by the governor and the intendant), the availability of such information to the public contributed significantly to the success of colonial theatres. Titles of works (with occasional plot summaries); performance dates; names of singers, actors, dancers, and instrumentalists; the décor; and other pertinent information were provided in a

TABLE 3. *Theatre Activity in the Colonies*

		RELATIVE EVENTS	PREMIERES OPERAS	PREMIERES PLAYS	REPRISES OPERAS	REPRISES PLAYS
SAINT-DOMINGUE						
Cap Français	1764–1779		145	195	177	144
	1780–1791		60	54	161	74
		1740: Earliest theatre attempts				
		1764: *Prospectus, la Gazette de S. Domingue*				
		1764: Cap Français Comédie inauguration; became public				
		1766: New building acquired				
		1784: Theatre enlarged				
Port-au-Prince	1762, 1775		16	12	24	9
	1778–1789		115	85	125	30
		1751, 1770: Devastating earthquakes				
		1762: First theatre built				
		1775, 1776: Theatres rebuilt				
		1778: Mesplès theatre built				
Léogane	1766, 1771–73, 1776		7	5	1	0
		1762–1772: First period of theatre				
		1786–1788: Second period (Labbé, *quarteron*, acquired a theatre)				
Saint-Marc	1764–1779		29	18	4	3
	1780–1787		18	12	8	3
		1770: Two female codirectors; premiere interrupted by an earthquake				
		1772: Theatre reopened under new management				
Les Cayes	1784–1785		9	2	2	0
		1765: Theatre opened				
		1788: First building for a theatre				
MARTINIQUE						
Saint-Pierre	1775, 1787–1788		18	3	0	0
		1750: Earliest theatre attempts				
		1770: Theatre built; could hold only 250 persons				
		1786, December: Inauguration of larger theatre				
GUADELOUPE						
Point-à-Pitre	1787–1788		5	0	0	0
TOTAL PERFORMANCES			422	386	502	263

section entitled *Spectacles*.[3] Praises, criticisms, and, occasionally, biographical sketches of artists and other aspects of a production were also included.

The earliest attempts of theatre production occurred in Cap Français around 1740, and consisted of a few plays performed by amateurs in private homes for the enjoyment of family and friends. During the next two years, these small ventures blossomed, producing larger and more varied programs to which influential members of the public were invited. The success of such daring innovations, however, was hampered by the immense costs associated with maintaining a theatre—even with an immense slave-labor force guaranteed by the heads of state specifically for the construction and maintenance of theatres. Cap Français (and all succeeding colonial theatres) followed the patterns of the Comédie-Italienne and other public theatres where concerts and all theatre productions (musical and spoken) occupied one building.[4] In order to ensure continuous success of the theatre, several businessmen agreed to finance productions for two years (1744–1746). Under the guaranty, the theatre was able to move to larger quarters and to import singers and dancers from France. Operas were added to the usual repertoire of little comedies and vaudevilles, marking the first documented evidence of musical theatre in the colonies.[5]

The Cap Français Comédie became public in 1764, and its continued success soon warranted larger quarters. The new facility, acquired in 1766, consisted of an oval-shaped auditorium that measured 120 feet long and 40 feet wide.[6] There were two tiers of boxes on each side, with ten boxes on each tier and six seats in each box. Of these, four boxes (two on each tier) were rented on a yearly basis. The loge of the king (represented by the governor) was on the right and that of the intendant on the left. The *Paradis pour les gens de couleur* ("only for mulatto men and women") consisted of four boxes in the rear gallery. The vast majority of attendees gathered on the parterre (main floor), and Cap Français established a format that other theatres followed rather closely. The parterre generally had a few benches lined on each side or, in some theatres, formed a semicircle. The center was left bare for standing.

Despite the grandeur and success of several performances, however, the Comédie still found itself immersed in debt. Thus, shareholders petitioned the king for financial relief in the "Mémoire concernant le Spectacle de la ville du Cap."[7] Emphasizing the benefits of having a theatre, they pointed out that such institutions "corrected and purified morals [necessary] for a civil society. The theatre softens character and inspires virtue." Everyone—from the busy entrepreneur to the common worker—benefited from attendance at the theatre because they were "fulfilled in an acceptable manner and their morals refined." Further, the authors concluded, there were "far less quarrels among citizens since the establishment of a Spectacle." Thus, the role of the performing arts as a main participant in the "process of refinement" (of both citizens and nonwhite subjects) became a vital part of the *cultural* political campaign, and this theme recurred in theatres throughout the life of French colonial rule in the Antilles.

The Cap Français Comédie went through several changes over the next decade. Several shareholders resigned, new patrons took their places, and there was a steady flow of changes in theatre directors and stage managers. Nevertheless, the Comédie continued to be successful. In 1784, a third row of loges, two balconies, and six loges for the *Paradis pour les gens de couleur* were added, bringing the total for the *Paradis* to seven loges for *mulâtresses* and three for *négresses*, with a total capacity of 1,500—very impressive for a city with an estimated population of 8,500 that were allowed to enter the theatre (7,100 whites and 1,400 *affranchis*); attendance by the enslaved, of course, was forbidden. Again, it is important to keep in mind that theatres in the colonies were constructed with much less expense than in France because of free slave labor; for, by this time, indentured servants were no longer in the colonies or, themselves, had become slave owners.

The level of success of the Cap Français Comédie can be measured by the number, frequency, and types of performances. The theatre was open all year, but with less activity in the hot and humid months of June through August and during closures for Holy Week and other religious observances. During the first decade and a half after the theatre became public (1764–1779), operas and plays were performed two or three times a week. Regular performance days were Sunday and Thursday, and benefit performances for the director, a particular *comédien*, or other performer(s) were held on Tuesday or, to a lesser degree, on Wednesday or Friday. By 1779, more than 145 operas and 195 plays premiered, and succeeding performances of many of these works totaled at least 321 (operas, 177, and plays, 144).

During the 1780s, those "glorious years" of French colonial rule about which Moreau de Saint-Méry spoke so eloquently, an additional performance day was added to the regular schedule of Sunday and Thursday. Benefits were also held more frequently—Tuesday and Friday or Saturday. It seems that Saturday became the preferred night for benefits around 1784, for they occurred almost every Saturday night from that year onward. There were several instances in which as many as three benefits were held in one week, bringing the total of all performances to six per week. Performance records also reflect the public's preference for opera over spoken drama, for during this decade, the Comédie produced approximately 60 new operas, 54 new plays, and a minimum of 235 repeat performances (operas, 161, and plays, 74).

Saint-Pierre

The news of the successful launching of theatre in Cap Français soon spread throughout the colonies. The second *comédie* was established on the tiny island of Martinique. As indicated above, the colony could boast of two flourishing cities: Fort-Royal (now Fort-de-France) and Saint-Pierre, both located on the western coastline. Administratively and militarily, Fort-Royal was the most important city in Martinique. Located in the bay midway between the northern and southern points of the island, Fort-Royal was strategically very significant. Quartered here were heads of government, the military, and the naval station.

For the present study, however, the city of Saint-Pierre is of more interest. Located north of Fort-Royal (nowadays, about a forty-minute drive from Fort-de-France on a curving, mountainous highway), Saint-Pierre is the oldest city in Martinique.[8] By the middle of the eighteenth century, the city had become the center of commerce and industry as well as a thriving artistic community. The "intellectual elite" flourished here amidst the "full blooming" of cultural activities that seemed to lean toward musical theatre and elaborate grand balls.[9] It was in this vein that, around 1750, a few businessmen used their own funds to import French actors to produce works similar to those performed in Paris. Although gazettes during the next few years (1750–1765) are rather scarce, modern research by French Antilles musicologists and historians suggest that early attempts to establish a theatre were successful.[10]

The Saint-Pierre Comédie continued on a very small scale, but the desire to establish a permanent and suitable theatre remained strong. In 1770 they built a theatre and again hired several actors from France. The difficulty was that the theatre could hold only 250 persons and, therefore, was insufficient to support performers and to cover other expenses of maintaining a theatre. Several officials, rich merchants, and other businessmen were unrelenting in their pursuit of a "grand Comédie." Repeatedly, they petitioned the two heads of state and the king to support the building of a larger facility.[11] Like their counterparts in Saint-Domingue, they regarded a thriving theatre as an extremely positive alternative to the increasing popularity of those rowdy cabarets and gambling houses. Finally, in January 1786, construction of a new theatre began, and the inauguration took place in December of that year.[12]

As in Cap Français, the Comédie was the main attraction in Saint-Pierre (see figure 8).[13] It became the showplace of the Lesser Antilles, and the description by a visiting Danish official attests to its magnificence and reputation:

> The main entertainment for the French in these countries is the theatre. There is a magnificent theatre in Saint-Pierre that surpasses in grandeur and in taste the most renowned European structures of this kind. It has a vast courtyard, and in front of the main door, there is a place where carriages [*porteurs de litière*] take the upper level upon arrival and the lower level when they return. It has four tiers of boxes; the first of which is surrounded by an outside gallery where spectators can amuse themselves while waiting for the spectacle to begin. People can also go out there between acts for a little air without losing one's place in the box. There is no separation in the tiers of boxes, and each person can take the seat that suits him best.
>
> The fourth tier is called "Paradise for Colored People" [*Paradis pour les gens de couleur*]. All those who cannot prove direct European lineage are relegated to this section.

FIGURE 8. *Saint-Pierre Théatre before the volcanic eruption in May 1902*

> One often sees here some *Christises*, whose skin is incomparably whiter than those of our people in Northern Europe.[14]

It is also interesting to note that the author seemed to be rather uncomfortable amidst the French colonial elite:

> It is a great inconvenience for us North Europeans to be suffocated in these huge assemblies by the odor of musk with which the fashionable society is scented. . . . To poison the air more, all around you, everyone has a fan with which they agitate this distressing vapor like a storm stirs up the dust, for it would be contrary to decency if a creole appeared at the spectacle without a fan.[15]

Evidently, our visitor did not share the French passion for perfume.

Saint-Pierre could boast of having one of the most impressive theatres in the Americas. Maurice Nicolas lauded it as "a miniature reproduction of the great theatre of Bordeaux."[16] While Nicolas does not provide a comparison of the two theatres, certain similarities can be gleaned from recent studies and archival documents.[17] The seating capacity of the Bordeaux Grand Théâtre (1,726) was twice that of the Saint-Pierre Comédie (800). However, the latter structure, like its model, was admired for its elegant statue-topped colonnades, monumental stairways, and four tiers of boxes. Although no photographs or paintings of the interior of the Saint-Pierre structure are available, we can use eye-witness accounts and other archival documents to observe some similarities between these two magnificent structures, such as the four tiers of boxes, the stage, the parterre, etc. (see figures 9 and 10).

Saint-Pierre Comédie was built on a hill overlooking a breathtaking view of the Caribbean Sea. However, in order to take full advantage of this sight (and to enter the theatre), one had to ascend four flights of stairs, the first of which consisted of five steps. The second stairway (thirteen steps) led to the halfway point, where a huge fountain was the centerpiece of a spacious landing. The third and fourth staircases were twenty-one and six steps, respectively. Two or three miles northeast of the Comédie is the volcanic Mount Pelée (now dormant) hovering over Saint-Pierre. On May 8, 1902, Mount Pelée erupted, covering most of the city. Subsequent eruptions on May 20 and intermittently up until the middle of August completely demolished Saint-Pierre and several nearby villages. Years of excavation, cleanup, and rebuilding ensued. Today one can visit the site of that once magnificent structure, climb the remains of that monumental staircase leading up to where the entrance used to be, and then gaze back westward at the magnificent view of the sea while Mount Pelée towers over your shoulder from the northeast (see figures 11–13). The theatre was never rebuilt, but one can stroll around the remains of the structure and descend a few steps for a closer view of the foundation, still intact with some columns, partitions, and flagstones clearly visible.

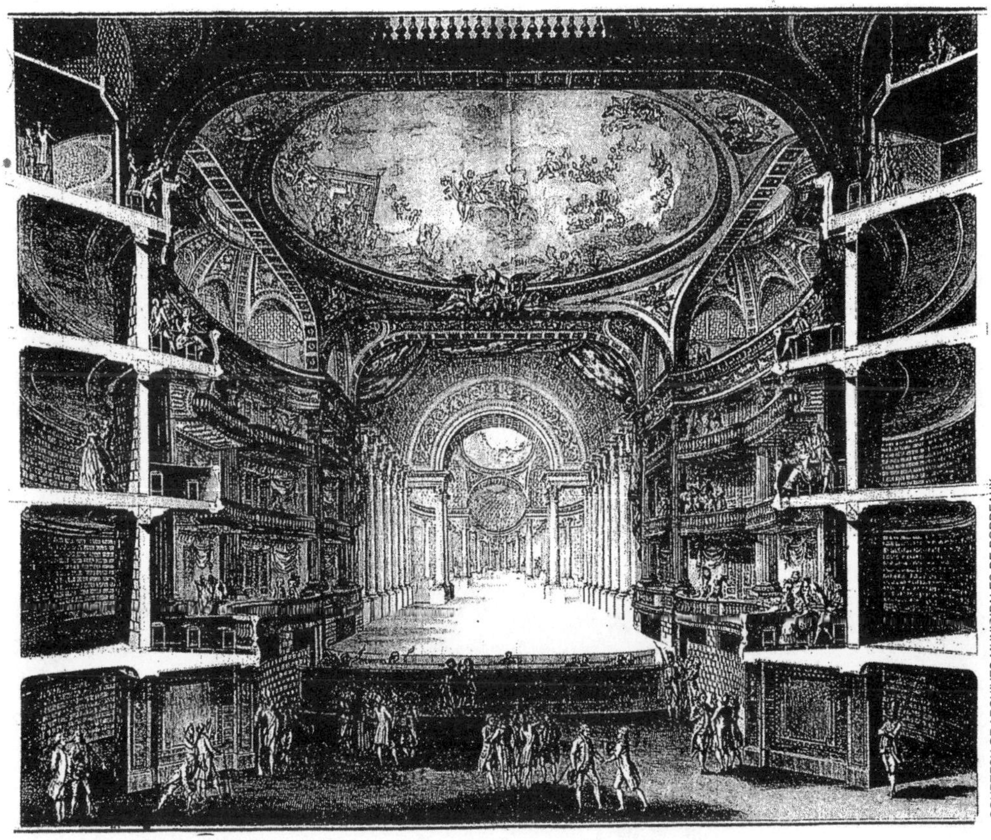

FIGURE 9. *Grand-Théâtre de Bordeaux, "A Perspective of the interior of the hall"*

There are only a few performance records for the subject period. Therefore, with the exception of one opera (*La Surprise de l'Amour*, performed August 4, 1775), all works mentioned in the present study were performed in 1787 and 1788. During this period, at least eighteen operas and three plays were mounted; there is no mention of repeat performances. Several contemporary and modern sources discuss the magnificence and success of the Saint-Pierre Comédie during the 1770s and 1780s, and it is, therefore, certainly safe to assume that several premieres and reprises were mounted.

Port-au-Prince

The next step in theatre development occurred in Port-au-Prince, nestled in the southwestern corner of Saint-Domingue. When the first comedies, operas, and vaudevilles were being produced in Cap Français, Port-au-Prince did not yet exist. It was around this same time,

PHOTOGRAPH BY THE AUTHOR

FIGURE 10. *Saint-Pierre Theatre today, main entrance*

PHOTOGRAPH BY THE AUTHOR

FIGURE 11. *Saint-Pierre Theatre, first landing and fountain*

PHOTOGRAPH BY THE AUTHOR

FIGURE 12. *Saint-Pierre Theatre, exterior gallery and entrances to first tier*

PHOTOGRAPH BY THE AUTHOR

FIGURE 13. *Saint-Pierre Theatre, inside the auditorium, exits to the outside gallery, and view of the Caribbean Sea*

however, that the intendant of Saint-Domingue initiated steps for the formation of a new city by proposing that two small neighboring parishes (Cul-de-Sac and Trou-Bordet) be combined to form one large parish. After several planning and negotiating sessions between the intendant and officials of the two villages, plans for the establishment of "the new city of Port-au-Prince" were approved in April 1749.[18] Construction of public buildings, houses, roads, etc., began immediately, with the two heads of state granting to builders "a sufficient number of slaves" to complete these tasks. A few months later, the king declared Port-au-Prince the administrative and political capital of the colony.[19]

Port-au-Prince also had its share of problems, similar to those experienced by officials and theatre enthusiasts in Cap Français. Plagued by earthquakes, hurricanes, fires, and floods during the first two decades of the city's existence, the people struggled continuously to rebuild the city and to strive for a permanent *comédie*. Two devastating earthquakes (in 1751 and 1770) destroyed most of the city, including 100 houses built in 1751 and 690 houses newly constructed by 1770. Nevertheless, the rebuilding continued, and by the latter half of the 1780s, there were almost 900 houses in Port-au-Prince. One of the city's most impressive accomplishments during this period appears to have been the completion of a road and a regular transport service that connected Port-au-Prince to Cap Français.[20]

Port-au-Prince opened its first theatre in 1762, almost two decades after the first theatre was established in Cap Français, and it seems to have been a rather modest attempt. Nevertheless, due to the rapid growth of the city, and the public's unrelenting desire for a suitable theatre, government officials and businessmen attempted continuously to improve the situation. In the late 1760s, a prominent engineer, M. de Saint-Rome, financed the building of a larger theatre measuring 72 feet long. However, the earthquake of 1770 seriously damaged the theatre as well as much of the city. Theatres were rebuilt in 1775 and in 1776,[21] but it was not until 1778 that the city's desire for a suitable theatre came to fruition. The two heads of state entered into an agreement with François Mesplès, a prominent businessman, to build a "grand home for the Port-au-Prince Comédie."[22] The seating capacity of the Mesplès theatre was 750, consisting of "nine boxes, each with seven seats; the orchestra; boxes for the governor and the intendant; five enclosed loges; two balconies; and twenty-one boxes of which fifteen were reserved for blacks and mulattos of both sexes."[23] The *Paradis pour les gens de couleur* was located on each side of the auditorium, second tier, parallel to the stage and the parterre, rather than in the rear balcony as was the case in the Cap Français and Saint-Pierre theatres. Nevertheless, the facility was pretty impressive, particularly for an audience of approximately 2,200 persons (1,800 whites and 400 *affranchis*) that were granted admission to the theatre (see figure 14).

Although Mesplès boasted of building "a very beautiful theatre," an anonymous theatre patron complained that the auditorium was "small, badly constructed, disagreeable, not favorable for the actors, and very uncomfortable for the public."[24] According to numerous newspaper notices and other eyewitness accounts, however, the inauguration of the facility

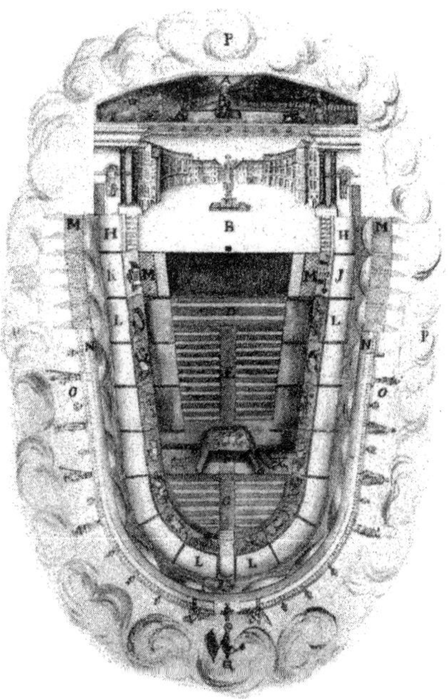

TABLEAU D'INDICATION pour l'interieur de LA SALLE

A. *Frontispice au dessus du rideau*
B. *Théâtre et décoration*
C. *Orchestre*
D. *Place séparée pour messieurs les Officiers de la garnison*
E. *Parterre garni de bancs*
F. *Loge de Messieurs les Officiers de la Juridiction*
G. *Amphithéâtre garni de bancs*
H. *Gradins adoptés pour Mrs. Du Conseil*
J. *Loge pour les généraux*
K. *Loge pour les Intendants*
L. *Loges indistinctes autour de la Salle*
M. *Loges grilles haut et bas*
N. *Deuxième rang de loges pour les gens de couleur*
O. *Bordure autour de la voûte*
P. *Voûte peinte en nuage*
Q. *Renommée au fond de la voûte en face du Théâtre*

JEAN FOUCHARD, *LE THÉÂTRE À SAINT-DOMINGUE*. PORT-AU-PRINCE, HAITI: IMPRIMERIE DE L'ÉTAT, 1955

FIGURE 14. *Port-au-Prince Theatre, plan and legend of the auditorium*

marked the beginning of the longest and most brilliant period of theatre in Port-au-Prince.[25] As in Cap Français, the public seemed to prefer musical theatre to spoken drama, for over 115 operas, as compared to 85 plays, premiered at the Mesplès theatre. There were more than 150 reprises (approximately 125 operas and 30 plays) during this period. The Mesplès theatre continued to produce a string of successes up until 1791, when the building went up in flames during the devastating period that marked the beginning of the end of French colonial rule in Saint-Domingue.

Guadeloupe

Successful theatres on a smaller scale were built in Guadeloupe and in the outer regions of Saint-Domingue. Documentation of theatre activities in Guadeloupe is rather scarce. By the early 1780s, the colony could boast of two theatres, both in bustling seaport cities: Pointe-à-Pitre, on the northern coast, and Basse-Terre, on the southern coast. Like Martinique and Saint-Domingue, the island was plagued with hurricanes and fires. Nevertheless, according to eyewitness accounts of visitors to the island, both cities maintained theatres throughout the century.[26]

Smaller Theatres in Saint-Domingue

In Saint-Domingue, theatres sprung up in the cities of Jéremie, Petit-Goave, Jacmel, Léogane, and Les Cayes (all located on the southern peninsula of the island), and in Saint-Marc on the western coast, halfway between Cap Français and Port-au-Prince. With a few exceptions, theatre activity in Jéremie, Petit-Goave, and Jacmel seems to have occurred in private homes and consisted primarily of visiting troupes. While there are only rare instances of information on specific performances, it does appear that these fairly remote sections of the peninsula enjoyed a vibrant theatre for more than a decade (1775–1790).

Les Cayes obtained authorization in 1765 to open its theatre,[27] and, despite some difficulties and numerous changes in directorship, continued to produce operas throughout the subject period. During their most successful period (1784–1785), nine operas and two plays premiered. In 1788, the first building constructed specifically for theatre productions was completed. The auditorium measured 118 feet long and 64 feet wide with two tiers of seven loges on each side. There was, of course, a *Paradis pour les gens de couleur*.

The first period of theatre in Léogane (1762–1772) consisted primarily of performers from the Port-au-Prince Comédie who performed in homes of the planter elite and rich merchants or in halls rented specifically for such occasions. Despite several efforts to establish a permanent theatre during this decade, citizens of Léogane had no facility built specifically for theatre performances and, thus, continued to welcome the Port-au-Prince performers for the next fourteen years.

It was in Léogane, however, that we encounter one of the most interesting and boldest examples of the enterprising capabilities of free colored people. By the early 1780s, a *quarteron* businessman, known only by one name, Labbé, had acquired considerable wealth. In 1786, fourteen years after the closing of the last theatre in Léogane, Labbé organized a theatre group composed of singers, musicians, and other artists from various cities in Saint-Domingue.[28] At his sole expense, Labbé procured a hall of 400 seats, 70 of which were in the usual gallery allocated for colored people. As was customary throughout the colonies, a military contingent, commanded by a white officer (in this case, a brigadier), was assigned to the Comédie. Under his direct command were three *maréchaussées* (a branch of the local police responsible for enforcing and maintaining public safety) and Labbé, a sergeant in the militia who headed the contingent of militia (ten *affranchis*). Labbé's post was located below the box reserved for the intendant. Although both whites and free coloreds served in the *maréchaussée*, local gazettes and Moreau are very specific in stating that Labbé was only in command of the contingent of militia (consisting solely of free coloreds). Therefore, it is reasonable to assume that the three *maréchaussées* were white men under the direction of a white commander (as was Labbé also).

It is interesting to note that whereas modern Antilles historians refer to Labbé as "*Monsieur* Labbé," he is known in archival sources as "*le nommé* Labbé." Despite his accumulated wealth and the enormous success of his theatre, Labbé was never accorded the title of "Monsieur" but still referred to as "*le nommé* Labbé." How ironic that a free colored man could acquire such wealth, finance a theatre, own several slaves, but still be tagged with a title reflecting the status of enslavement. Labbé relinquished the enterprise two years later (1788), sold everything, and disappeared from all theatre activities. The reasons for such abrupt departure from a flourishing business remain a mystery. Perhaps such a bold enterprise by a colored man was just a trifle more than colonial authorities could tolerate.

In Saint-Marc, we encounter another unique event. In 1770, two women codirected the Comédie: Madame Francheville, a fashion designer, and Mademoiselle Marthe, an actress.[29] Unfortunately, this historic venture by two women lasted only a short time. An earthquake interrupted the premiere;[30] a panic-stricken public fled the theatre and refused to attend future performances in the building. Two years later, the city inaugurated a newly constructed theatre, under new management, at a different site, and with a seating capacity of 500 that included a section for colored people "without distinction of nuances"[31]—referring to skin color. In other words, the seating of colored people was not to be determined by how light or how dark one's skin was. Saint-Marc, located on the western coast, was part of the frontier society. Thus, the seating arrangement appears to have been a reflection of the makeup and customs of that society, a system where mixed-race families thrived, and racial labels rarely were hurled at them—a stark departure from any *Paradis* in other theatres.

From this point on, the Saint-Marc Comédie seems to have been fairly successful, despite several changes in directors and financial backers.

The Audience

The composition and seating of spectators in all theatres adhered strictly to the established social hierarchy. The best seats in the house were always reserved for representatives of the king: the governor and the intendant. Each official had one loge (six to eight seats) on the first tier (the governor on the right side of the theatre and the intendant on the left). On the same tier, a few boxes were allocated to top officials under the two heads of state—the military alongside the governor (on the right) and administrators with the intendant (on the left). Members of the judiciary usually had loges on both sides, reflecting their role as impartial representatives of the court. Generally, these boxes were enclosed structures for maximum privacy and security. The remaining boxes on the first tier, as well as most of those on the second tier, were rented on an annual basis to aristocrats of colonial society (rich *colons*, merchants, and other businessmen).

As indicated above, the vast majority of attendees gathered on the parterre. Spectators in this area generally were a mixture of whites with varying backgrounds. The parterre was a favorite venue for musicians, painters, sculptors, and architects to mingle, to discuss their trade, and to criticize their competitors. The parterre was also one of the favorite meeting places for marines, soldiers, and other members of the military from well-to-do families who would gather here to boast of their latest exploits. Then, there were those rowdy young men, sons of the elite spoiled by the endless doting of their parents, who "talked too loud and made indecent remarks."[32] These groups were in stark contrast to the white creole women, whose presence was said to transform the parterre into "a garden filled with perfumed roses."[33] This was also in stark contrast to usage in France, where only men were admitted in the parterre. Further, the Parisian parterre was noted for jostling crowds, loud arguments between spectators, and other rowdy behavior, for which it became known as "the pit" or even "hell."[34] In the colonies, however, what seems to have given married women in the parterre such a tantalizing aura is that they were never accompanied by their husbands, but entered on the arm of a friend, for to go to the theatre with one's spouse was considered "bad taste."[35] Besides, it seems that these women "changed this accessory [a husband] so easily, . . . by marrying frequently, up to ten times."[36]

Located far above the lively parterre was the *Paradis pour les gens de couleur*, the section reserved for a "select portion" of *affranchis* from the upper level of the colored hierarchy. As indicated above, they were illegitimate children of former owners (rich white planters), or descendants of such unions; and, as legitimate heirs of the father's estate, they became part of the powerful and rich planter elite (the colonial aristocracy). In the South Province, however, many of these free coloreds were legitimate children of mixed-race marriages, due to customs dating back to the first settlements as indicated in the previous chapter. More significant for the present study, however, is that from all outward appearances, they seemed to have immersed themselves in French culture. Not only did such an arrangement ensure absolute respect for the social hierarchy; it also underscored the French view of the performing arts as a positive motivating influence on the individual.

This arrangement also engendered hostilities within the black and colored sectors—particularly in Cap Français, where free colored people were first allowed in the theatre in 1766, two years after it was opened to the public. Seats in the *Paradis pour les gens de couleur* were reserved for mulattos only (female and male children of white men and black women). In June 1775, *négresses libres*[37] were admitted into the theatre in order to be with their daughters. Such black women were "special friends" (concubines) of very influential white men, as well as mothers of young women—many of whom, for the most part, were also mistresses of rich whites. According to Moreau de Saint-Méry, the mothers chose him to draw up their request for entry and to be seated near their daughters.[38] However, their presence at the theatre annoyed free colored women, who objected to free black women being in the same box, and threatened to yield all seats to them if such arrangements continued. Authorities finally solved the problem by placing the two classes in separate boxes. When the Comédie was enlarged in

1784, the *Paradis pour les gens de couleur* consisted of seven boxes for free colored women and three boxes for free black women. While such allotted seating arrangements ensured respect for the social hierarchy, it also illustrated very clearly two major problems still confronting authorities: the French male's insatiable fascination with black and colored women, and the lengths to which they would go in order to please them.

Repertoire

During the subject period, more than 400 operas premiered in the colonies—all composed by whites (French and creole). Of this number, at least 101 works (musical and spoken dramas) included some type(s) of African presence (see appendix 7). These include

- *affranchis* and the enslaved performing as soloists in both instrumental and vocal pieces;
- *divertissements* in which slaves performed French court dances and a variety of "proper" songs (French *airs* and *ariettes*)—all of which glorified the power of France through their texts, movements, and gestures;
- insertion of dances (all composed by whites) based on African culture at the end of an opera or play and at the end of the program;
- entrepreneurial theatre ownership by a free colored person;
- *créole* parodies: operas based on a preexisting French opera or play, drawing on the themes and characters of that work, but incorporating *créole* songs and dances instead of the original pieces;
- operas written in *créole* by local composers; and
- operas based on colonial lifestyles of both *affranchis* and the enslaved.

Such productions were a reflection of the times—or, more precisely, a means of escape for everyone. Whites became increasingly anxious as the number of slave revolts and runaways continued to mount. Government officials struggled to quell these tumultuous events, as well as a myriad of other problems confronting them on a daily basis. Thus, the musical theatre assumed a very significant position in the cultural political campaign, not only by its rules of admittance and seating arrangements, but also by the types of operas presented. The repertoire reflects the strong influence of the *philosophes*, as was also the case in France during the second half of the eighteenth century. Primarily, themes revolved around the virtues of innocent love and the pursuit of pleasure. The contrast was drawn between the innocence and serenity of the natural state—a world void of the establishment and abuses of political societies—versus the misery, corruption, and other intricacies of court and city existence. Therefore, most of the repertoire consisted of elements of the *pastorale*. Such themes focused on peace, tranquility, virtuous love, and the pursuit of pleasure, the opposite of what was actually occurring in the colonies (the insatiable attraction of the public to rowdy cabarets and gambling, and the increasing non-virtuous behavior of French men toward black and colored women). Thus, absent from these works were any themes based on France's relentless quest for overseas domination. There were no long, five-act operas, no prologues and *divertissements* glorifying the power of the monarchy, and no mythological deities meddling in the affairs of mortals, or resolutions accomplished by these immortals as they descended from the skies in huge chariots to put things in order (in the name of the king). There were no references to any of the major contemporary problems, such as the tyranny, exploitation, greed, and embezzlement by a string of heads of state, seeds of discontent within the slave population (numerous runaways, revolts, and rebellions), and the growing popularity of cabarets (brawls, noisy crowds, and other disturbances).

Instead, the settings generally included pleasant landscapes, such as beautiful gardens, the seacoast, and peaceful woods. A program generally consisted of one-act operas, with two or three being performed on a given night and coupled with a play, or a two- or three-act opera preceded by a play, primarily by Molière or Voltaire.[39] *Symphonies* were performed between pieces or acts and at the conclusion of the program. The mood was gay, light, and serene, with very few works requiring a long attention span. Thus, no colonial theatre produced any *tragédies lyriques* by the founder of French national opera, Jean-Baptiste Lully, or any works in this genre by his successors. Performance records reveal that colonial society preferred shorter and simpler operas, such as the *opéra-comique*, *opéra-bouffon*, *ballet-héroïque*, *pastorale*, and *pastorale-héroïque.* Only on rare occasions were three- or four-act operas produced, and these were works based on fairy tales that transported audiences to a world of fantasy and make-believe—a world in which they could more easily find an escape from reality.

A Typical Evening at the Opera

A performance generally would start at 6:00 P.M. or, less frequently, at 5:00 P.M. if the program was rather long. The evening commenced with a serious opera or play, generally followed by another opera, shorter and lighter in nature. Instrumental music and dances were inserted between acts of an opera or a play, between the two pieces, and also at the conclusion of the program. Further, officials agreed, what could be more delightful and pleasurable than to conclude the program with the refined and culturally uplifting artistry of a French *symphonie* and dance! This format became a standard, for officials wanted the audience to leave the theatre in a very contented mood. A patron underscored such reasoning in a critique of the production of a serious five-act drama, *Jenneval, ou le Barnewelt français*, followed by a light opera, *Les Vendanges de Puteaux, ou le double déguisement*:

> The moral effect that results from the first of these two pieces has enjoyed commendations from the public in all theatres where it has been given; but the sad impressions that it leaves in the hearts of spectators beg to be dispelled by a second piece in which gaiety smoothes the brows of spectators and leads them from the painful course through which their attention has just traveled in the first piece. It is for these reasons that Mlle. Martha [beneficiary] chose the opera, *Les Vendanges de Puteaux*, for the lightest and most pleasing gaiety.[40]

A superb buffet with all types of *hors d'oeuvres*, main dishes, desserts, chocolates, and beverages generally followed the performance. After dinner there were more sumptuous activities. On special occasions, such as a benefit performance, a huge fireworks display was given in front of the theatre. Models for such events were provided by Italian troupes (in Paris), which as early as the last decade of the seventeenth century had used firework displays at the Bourgogne Theatre in order to stimulate attendance. However, in the eighteenth century, it seems that these events were held inside the theatre. In a comprehensive study on the Italian Theatre in Paris, Brenner informs us that, according to theatre records, "a metal shield or some contrivance was brought out upon the stage and the fireworks were set off in it."[41] Further, Brenner suggests, such precautions apparently were effective, "for no fire is ever reported." In colonial theatres, however, the danger of fires from such events loomed much larger than in Paris, due to the hot and humid climate, poor ventilation, the small size of theatres, and the duration of such events (frequently up to two hours).

At the conclusion of fireworks, the audience would reenter the theatre for a light one-act opera or an *intermède*.[42] To top off the evening, the festivities culminated with a *grand bal* that lasted until the wee hours of the morning, especially when the performance was a benefit for the director or one of the performers, closely following a tradition established in France. However, in Paris, there were also "standard benefit evenings" solely for the Opéra and, on other occasions, for singers and dancers.[43] Further, benefits were given as rewards for long service (usually on the eve of retirement), as charity for a widow(er) and family of a singer, for persons connected with the theatre who died in service, and as charity for other worthy causes, such as aid to the poor during harsh winters. In such cases, a portion of the proceeds went to the beneficiary, while the theatre kept a certain amount to cover basic expenses. In the colonies, benefits were given more frequently and, primarily, on an individual basis for leading singers, musicians, dancers, and the director. The beneficiary was responsible for all preparations (choice of operas or plays to be performed, actors, singers, costumes, décor, etc.). Receipts for the performance were divided between the theatre and the beneficiary, and all receipts for the *grand bal* were usually handed over to the beneficiary.

We can now see that music became an essential ingredient in defining the national character and culture of the French colonial empire, for it was through the musical theatre that many free colored people attempted to shed the shackles of enslavement status. For colonial authorities, this so-called "process of refinement"—a phrase used ad nauseam by defenders of the system—played a significant role in the monarchy's cultural political campaign. It is against this backdrop that the glowing reputations of young black musicians, the incredible singing careers of two colored sisters, the tireless determination of their white benefactors, and the daring innovations of a colored entrepreneur unfolded. Furthermore, these black and colored artists, despite being born in, living in, and held hostage in a society built on human bondage (of them and/or their ancestors), were able to excel on the hallowed stages of concerts and theatre (musical and spoken). However, they did, and we will now explore how this was accomplished, and to what heights these struggling artists actually reached.

CHAPTER 4

INTRODUCING THE STARS

As discussed above, slaves were very useful in strengthening the economy of colonial society by filling various occupations. They were also well prepared for performing in concerts and operas, for they had been thoroughly trained in the *galant* dances of the French court and had learned a variety of musical techniques from missionaries and other artists imported from France. Many were also trained musicians, which heightened their value socially as well as economically. In fact, musical events were so important for colonial aristocrats that displaying one's slaves who could perform well on the violin or other European instruments enhanced considerably the prestige of the slave owner's house. According to colonial authorities, granting permission for slaves to perform in concerts and operas helped to maintain the peace because, they deemed, it guaranteed the enslaved would not entertain unruly thoughts of escape or revolt against their owners. Although most performers were white artists trained in the colonies or imported from Paris, authorities felt that allowing a few slaves to participate in these productions also made it easier for authorities to reinforce absolute respect for the social hierarchy, because all songs and dances glorified the power of France through texts, movements, and gestures. This, of course, promoted French culture because they performed only French music, French songs, and French dances. Therefore, inevitably, with the support of several colonists, a few young black musicians were able to play in opera and concert orchestras as early as the 1760s.

Entrée 1: The Young Blacks

A perusal of the first five years of newspaper publications in the colonies reveals that several young slaves were very talented musicians. In almost every issue, there are sections in which *colons* and other slave owners submitted notices of business and personal goods for sale, or of rewards for runaway slaves. In both cases, the owner provides explicit descriptions of slaves, e.g., height, color, age, scars (particularly those inflicted during the initial branding stage by the new slave owner or resulting from punishment), and type(s) of work/trades in which they were experienced. For those slaves who were musically talented, the instrument they played and the extent of their proficiency were clearly pointed out in order to increase their value. The preferred instrument was, by far, the violin. However, the ads also reflect that several slaves were well trained on the trumpet and the horn.[1]

Noteworthy among the first known core of black musicians were three slaves (ages fourteen, fifteen, and seventeen) who played the violin, read music on all clefs, and had performed in several opera productions. Their owner, preparing to return to France, put them up for sale in February 1764, marketing them as a trio of extremely talented violinists. In his advertisement, he stated that the three blacks had played in the opera orchestra in Cap Français for at least two years and would lose their value if separated. Therefore, he offered them for sale as a unit.[2]

A few musicians attained prominence as featured soloists. Three names stand out: *le nommé* Rivière, *le nommé* Joseph, and *le nommé* Julien. All were violinists who performed between acts of operas or plays, or at the end of the program.[3] The first mention of Rivière occurred in December 7, 1779 (*Supplément aux Affiches Américaines*) as a soloist at the Port-au-Prince Comédie. It seems that Rivière also played the mandolin, and two years after his 1779 performance, he was featured in a concerto for mandolin and guitar.[4] Joseph performed with the Cap Français Comédie for at least three years in the 1780s. Julien was a featured soloist in Cap Français in 1781, spent a couple of years in France, and then returned to Saint-Domingue. In 1783 he was performing at the Port-au-Prince Comédie. However, after he returned to the colony, the gazettes no longer referred to him as *le nommé* Julien, but as Julien, *le jeune griffe* ("the young half-breed"), reflecting his elevation to a slightly higher step on the social ladder, probably due to a combination of personal traits: mixed blood and the newly acquired free status as a result of that very prestigious experience of a sojourn in Paris.[5] Nevertheless, regardless of how well and under what circumstances these musicians were trained and performed, the demeaning titles of slave status always accompanied both *affranchis* and the enslaved. Curiously, in Moreau de Saint-Méry's glowing description of Saint-Domingue during its glory years of the 1780s, there is no mention of slave musicians. It seems that for this author of several thousand pages devoted to lifestyles, laws, and other conditions in his adopted home, these musicians were not important and, therefore, did not exist.

Nevertheless, we know that these musicians contributed significantly to colonial opera, for their performances are well documented in several gazettes—but always with that degrading tag of slave status. Since there are no critiques of their performances—just listings of their names and pieces performed—we must look at other ways to determine the quality of their performances and the level of esteem they acquired.

Although it does not appear that these musicians were held in high esteem by the colonial elite, this was certainly not the case among other musicians, artists, and patrons of the theatre. In fact, the one thing that all three musicians had in common is that they were featured soloists in benefits for some of the most important figures in colonial opera. As noted in the previous chapter, benefits were very lavish affairs that paid tribute to the director, a singer, or other performers. The beneficiary was responsible for all preparations (choice of operas or plays, actors, singers, costumes, décor, etc.). This was the beneficiary's time to really shine, i.e., to give their best performance, to produce the best musical and scenic displays, and to select the best performers. Therefore, we can certainly conclude that it was the beneficiaries—to whom the Comédie paid special tribute—that specifically chose Rivière, Joseph, and Julien to perform in these special events.

The first notice of a slave musician performing as the featured soloist with an opera orchestra appeared on December 7, 1779. The *Supplément aux Affiches Américaines* announced that the Port-au-Prince Comédie would present two short operas and a violin concerto by the orchestra with *le nommé* Rivière as the featured soloist.[6] The concerto was based on an *ariette* taken from an opera, *Le Tableau parlant* (The Speaking Picture).[7] The event was arranged by Mr. Depoix (beneficiary), consistently lauded as a "brilliant" actor and singer who "always searched for ways to please the public [and] spared nothing for decorations."[8] In 1781 Depoix departed for Saint-Marc, where he performed for about a year and received similar praise. He returned to Port-au-Prince, continued a very successful career, and in 1784 was appointed codirector of the Port-au-Prince Comédie, a position he only held for a short time because he had previously made plans to move to France.[9]

Two luminaries selected Joseph as solo violinist in benefit performances. The first one, Mr. Durville, was an actor at the Cap Français Comédie. Throughout his long and successful career of eleven years (1776–1787), his name appears numerous times in the gazettes, where he was noted for excellent work in tragedies and hailed as one of the best interpreters of tragedies by Racine and Voltaire. Our second artist, Mr. Regnault, an actor, a singer, and a violoncellist, was active in the theatre from 1778 to 1791. During the first half of his career, he performed in Port-au-Prince and in Saint-Marc, and by the middle of the 1780s he seems to have settled in Cap Français, where he was appointed music director of the Comédie.

As a result of the supreme work and devotion of these two men, the Cap Français Comédie held several benefits for them. One of these events took place on Saturday, January 25, 1783, a very prime night for benefits in the 1780s. Durville, the beneficiary, chose Joseph, "a musician attached to the orchestra," to play several violin solos and a concerto with the orchestra.[10] It appears that Joseph remained with the orchestra for a few years, for on Saturday, February 11, 1786, he performed in another benefit. The beneficiary was Regnault; he selected Joseph to perform between the two operas performed that night.[11] Here again, Joseph was the star attraction, performing a violin concerto.

As indicated above, our third violinist performed in both theatres. The first mention of Julien appeared on November 20, 1781, in the *Affiches Américaines,* announcing that he would be one of the featured soloists in an upcoming benefit for Mr. Fontaine, director of the Cap Français Comédie. The program consisted of an opera and a play, which was held seven days later. Fontaine selected *Diable à quatre, ou la double metamorphose, opéra-comique*, in three acts, composed by François-Danican Philidor (1726–1795) on a libretto by Michel-Jean Sedaine (1719–1797). The second piece was *Janot, ou les battus payent l'amende*, a *comédie* written by Dorvigni that had been "very successful in Paris with more than 140 performances."[12] The director was also responsible for coordinating and presenting concerts. Although such events usually were presented alone (without an opera or play on the program), on this particular night, Mr. Fontaine did, indeed, present a full concert. During the *entr'acte*, the orchestra performed a concerto for violin "based on an *ariette* from *Le barbier de Séville*," the popular drama by Pierre Augustin Beaumarchais (1732–1799).[13] Julien was the soloist. The second orchestral offering was "a *divertissement* arranged by the director." The "concert" concluded with a concerto for violin and violoncello with Messrs Petit, violinist, and Charles, cellist.[14]

We hear of Julien almost two years later. It appears that he recently returned from France and is now in Port-au-Prince.[15] The Comédie gave a benefit for Mr. Petit, who had also left Cap Français, moved to Port-au-Prince, and was now first violinist in that orchestra. Mr. Petit selected one dramatic work, *Zémire et Azor*, a *comédie-ballet* in four acts, and one of the most popular operas produced in the colonies as well as in Paris.[16] Between the first and second acts, Petit was the soloist in a concerto for violin composed by Jarnowic, his former teacher.[17] After the third act, Petit and Julien played several duets. The program ended with a dance by Mr. Acquaire, a brilliant dancer, actor, and singer who later would become director of the Port-au-Prince Comédie.[18]

Two weeks later, Julien was performing again—and with Mr. Petit. This time, it was a benefit for Mr. Acquaire. Like Petit, Acquaire selected one dramatic work, *La Belle Arsène*, a *comédie-féerie* in four acts, which was performed numerous times in Paris and in the colonies.[19] Between acts 2 and 3, Julien and Petit again were the featured soloists in a concerto. The program concluded with a dance by "two young amateurs from this city" (students from a local dance school).

The multiple productions in which Julien performed pose some interesting points. First, all three benefits were held in honor of three of the most important figures in Saint-Domingue colonial theatre. Second, Julien always appeared on the same program with Petit, in both Cap Français and in Port-au-Prince. What was the relationship between the two violinists?

What were the circumstances surrounding Julien's training in France, with whom did Julien study, and what, if any, was the involvement of Petit in this sojourn? Curiously, there is no mention of Petit in the gazettes for almost a year (May 1782 to March 1783), during which time Julien was probably in France. Was Petit there also? We know that slave owners had to obtain permission from officials to take their slaves to France for training (or appoint the appropriate caretakers to accompany them). Further, according to French law, slavery was "not admissible" in France, and "jurisdictionally, once allowed into the country, slaves became free."[20] Therefore, it is certainly logical to conclude that Julien returned to Saint-Domingue as an *affranchi*, and hence the gazettes no longer attached that degrading slave-status tag "*le nommé*" to his name. However, the ruling powers could not let it go; they branded him as a "half-breed" (*griffe*).

Unfortunately, we can only speculate on the number of performances, tenure in the orchestra, and training of Julien and his two counterparts, Joseph and Rivière, because gazettes do not provide such information. However, we can certainly assume that all three were excellent violinists. Why else would some of the most prominent figures in colonial society select them—on multiple occasions—as primary soloists in special events? Further, it is quite interesting that in the hundreds of travel narratives of officials and other visitors to the islands that comment on lifestyles (including opera performances) in the colonies, performances by black musicians are rarely mentioned. These extremely talented musicians made significant contributions to colonial musical theatres; but it seems that to the upper levels of the established hierarchy, they were, in fact, invisible.

The same policy of "invisibility" also occurred in Martinique and Guadeloupe. Although newspapers for the two colonies during the subject period are rather scarce, modern research by French Antilles musicologists and historians indicate that while Parisian society frequently critiqued musicians performing in France, such analyses are conspicuously absent when it comes to black musicians in the Antilles. These scholars also suggest that slave musicians in the two colonies were equally talented as their counterparts in Paris. One scholar states:

> We associate the talent of musicians working in Paris with those in the Antilles, because they were from the same school. . . . [Like their Parisian counterparts, Antilles musicians] ornament their melodies with grace notes, syncopation, accents, and other rhythmic subtleties."[21]

Antilles musicians were main topics of discussion by "the refined, eclectic aristocratic society [in the Antilles]," particularly after observing performances by "the Juliens" at concerts and at lavish balls.[22] Rosemain further suggests that the contemporary crop of Antilles musicians was comparable to the talents of "a certain Julien," orchestra director, who "had known glory under Napoleon I," and was highly praised by Parisian society.

Accomplishments of musicians in all three colonies were exceedingly significant. Their presence in concert and opera orchestras as early as the 1760s helped to prepare the way for the debut of the first colored singer. Although these talented young men had no singing roles, the presence of blacks in these prestigious orchestras appears to have been accepted quite well by white audiences.

Entrée 2: Minette, Lise, and the Acquaires

The incredible singing careers of two *métive* sisters,[23] Minette and Lise, began almost seventeen years after the first performances by black musicians in opera orchestras. Unfortunately, information on the early childhood of the sisters is sorely lacking. We do know that the sisters lived in Port-au-Prince with their mother—a former slave who had gained her freedom upon the death of her owner, the father of the girls. According to Fouchard, she supported herself and the children on the meager returns she earned by setting up a booth where she sold flowers, scarves, soap, and a variety of trinkets.[24] It seems that Minette and Lise loved to sing while playing or working at their mother's booth, and everyone marveled at the clarity and charm of their young voices. When Minette was about thirteen years old and Lise eleven, their lives were changed forever. A white woman who lived near their mother's booth had heard the girls sing and was amazed at the incredible sounds flowing out of the mouths of these two frail little bodies. This woman, Madame Acquaire, asked the mother to send the girls to her for singing and diction lessons.

Madame Acquaire was a leading singer at the opera and also gave vocal and dancing lessons in her home. There seems to be no information on Madame's early life and career prior to performing in Port-au-Prince. Her husband also performed at the opera, primarily as a dancer and occasionally as a singer. Mr. Acquaire was born in Port-au-Prince and seems to have never left the island. From 1772 to 1787, he performed in four cities in Saint-Domingue (Léogane, Cap Français, Port-au-Prince, and Saint-Marc) and was appointed director of the Port-au-Prince Comédie in 1787. The Acquaires had leading roles in numerous operas and were greatly admired by audiences. Nevertheless, much of Mr. Acquaire's energies seem to have been consumed by the gambling tables. This obsession seems to have been an ongoing weakness in his otherwise long and successful career in the theatre. Mr. Acquaire's mother paid his gambling debts on several occasions; but in 1776, coming to his rescue again, she forewarned the public that she would no longer be responsible for any debts her son incurred in the future.[25]

After a few months of lessons, Mme Acquaire apparently decided that Minette was ready to be presented to the public. Although the Acquaires were very successful at the Comédie, they had to be quite aware of the huge risk they would be taking in sponsoring a colored singer for an appearance on the hallowed concert stage. However, the disastrous state of their personal finances, caused in part by Mr. Acquaire's gambling losses, seems to have been a major factor in their decision to undertake such a bold venture. The year was 1780. The directors of the Comédie had scheduled a special concert for Christmas Day. Six days prior to this, the newspaper announced "une jeune demoiselle [a young girl] will sing several grand ariettes and duos."[26] No one provided the identity of this "young girl." It was Minette, now fourteen years old.

As with the young black musicians, no critique of Minette's concert debut appeared in newspapers or in other types of eyewitness accounts. Although there is no mention in the gazettes of her performance, we can, logically, assume that Minette performed exceedingly well, for as we shall see, it is certain that Mme Acquire immediately began to prepare for more daring ventures. First, the primary item on her agenda was to train Minette for her opera debut. Second, the Madame also remained faithful and committed to training her other protégée, Lise. Opera in Saint-Domingue was on the threshold of a major historical breakthrough.

CHAPTER 5

BREAKING THROUGH THE BARRIER

Throughout the early stages of theatre development in Port-au-Prince, performances continued with some irregularity, primarily due to several changes in directorship. However, conditions changed dramatically under the stewardship of François Saint-Martin, an actor, singer, and entrepreneur. He was appointed director of the Port-au-Prince Comédie in 1777, a position he held until his death in June 1784. During this period, he also undertook directorship of theatres in Saint-Marc (1782–1784) and in Les Cayes (1783). In addition to discussing the bold innovations of Saint-Martin, it is also important to note the extent to which the repertoire of each theatre was influenced by views of the *philosophes*.

Saint-Martin is an important figure in the present study, for he played a major role in the careers of Minette and Lise. Under his directorship, the Port-au-Prince Comédie ventured boldly into an arena not seen anywhere in the world, not even in the grandest and most publicized theatres in the colonies (Cap Français and Saint-Pierre). Aided by the support and guidance of Saint-Martin and Mme Acquaire, the City of Port-au-Prince introduced the first colored singer to the world of opera.

Phase 1: Year of *La Débutante*

On February 13, 1781, the Port-au-Prince Comédie honored Mme Acquaire with a benefit. It was at this event that Mme Acquaire, with the full consent of Saint-Martin, chose to present Minette to the opera public—just seven weeks after Minette's concert debut.[1] The first work on the program was *Isabelle et Gertrude, ou les sylphes supposés*, a one-act opera that had been in the Paris repertoire since 1765 and a staple in colonial repertoires for the past fourteen years.[2] The opera was based on a poem by the great *philosophe* Voltaire, "Gertrude, ou l'éducation d'une fille" (1763). Isabelle, a naive fifteen-year-old girl, discovers the joys of virtuous love with Dorlis, a sensitive young man of twenty-one years. Gertrude, mother of Isabelle, objects to the union of the young couple because of Isabelle's age; she also plans to send Isabelle to a convent. Dupré, the scorned suitor of Gertrude, describes the mother as "a female *philosophe* . . . and a prude, although still a lovable woman, [who] speaks only of morals and virtue and has an aversion for all men" (scene 2). After seeing Gertrude and Dupré together in the garden, Isabelle asks her mother why she was meeting with Dupré. In a long, drawn-out scene, Gertrude lies to her daughter, telling her that the voice she heard as Dupré was not actually his, but that of one of the good genies "who borrows the organs of men and appears to us under a figure that is familiar to us, like that of a parent, or of a friend" (scene 10). The naive Isabelle, of course, believes her mother, and later, when Dorlis appears, Isabelle is frightened, then confused, because she does not know whether it is Dorlis or an apparition. He finally assures her that it is he, and not an apparition. After more secret meetings and wooing between the two couples, Gertrude finally submits to Dupré and both agree to the wedding of the young couple. In the last scene, we find a very happy Isabelle; but she is still confused about how their problems have been resolved. ("I do not understand any of this, but, like my mother, I also submit [to love].")

Minette made her debut in the role of Isabelle, alongside Mme Acquaire as Gertrude. Mme Acquaire's choice of *Isabelle et Gertrude* for the occasion was, indeed, very appropriate for several reasons. The plot, themes, characterizations, and settings reflect the deep influence of views of the *philosophe*s. With regard to the two main singers, the strong presence of Mme Acquaire as Gertrude, protector and supporter, must have been tremendously helpful to the aspiring young *débutante*. Further, the characterization of Isabelle (innocent, naive, and confused) was certainly suitable for a colored *débutante*, and one that white audiences could easily accept.

That blissful and idealistic view presented by *Isabelle et Gertrude*, however, was short-lived; for the next item on the program was *Thérèse et Jeannot*, *parodie créole* (creole parody). As indicated above, the creole patois implied slave status, and creole parodies in eighteenth-century French Antilles society generally adhered to a particular scheme. These were musical dramas created by a person born on the island, and were based on an existing opera or play. Creole texts, songs, and dances usually replaced original French versions. These works dramatized lifestyles in the French Antilles colonies—as seen, of course, in the eyes of the French—ranging from the authoritative, superior, and protective nature of the French to the inferior and "childlike" nature of black and colored populations. *Thérèse et Jeannot* was based on *Le Devin du village* (The Village Soothsayer), a one-act *intermède* composed by Rousseau, the *philosophe*.[3] All characters were played by whites *à visage noir*—that is, in blackface. Mme Acquaire had the role of Thérèse, and Mr. Acquaire that of Jeannot. At the conclusion of the parody, Mr. Acquaire performed a "creole dance" (*pas créole*). Although Mme Acquaire and Saint-Martin are to be lauded for taking the first steps in cracking the racial barrier in opera, it appears that they also deemed it necessary to leave the audience with a firm sense of superiority that, undoubtedly, was accomplished with the creole parody and dance. *Thérèse et Jeannot* and other creole parodies are thoroughly examined in the next chapter; for now, let us return to the program.

After the creole dance, everyone departed the theatre for a sumptuous dinner. However, the evening was not yet over. After dinner there was a spectacular fireworks display in front of the theatre. Then everyone reentered the theatre to see *Pygmalion, scène-lyrique*, a light, one-act work composed by Rousseau. A grand ball followed and, as was customary, no blacks or coloreds were allowed to attend, not even Minette, with applause undoubtedly still ringing in her ears. Besides, these balls lasted until the wee hours of the morning, and *affranchis* were under a 9:00 P.M. curfew!

Conspicuously absent in gazettes and essays on the theatre is any critique or other mention of the debut. Nevertheless, we can certainly assume that Minette was accepted very well by the audience, for within the next three weeks, she repeated her role in *Isabelle et Gertrude* and appeared in two more operas, *Silvain*, and *Le Maître en droit, ou le tuteur dupé*, both of which had been performed numerous times in Paris.[4] In addition, two months after her opera debut, Minette was back at the Concert Spirituel, where she sang two *ariettes* at an Easter concert. Thus, it appears that within the walls of the theatre and the concert hall, artistry and talent were the conquerors and racial prejudice the loser.

During the remaining eight months of the year (May through December), Minette's repertoire reflects an astounding number and variety of operas. She sang in eleven different operas, with subject matter ranging from the simple pastoral to the rather complex supernatural.[5] She also appeared in one play.[6] French and colonial audiences expected opera singers to be good interpreters of character, musically and textually. In the colonies, expectations were taken to a much higher degree, for it was customary for opera singers to assume acting roles in plays also. Such dual artistry, when performed well, could enhance their reputation considerably. Thus, in contemporary documents, these artists are generally referred to as "actrices" or "acteurs," regardless of the genre in which they were performing.

Equally remarkable is the manner in which Mme Acquaire guided Minette through a careful selection of roles, appropriate not only for her young voice, but also as an appeal to the public for acceptance on the basis of artistry and talent. Two weeks after the Easter concert, Minette again sang alongside Mme Acquaire in a one-act opera, *On n'avise jamais de tout* ("You can't think of everything"). Minette's role was similar to that in *Isabelle et Gertrude*: an innocent young girl (Lise) in love with a sensitive young man (Dorval). However, *On n'avise jamais de tout* includes more complex obstacles to the union of the young innocents. The primary impediments are Mr. Tué, Lise's guardian, who conspires to marry the girl for her money, and Marguerite (Mme Acquaire), the governess who works for Tué and keeps Lise hidden from Dorval. Through a series of incidents reflecting Dorval's honorable intentions and noble character versus Tué's despicable lust for wealth, the *Commissaire* forces Tué to consent to the young couple's marriage. Thus, greed, denounced by the *philosophe*s as one of the primary ills of contemporary society, succumbs to virtuous love and honor.

The next three productions in which Minette appeared (June 5 through September 11) cast her in a completely different type of opera. We now cross over into the world of the fairy tale with all its enchantments, spectacular transformations (characters and scenes), magic articles, and the supernatural, e.g., evil fairies versus good fairies. The first of these, *Zémire et Azor*, was based on the beauty-and-the-beast tale. Minette had a minor but important role as one of Zémire's sisters, again alongside Mme Acquaire as Zémire. An evil fairy has put a curse of an extremely terrifying ugliness on Azor—heretofore, a handsome Persian prince. When Zémire first meets Azor, she is quite frightened by the sight of him. Azor tries to calm her fears and then starts to woo her. Zémire is surprised at the "charming language" pouring from the mouth of "this horrible figure" (III, 5). When Zémire finally recognizes that Azor is a "very noble person," she consents to abandon her father (Sander) and her two sisters (Fatmé and Lisbé) and to remain with Azor. Thus, with such proof of Zémire's unconditional love for him, the evil fairy's spell is broken. Azor regains his handsome features, Zémire is reunited with her family, and all celebrate the union of Zémire and Azor through the power of love. *Zémire et Azor* is truly a journey into fantasy land. There are elaborate scene transformations (from the magnificent palace of Azor to the simple country house of Sander, and then to Azor's palatial gardens). No less spectacular is the mode of transportation Azor provides for Sander's return home (a huge cloud). Azor tests Zémire's promise of love by giving her a magic ring that she could use to escape from him and return to her family. The opera provided colonial audiences with quite an elaborate escape from reality.

The next two performances also featured "fairy-tale" works, and again we encounter the influence of the great *philosophe*. The first of these, *La Belle Arsène*, was based on a poem by Voltaire, "La Begueule" (1772). In the performance on August 14, Mme Acquaire had the primary role (Arsène) and Minette was Mirsis, a minor nature goddess. Four weeks later (September 11), the Comédie held a benefit for Mr. Acquaire. The first item on the program was *La Fée Urgèle, ou ce qui plait les dames* ("Urgèle the fairy, or, what do women want"), drawn from Voltaire's poem "Ce qui plait les dames" (1763). Mme Acquaire was the leading lady (Marton), and Minette undertook the role of Robinette, confidant of Marton. After the opera concluded, Mr. Acquaire and Minette performed an *allemande*, a court dance.

The benefit concluded with *Pygmalion*, composed by Rousseau, which, again, presented Minette in a different view—not as a singer, but as an actress. Pygmalion, a sculptor, falls hopelessly in love with his statue (Galathée), whom he has positioned on a pedestal. He begs Venus, goddess of love and beauty, to bring her to life, and his wish is granted. Galathée (Minette) starts to move and then descends from the pedestal. Pygmalion, speechless, kneels at her feet. Galathée makes a few steps, touches a block of marble then herself repeatedly. During each movement, she utters a few words ("I," "It is I," or "It is no longer myself . . ."). She approaches Pygmalion and places her hand on his shoulder. He recoils, then takes her hand and kisses it. Sighing, she repeats, "Ah! Still I." Pygmalion then vows to live only for her. The decision to end the program with *Pygmalion* was, indeed, a wise one, for the work was a fitting conclusion of an evening designed to transport the audience to a world of fantasy and bliss aided by supernatural beings.

Protector and protégée appeared together onstage in all three fairy-tale operas. Further, we know that by the time Minette appeared in *La Belle Arsène*—six months after her opera debut—Mme Acquaire's careful planning and guidance had garnered some very positive results, for, according to a critic, "*la jeune personne* [has] already played several roles to the satisfaction of the public."[7]

As further evidence of Minette's success, the Comédie held a benefit for her in October. It seems that Mme Acquaire and Saint-Martin decided it was now time to give Minette the lead role in a large-scale opera. The work chosen for this event was *L'Amoureux de quinze ans, ou le double fête* ("The fifteen-year old lover, or the double fête").[8] Minette's character, Lindor, is a fifteen-year-old boy in love with Hélène (Mme Acquaire), the beautiful eighteen-year-old daughter of the Baron. While we still witness in this work the innocence of youth similar to that in operas mentioned above, *L'Amoureux de quinze ans* also focuses on the impatience of youth and the "good father" image (*le bon père*) so prevalent in French society. Lindor goes through a series of emotions—impatience as he attempts to convince his father, the Marquis, of his maturity despite his young age ("Oh, how cruel it is to be only fifteen years old"); sadness as he laments over his love for and desire to marry Hélène; and hurt when he learns of the intent of Hélène's father to send her to a convent. The two fathers get together and compliment themselves and each other on what "good fathers" they have been—nourishing, protecting, and guiding their children. They agree that the *divertissement* Hélène has planned should be a double fête because the festivities are for both of them. However, as the festivities progress with lots of dances and songs about love, the good fathers soon realize they have ignored the true feelings of their children. Lindor's father regrets having dismissed his son's deep feelings for Hélène, and the Baron finally accepts the fact that Hélène loves Lindor and does not want to go to the convent. Being such good fathers, the two men finally grant permission for the young couple to be married. Reactions to this opera were very favorable, for the "good father" image had been transferred to the colonies. In this society, however, the *colon* was seen as the ultimate *bon père*—caretaker and protector of his slaves and colored descendants (*affranchis*).

Three weeks later, Minette was the leading lady in *Toinon et Toinette*, and a month after that she had a lead role in *Sara, ou la fermière écossaise*. Her debutante year concluded with two masterful performances in large-scale spectacular operas: a repeat of her role in *La Fée Urgèle* (with Mme Acquaire) and a new role in the premiere of *Le Jugement de Midas*.[9] The latter work represents a departure from the pastoral and fairy-tale subject matter so prevalent in colonial theatre. Instead, it reflects the continuous debates of the century regarding the merits of contemporary versus traditional compositional styles. The opera was based on a tale from Greek mythology in which Apollo, god of the sun, music, and poetry, and Pan, god of woods and fields, dispute the merits of the other's musical preferences. Midas, king of Phrygia, was the arbiter of their dispute. Grétry and D'Hêle, however, chose to modernize the plot by replacing some of the deities with simple, everyday characters. Midas is a bailiff and Pan a butcher. Apollo, disguised as a shepherd, describes the music of his rivals as being similar to that of a *coucou* (cuckoo) and an *hibou* (owl) and compares it to his own, which, he maintains, is similar to a *rossignol* (nightingale). The love theme must be present, however, as in all French operas of the period. Thus, Apollo, always the consummate lover, first woos Lise (Mme Acquaire) and then, in the next scene, Chloé (Minette). In the meantime, Midas, a proponent of the old style, rules that the voices of the cuckoo and the owl are superior to that of the nightingale. Because of this lie and deception, Midas's ears are then enlarged to the size of those of a donkey. Mercury, messenger of the Olympian gods, enters with Apollo, who then reveals himself. Midas asks that his ears be diminished, but the gods refuse, saying that he must serve as an example to "false connoisseurs." According to the Parisian audience, the author, a proponent of the contemporary style, "actually had ascribed the donkey ears to friends of Rameau," patrons of the old style.[10]

Phase 2: The Sisters, 1782–1785

During the next four years, Minette continued to develop her craft under the guidance of Mme Acquaire. She expanded her repertoire with lead roles in thirteen operas and in two plays.[11] When she was not performing in an opera or a play, she sang one or several *ariettes* between acts of a play or between pieces (usually a play followed by an opera). She also performed in Christmas and Easter concerts, where she would sing at least two *ariettes* and then a duo with Saint-Martin. In addition, these concerts usually concluded with a "superb trio" featuring Minette, Saint-Martin, and Mr. Durand, "*pensionnaire* of the King and the Académie Royale de Musique."[12]

We also see other evidence of Minette's acceptance by the public, for the Comédie held four benefits for her during this phase.[13] The program of the first benefit consisted of one work, a repeat performance of *Zémire et Azor*. However, instead of the minor role as Zémire's sister in the 1781 production, Minette now had the lead role, Zémire. For the second benefit, she was complimented as one "always anxious to earn the favor of the public." According to the critic, this was reflected in the choice of *L'Infante de Zamora*, *opéra féerie*, a work "approved for its good taste [instead of] one of those ephemeral productions that have corrupted and degraded our lyric stage for some time by focusing on day-to-day events of private society."[14] It is evident the writer is a proponent of traditional French opera, for he appears to be unimpressed with works that were infused with social commentary, bourgeois morality, and other Enlightenment ideals espoused so eloquently by the *philosophes*. Thus, our critic is more comfortable in the world of fantasy and make-believe—a world in which he can more easily find an escape from reality.

Curiously, however, three weeks later Minette performed in *Les Raccoleurs*, a far departure from the usual works of "good taste" or bourgeois morality.[15] This opera was a *poissard* work, a genre that portrayed a very low class of people notorious for their foul language and gross manners. Characters were drawn from day-to-day life at the fish market (haranguing fishwives, vendors, peddlers, innkeepers, etc.). The event was a benefit for Mme Acquaire. However, the Madame did not appear in this opera, and we have to wonder why she selected such a work for Minette. Fouchard maintains that "even though the *poissard* style deviated from Minette's particular tastes," she agreed to accept the role only to please Mme Acquaire.[16] Gracious as this may sound, it is pure conjecture by Fouchard, for Minette undoubtedly was in no position to pick and choose. Despite numerous successful performances thus far, she was still only a sixteen-year-old *métive*.

In 1784, there were several important developments in the careers of the two sisters. It is around this time, three years after Minette's first opera performance, that Lise made her opera debut at Les Cayes Comédie, several miles southwest of Port-au-Prince. Sources do not indicate an exact date and program for this event. However, eyewitness accounts of Lise's first performance described it as "quite dazzling" and predicted for her the same kind of success her sister had attained. According to Moreau de Saint-Méry, her debut and subsequent performances were well acclaimed and "promised to add to the theatre annals of the colony an example as pleasing as that of her sister."[17] Since Saint-Martin was director of the Les Cayes Comédie at this time, it certainly can be assumed that Lise's debut occurred as a result of his support and the guidance of Mme Acquaire. Unfortunately, we cannot follow the career of Lise during the remainder of this phase, for her name does not appear in sources for almost two years.

It is interesting to note that everyone still referred to Minette as "the young person" or "the young debutante." Thus, we see that while attaining extreme heights of popularity in the colonial world of opera, Minette could not shed the shackles of enslavement status. Apparently, as far as the white public was concerned, she was still a "*nommée*." It was not until December 8, 1784—four years after she first appeared on the public stage, the conclusion of her fourth year at the Comédie, and three weeks prior to her next benefit—that "the young person" was actually identified as "Demoiselle Minette." The occasion was the production of *Acajou*, another "fairy-tale" opera.[18] Minette was the beautiful princess Zirphile, in love with Acajou, a prince (Mme Acquaire in male disguise). Mr. Acquaire, disguised as a woman, was Harpagine, the evil fairy, determined to keep the young couple separated. The plot contains the usual elements for this genre: good fairies vying against bad fairies, genies, a magic ring, enchantments, etc. In the end it is, of course, the good fairies that come to the aid of the young couple by outsmarting their rivals (the evil fairies).

In the same year, Minette suffered a humiliating disappointment. Saint-Martin had signed her to a three-year contract in November 1781—nine months after her opera debut. Unfortunately, Saint-Martin died in June 1784, three years after the formation of this document. On his deathbed, he dictated his will, in which he acknowledged the contract and that Minette had never been paid. Benefits had been given in her honor; but, unlike other artists who received a large portion of receipts for benefit performances, Minette had received nothing. Further, Saint-Martin stipulated that Minette was to be paid the three years of salary owed to her plus receipts from previous benefits held in her honor. There seems to be no evidence that his wishes were carried out. In other words, despite a theatre always filled to capacity to hear her sing, Minette, the "*mestive libre*" (as she was described in Saint-Martin's will), was still a slave.[19] The matter (and the money) remained in the hands of the Commissaires (governing body of theatres consisting of government officials, *colons*, and other influential white businessmen).

The death of Saint-Martin had other adverse effects on her career. Conspicuously absent in contemporary documents is any further mention of Minette appearing in those special Christmas and Easter concerts given by the Concert Spirituel, or any other concerts until late in her career.[20] There were no more *ariettes*, duos, or "superb trios" with the director and leading male singers. During the remainder of this phase, Minette's schedule of performances also changed dramatically. She appeared in only four operas, performing twice in 1784 (December 7 and 21) and once, almost a year later, in 1785 (October 11). The last two performances were benefits for her, but again, there is no indication that she received any of the proceeds from these events.

Equally disturbing was the onslaught of negative criticisms that began about a year after Saint-Martin died. Generally, up to this point, critics were quiet or fairly supportive. As indicated above, by July 1781—just five months after her opera debut—it was very evident that Minette "had played several roles to the satisfaction of the public."[21] Subsequently, a few critics also indicated that Minette's performances were "generally successful," and complimented her on the "ardent zeal, . . . grace, and vivacity" that she displayed, all of which became hallmarks of her performances.[22] However, such compliments were almost always accompanied by admonitions that she had little talent and, therefore, must always "solicit the indulgence and kindness of the public, . . . for it is through that alone that she can hope to obtain any success."[23] Over the next few years, criticisms increased dramatically and became more caustic.

Phase 3: The Mature Years of the Sisters (1786–1789)

Lise, like her sister, had a brilliant career, acquiring leading roles in some of the most successful operatic productions in the colonies.[24] While Minette performed only in Port-au-Prince, Lise spread her fame to at least three cities (Les Cayes, Léogane, and Saint-Marc). Her first appearance during this phase occurred on February 6, 1786, in Saint-Marc. She had lead roles in *Le Tonnelier* (The Cooper), *opéra comique*, and in *Les Amours de Marabalais, parodie Nègre du Devin du village*.[25] The evening presented quite a mixture—something for everyone's taste. The first item on the program was Rousseau's *Le Devin du village*, an extremely popular work.[26] As indicated above, Rousseau was a strong critic of his own society and its moral degradation. The composer underscored these same views in *Le Devin du village*, for the work focuses on the triumph of rustic simplicity and virtue (the original state of nature) over corruption and moral degradation (deviation from that state). After the conclusion of this work, some amateurs from a local dance studio performed an *Anglaise*, a court dance.

The next item on the program was *Le Tonnelier*. To encourage public attendance, Lise was introduced to the Saint-Marc public as "Demoiselle Lise, sister of la Demoiselle Minette," which we can assume as further proof of acceptance and popularity of the sisters.[27] The plot of *Le Tonnelier* is pretty straightforward. Colin loves Fanchette (Lise), but Martin, her stepfather and a cooper, has his own plans for her—as his future wife. However, Martin owes Gervais, Colin's uncle, a great deal of money; and Colin convinces his uncle to demand payment from Martin with the stipulation that should he not repay him immediately, the only way he can prevent being sent to prison is to consent to the marriage of Colin and Fanchette. Thus, *Le Tonnelier* is one of those uncomplicated one-act pieces in which innocence, virtue, and honorable intentions of simple village people overcome the conniving and deceitful actions of others—another example of the influence of the *philosophes*.

The last item on the program was *Les Amours de Marabalais, parodie Nègre du Devin du village*, another creole parody. Unfortunately, there is no information on the plot, composer, or librettist.

Despite achieving numerous successes by this time, Minette and Lise were praised on the one hand, then criticized severely, and constantly reminded of their low-rung status on the ever-present ladder of colonial society. Nevertheless, we can also look at the continuing barrage of criticisms against the sisters as further proof of their exceptional talents and increasing popularity. For example, Lise took part in an amazing event during this period. In fact, it was one of the most interesting and boldest examples of the enterprising capabilities of free colored people during the subject period. On February 19, 1787, Mr. Labbé, that rich *quarteron* entrepreneur and director of the Léogane Comédie, welcomed Lise with a benefit in her honor. This was a truly remarkable event—a *colored* woman starring in an opera house *financed and* directed by another colored person.

The main item on the program was *L'Épreuve villageoise*, an opera that had featured Minette in the same lead role on October 11, 1785. Both events were benefits for the sisters. The plot of *L'Épreuve villageoise* is a typical pastoral: André, a sincere, honest young man, loves Denise, a pretty young village maid, who loves someone else. Criticisms of performances of both sisters in this work, two years apart, were very similar. They criticized Minette, "who dare[d] to offer only her zeal; how can one please when one is without talent? All hopes lie in the indulgence of her judges; it is from them alone that she can expect to obtain any success."[28]

Now, compare this with a criticism of Lise's performance in the same opera two years later.

> By favoring this Spectacle, the young Lise dares to beseech from the public the continuation of indulgence with which it has honored her until this day. She will regard this kindness *less as a prize owed to her talents* [emphasis added] than as an encouragement to make them blossom.[29]

Further, both critics credit the widespread acclaim of *L'Épreuve villageoise* in Parisian and colonial theatres, and not the talents of Minette and Lise, as a "very sure prediction" that the public would "indulge" a performance by each sister.

While there are only a few mentions of Lise during the remainder of this phase, it does appear that she was very successful in Léogane, for Labbé sponsored another benefit for her on January 22, 1788. Two items on the program, *L'Amant statue* and *Les Deux tuteurs*, had been performed by Minette. In fact, Minette's appearance in *L'Amant statue* at the Port-au-Prince Comédie occurred just three days prior to Lise's benefit.

Two weeks later, Labbé presented Lise in a lead role in *Le Faux Lord*, which, over the previous five years, had been performed forty-eight times in Paris.[30] *Le Faux Lord* is another example of one of those theatrical offerings of "good taste." Lise's character (Irène) is a young maiden whose rich and greedy father (Anselme) refuses to allow her to marry her beloved (Léandre) because he does not want to "waste money" on a dowry. Through a series of disguises, the cunning and wit of village people triumph over the greed and conceit of the authority figure (Anselme).[31]

Looking at performance records of Minette and Lise, it certainly appears that during their short careers, each sister became the main attraction in the southern and western parts of the island. However, shortly after Lise's 1788 performances in Léogane, Labbé sold "all decorations, music, and clothing that are necessary to the theatre," relinquished his theatre, and disappeared from all theatre activities.[32] As indicated earlier, reasons for such an abrupt departure from a flourishing business remain a mystery. One must remember, however, that the decade of the 1780s, considered to be the golden period of French colonial rule, was a very unsettling period when numerous laws restricting freedoms of *affranchis* continued to be imposed on these persons.

Equally puzzling, there is no further mention of Lise performing anywhere in the colony.

While the nineteen-year-old Lise was being honored in Léogane, Minette continued to expand her repertoire by capturing leading roles in some of the most popular operas. During this last phase, she appeared in eight new operas and repeated her former roles in nine.[33] On two occasions, she also had a large role (Cherubino) in one of the most successful plays of the period, *La Folle journée, ou le mariage de Figaro*. Of these nineteen appearances, sixteen occurred in the first two years (1786 and 1787), two in 1788, and one in 1789. The Comédie gave three benefits for Minette (March 6 and May 3, 1787, and September 12, 1789), and as usual, there is no record of any payment to her. Nevertheless, she continued to achieve unprecedented success.

Some writers continued to be very critical and even belittling. Minette was often compared to opera divas who hailed from France, particularly Madeline Marie Safizot Marsan, the leading singer in colonial theatres. Madame Marsan had performed in opera houses in France and in Germany for several years. In May 1775, she departed Bordeaux, France (with her two children, ages six years and fifteen months) to join her husband in Saint-Pierre, Martinique. She was then twenty-nine years old. During the first three months of her residence in Saint-Pierre, she attained a string of successful performances in that city. The public hailed her performances as being "so seductive [and] captivating spectators believed they were transported from Saint-Pierre to Paris."[34] Five years later, she was performing at the Cap Français Comédie, where she first appeared in *Silvain* (April 25, 1780), an opera composed by Grétry on a libretto by Marmontel. From that point on, she received innumerable praises from Cap Français audiences.[35] Mme Marsan, a seasoned veteran of opera, received the most glowing tributes bestowed on any opera singer. In order to garner attendance at the Cap Français Comédie, theatre directors and newspaper editors frequently assured the public that the Madame would play a particular role. They also reminded the public that she accepted these challenges because she was "always anxious to please the public, [even] when she had the most insurmountable obstacles against her."[36] When Mme Marsan performed the title role of *Nina, ou la folle par amour*, one critic lauded "this adorable actress" as being equally talented as any of the most celebrated actresses at the Opéra-Comique and Comédie-Italienne.[37]

Conversely, Minette, very young and the daughter of a freed slave, was derided for her "slim weak frame." She was scolded for her "weak organs [and] moments of abandon [in which] expression was lacking." Editors and other critics felt compelled to remind Minette constantly of *her place* within society and consistently pointed out that "the public is responsible for her talents, [whereas] her faults are hers alone."[38] It is interesting to note that such attacks on her appearance, artistry, and talents were actually targeted at her choice of operas for benefits held for her on March 6 and May 3, 1787 (*Nina, ou la folle par amour* and *La Belle Arsène*, respectively)—the same two pieces about which critics opined that only someone of Mme Marsan's stature could do them justice.[39] When Minette appeared in the title role of *La Belle Arsène*, Mme Acquaire received a special tribute for her support and guidance of Minette.

> Aujourd'hui, aidée des conseils de l'Actrice qui a guidée ses premiers pas dan la carrière épineuse du Théâtre, . . . elle se hasarde à le jouer.
>
> (Today, aided by the advice of the actress who has guided her first steps in the contentious career of the Theatre, [Minette] dares to perform [the title role]).[40]

Nevertheless, critics were quick to describe her performance as "unsubstantial" and her career as "precarious."[41] Two months later, in a benefit performance for her, Minette again sang the title role in *Nina, ou la folle par amour*. Critics opined that even though a minor portion of Minette's success "can be attributed to her talents," she was still taking quite a chance to attempt such a demanding role.[42] After all, they had already pointed out that Nina belonged to the province of the great mature French divas—and not to a young *créole métive*.

While such criticisms illustrate a degree of racial prejudice, they unwittingly praised Minette's talents, for critics had to elevate her to the status of operatic diva while attempting to detract from her performances. If, in fact, Minette performed so badly, why even bother to mention her name in the same breath as that of Madame Marsan? The answer is quite obvious. Critics had to make Minette's success appear less important and rather inconsequential in order that her white counterparts and white audiences could continue to feel superior.

Shortly after Minette's benefit performance in *La Belle Arsène*, Mme Acquaire left Saint-Domingue and returned to France. During the remainder of that opera season (May through July), Minette appeared in four operas that, according to the gazettes, had been scheduled several months prior to Mme Acquaire's departure. From that moment on, it appears that the Comédie chose to present Minette very sparingly—only three operas in two years (1788 and 1789). With the death of Saint-Martin and the departure of Mme Acquaire, the remarkable careers of the sisters suffered considerably and, in fact, dwindled to an end.

CHAPTER 6

THE ESCAPE FROM REALITY CONTINUES

In the two decades preceding the French Revolution, colonial authorities continued to search for ways to ensure that citizens "taste the fruits of peace" similar to that enjoyed by those living in France, as espoused by the regent of France at the beginning of the eighteenth century. They recognized that encouraging and supporting the production of elaborate musical and dramatic activities could be tremendously useful in meeting their goals. As indicated above, theatre architecture, décor, and costumes in colonial theatres were just as elaborate as those displayed in Paris and in other European cities. Plays and operas at their height of popularity in Paris were performed in the colonies soon thereafter with all the pomp and magnificence of Parisian productions. Thus, by the 1780s, the theatre played a vital role in providing diversionary entertainment for the populace, for it had become the primary form of entertainment for persons on the upper levels of colonial society.

Emergence and Significance of Creole Operas

Colonial theatres carried the escape from reality much further than their Parisian counterparts. They produced a variety of operas utilizing the creole patois and subjects from colonial society. Basically, these works can be divided into two categories. The first type consists of operas written by French composers, produced in France, and later produced in the colonies, at which time local (creole) composers added creole or their version of African elements. The second category consisted of parodies of French operas or plays, and works composed by creole musicians that were based strictly on particular aspects of colonial lifestyles. I ask the reader to keep in mind, however, that all French and creole texts, dances, and music were composed by whites; titles applied to the dances are also those of whites. Thus, such pieces reflect *perceptions* of whites as to what constitutes African cultural elements.

In the first category, additions or other changes to an original French opera or play were incorporated for the sole purpose of making such works more suitable for colonial taste. Generally, such revisions occurred in the *divertissement*, the section that featured various types of dances and songs. French court dances, such as the *bourrée*, *chaconne*, *gigue*, and *menuet*, were followed by dances (presumed to be of sub-Saharan African origin) with titles such as *calenda*, *pas de nègre*, or *pas d'esclave*. Critics and composers generally added a descriptive phrase when using such dances, such as *danse nègre* or other notations, particularly when such dances were performed by white *comédiens*. For example, in a production of *Zémire et Azor*, a white creole was the featured dancer in a *pas de nègre*, "that grotesque genre."[1] Occasionally, producers went to extreme lengths to describe both performer and subject, such as in the premiere of *Le Mariage par lettres de change, ou le Negociant du Cap*, *comédie*, in one act:

> An amateur known for perfectly imitating the gestures and language of Negroes will assume the role of Figaro in the costume of a slave valet, with a *divertissement* and some creole couplets.[2]

Creole and African dances were also inserted between acts or at the end of a program that, in some cases, presented quite a contrast between two very different societies. Such was the case in a production of *Soliman second, ou les trois sultanes* (Soliman II, or The Three Sultanas). In the original version, an elaborate Turkish ballet was performed at the end of the opera. When the work was performed in Saint-Domingue, the Turkish ballet was kept intact. In addition, however, the program concluded with a *pas de nègre*.[3] Thus, the contrast was drawn between the East and the West, while at the same time, it allowed the white colonial audience to leave the theatre with its sense of superiority intact.

A unique example of the manner in which an entire work was revised to suit colonial taste can be seen in the colonial production of *La Négresse, ou le pouvoir de la reconnaissance*. As discussed above (Introduction), the work focuses on opposing views of mixed marriages and European exploitation versus the "kindness, hospitality, and natural goodness" of Africans. When the work premiered in Port-au-Prince, it appeared under a new title, *Les Créoles africaines, ou les effets de l'amour*.[4] The phrase "*créoles africaines*" replaced the term "*négresse(s)*," and all French *airs* (vocal and instrumental) were replaced by creole songs and dances. As discussed above, the *calenda* in *La Négresse* was actually a typical French court dance (duple meter, dotted rhythms, and binary form). However, since the announcement for *Les Créoles africaines* stated that creole pieces replaced the original French, it is certainly safe to assume that the *calenda* performed at Port-au-Prince Comédie was, indeed, an African-based dance piece. Nevertheless, it seems that *Les Créoles africaines* did not achieve very much success in the colony. This is very understandable, particularly in view of its focus on mixed marriage, white exploitation of blacks, and anti-slavery sentiment. Further, as we have seen, genuine acceptance of miscegenation was not welcomed by colonial authorities, even though the practice occurred repeatedly throughout the colonies. In fact, miscegenation continued to be one of the most troublesome issues confronting colonial authorities.

Local Compositions Based on Colonial Lifestyles

In the second category, local composers based their works on particular aspects of colonial lifestyles. Some were parodies of French plays and operas, or creole translations of such works, while others were original pieces written in creole by local composers. The creole parody, a musical drama based on a preexisting French opera or play, seems to have been the preferred type. The parody used themes of the original piece, but French personages, *airs*, *ariettes*, and court dances were replaced by creole characters, songs, and dances.

As indicated above, the creole patois implied slave status, and for this reason alone, it is curious to find several productions of a European classical form, opera, in the language of slaves mounted on the hallowed opera stage. According to numerous eyewitness accounts and other contemporary sources, several whites, especially those born on the islands, learned to speak creole (in addition to their own French language), primarily to converse with their slaves. In other words, by the second half of the eighteenth century, creole had become more acceptable in certain circumstances. It aided the *colon* in maintaining control over the enslaved, and later served as a useful tool to entertain whites at the expense of persons of African descent.

On the other hand, a substantial number of whites acquired a deep appreciation for many aspects of creole culture. Moreau de Saint-Méry admired the "infinite grace" with which certain images could be expressed in creole.[5] White creole men were susceptible to the "intoxicating and natural beauty" of black creole women and also hailed the mulatto ball as "the event of the season."[6] Persons of African and European descent existed harmoniously side by side, albeit quite fleetingly, in cabarets, giving birth to French Antilles creole music and dance. Many of their songs of love, discontent, joy, voyages, and other memories of the past found their way onto the stage of classical theatre.

Such views provided fertile ground for several local composers. One name, however, stands out: Claude Clément, known as "the great Clément, . . . doyen of all actors in the colony."[7] Clément was born in Cap Français and became one of the most revered *comédiens* and composers in the colony. He spent about four years (1763–1767) in Port-au-Prince, where he served as codirector of that young theatre for one year, and then relinquished his unsuccessful tenure. He then performed for a brief period in Saint-Marc before returning to Cap Français, where he continued a very long and successful career. As a singer and actor, Clément was one of the most revered performers in Cap Français, and Clément the composer seems to have captured the imagination of the audience with his creole operas and plays. According to Fouchard, Clément was the first composer to use the creole patois on the hallowed stage of colonial theatre.[8] As a tribute to Clément's thirty years of dedicated service to the theatre, in 1786 Cap Français bestowed upon him the title *maître de la Comédie*.

Clément produced the most widely acclaimed works in each of the above-mentioned subgenres. On March 9, 1779, the Cap Français Comédie held a benefit for him. The first item on the program was the premiere of *Lundi au Cap, ou les recouvremens* (Monday at The Cap, or The Recoupments), an original composition by Clément dramatizing commercial activities on the docks (buying, selling, bartering, settling debts, etc.) that occurred on a particular day of the week (Monday).[9] A ship captain from Bordeaux, a provincial port in the south of France, is the main personage. He barters with local merchants for several barrels of wine and other goods. One of the most innovative and striking elements in this work is the use of two very different languages—one contemporary and the other ancient—that serves to heighten the contrast between the two locales as well as between the characters. Clément used *créole* for lower-class merchants and slaves, while for the captain from Bordeaux, *provençal*, the ancient language of troubadours, is applied.[10]

For his creole parodies, Clément chose some of the most popular operas of the day. One such work was *Blaise et Babet, ou la suite des trois fermiers* (Blaise and Babet, or The Continuation of The Three Farmers).[11] Clément described his parody *Julien et Susette* as a *traduction nègre* (black translation) of *Blaise et Babet*.[12] He replaced titles of two of the main characters in *Blaise et Babet*, the village lord and a count, with the *Commandant du quartier* (district commander) and the *Chevalier*, respectively. Occasionally, both characters speak in French, but more often in creole, particularly when addressing their slaves. However, Clément was very emphatic in pointing out that the roles of all personages basically remained the same as those in *Blaise et Babet*. He changed the titles solely due to the locale—a colony rather than a French village as in *Blaise et Babet*.

Clément's most widely acclaimed work was *Thérèse et Jeannot, parodie-nègre*, in one act. The work was based on Rousseau's *Le Devin du village* (The Village Soothsayer), a mainstay in colonial repertoires throughout the subject period. The first performance of *Thérèse et Jeannot* occurred in 1758 at the Cap Français theatre. Clément retained some of the music of *Le Devin du village*, but replaced most of the French verses with creole texts that were, of course, more suitable for colonial audiences; or in some instances, he translated the original French text into creole. The village dances in *Le Devin* were replaced by the *calenda* or other African-based dance rhythms with titles of *danse créole*, *danse nègre*, and *pas de nègre*.

The plot and the use of three personages in *Thérèse et Jeannot* are basically the same as that in *Le Devin*: two sensitive young lovers who seek the help and advice of an older and wiser adult. Clément, however, skillfully molds *Thérèse et Jeannot* to appeal to the colonial audience. Colin and Colette (shepherd and shepherdess), the young lovers in *Le Devin*, are replaced by young creoles (Thérèse and Jeannot). The Soothsayer now becomes Papa Simon "in the true costume and color of the slave."[13] The Soothsayer resides in a house surrounded by the serenity of trees and fountains, whereas Papa Simon's home is a shanty in a barren landscape. In order to further satisfy the tastes of colonial society on a more appealing and broader scale, all characters were played by white people *à visage noir*—that is, with blackened faces. Such adaptations were generally defined as "necessary [and] analogous decorations."[14] It also seems that in the 1790s this form was transmitted to French theatres in the United States and, thus, influenced black minstrelsy, an extremely popular form that emerged later in the 1820s and reached its height during the period 1840–1870.[15] The primary difference between the two traditions is that the French "blackened face" was used in a classical musical form, whereas in the United States, black minstrelsy was a popular entertainment.

Further, during the 1780s, the decade of which Moreau de Saint-Méry spoke so eloquently, it seems that leading ladies vied to perform in this parody. In Cap Français, Mme Marsan generally had the role of Thérèse, and in Port-au-Prince, it was Mme Acquaire who excelled as Thérèse. Mr. Acquaire frequently had the role of Jeannot, as well as performing creole dances alone or with "an amateur." The parody was highly acclaimed, subsequently performed throughout the colony, and remained in colonial repertoires for thirty years.

Thérèse et Jeannot usually was performed with a light opera or, less frequently, with a play. Like all creole pieces, it was the last major item on the program. In addition, some type of creole dance followed the parody, which served to further enhance the mood created by the *parodie nègre*. The format was certainly in keeping with the desire of directors and other authorities that the audience depart the theatre in a pleasurable mood and with their sense of superiority very much intact.

Several *créole* operas and plays were produced during the 1780s and garnered an appreciable amount of success. The Saint-Marc Comédie opened the new year of 1786 with a play, *Les Nègres de place, ou le commerce de nuit.* Following a practice established by the Cap Français Comédie, they described the work as "a comedy in the language and costume of Negroes in which an amateur, known for perfectly imitating slaves in their idiom and in their manners, will fill the principal role."[16]

A few months later (November 14, 1786), Port-au-Prince mounted the same work. Again, it is made very clear that in order to enhance the imitation of slaves "*en langue créole*," the white actors will appear *à visage noir* (with blackened faces):

> The color and costume of Negroes, as well as those of the white tavern-keepers, Reinfort & Tienbon, will be observed with exactitude. This piece has already been performed several times at theatres in the colony and has amused the spectators very much.[17]

The quote also emphasizes the popularity of this work "*en créole langue*."

Arlequin mulâtresse protégée par Macanda, a *comédie* written by Mr. Acquaire, had premiered earlier in that year (March) at the Port-au-Prince Comédie.[18] Additional premieres included *Les Amours de Marabalais, parodie Nègre du Devin du village*; *Les Nègres de Place, ou les commerçans de nuit*; *Arlequin chez le restaurateur des Halles*; *Le Mariage par lettres de change, ou le négotiant du Cap*; and *Julien et Zila*, a creole translation of *Blaise et Babet*.[19] Unfortunately, the names of composers, librettists, and other information regarding plot, setting, and characterization for these works are very scarce, primarily due to the destruction of theatres in the 1790s. Contemporary documents that do exist, however, reflect that creole productions only featured white performers *à visage noir*—except in one instance. On February 6, 1786, Lise had the leading role (Thérèse) in *Les Amours de Marabalais, parodie Nègre du Devin du village*, produced by the Saint-Marc Comédie. There is no record of Minette performing in any of these works. It is also quite possible that when choruses of slaves were indicated, the enslaved were used in *divertissements* due to the immense cost of maintaining a theatre. However, this is more conjecture than fact, for, as I indicated at the beginning of the present study, theatres went up in flames in the disastrous turmoil of the early 1790s, resulting in total destruction of physical structures and of an indeterminate amount of documents (scores, librettos, and records about day-to-day operations).

There is no indication that theatres in Guadeloupe and in Martinique produced any creole operas or plays. It appears that such works were solely phenomena of theatres in Saint-Domingue.

Conclusions

Creole operas brought much pleasure and delight to white audiences. It is quite interesting to see the creole patois, with its strong association with African culture, elevated to the point of being featured in theatres of the classics. On the one hand, such productions supported the French view of their music as superior over other cultures, and thus culturally uplifting. When we look at the other side of the coin, however, it is evident that these works mocked and ridiculed African cultural traditions. This type of entertainment seemed to ensure that white audiences, after seeing the "inferior" slave culture denigrated, would leave the theatre contented and reassured of their superiority. Nevertheless, there is a somewhat positive side to this incessant need of the French to disparage the nonwhite sector, for, ironically, such performances also elevated African culture. The widespread popularity of creole operas and the prominence of such productions in colonial theatre repertoires (particularly in the 1780s, that "glorious decade" of French colonial rule) provide indisputable and substantial proof of the deep influence that the African presence exerted on the daily lives of whites—socially as well as economically. It is truly amazing that the French would spend such huge sums of money to imitate the style of those they considered to be inferior and practically worthless (except, of course, for their unquestionable value as a free labor force).

CHAPTER 7

FINALE: THE BEGINNING OF THE END

Throughout the 1780s, that glorious decade of colonial theatre, interest in black creole culture increased dramatically. The creole patois—with its strong ties to African culture—was prominently featured in theatres throughout Saint-Domingue. Equally significant, the increasing popularity of creole productions occurred simultaneously while the colonies were seething with discontent, the results of which deeply impacted theatre activities. In order to fully appreciate the connection between colonial dissension and the theatre, we must first explore the primary causes for such conditions.

Moral Grounds versus Economic Prosperity

For *colons* and other white authorities, the most problematic issues emanated from the nonwhite sector. First, there were incessant appeals of *affranchis* for equality, granted to them over a century ago in the *Code Noir*. In addition, the enslaved were becoming more aggressive and disruptive in their quest for freedom. Their cries for equality and freedom were heard on both sides of the Atlantic. In Paris, there were several persons whose interest in, and appreciation of, black creole culture took an entirely different path from that reflected in theatres of Saint-Domingue. They were influenced by abolitionist movements in England and in the United States, as well as by the incessant attempts of the *philosophes* to promote concepts of equality and liberty. French writers and other professionals strove to gain and to ensure political rights for *affranchis* (as promised to them in Article 59, *Code Noir*), to eliminate the slave trade, and to abolish slavery. Antoine-Nicolas de Condorcet (1743–1794), philosopher and advocate of educational reform, condemned slavery as "a crime against humanity" and declared himself "the enemy of slave trading and slavery."[1] The Abbé Henri Grégoire (1750–1831), prelate and member of the National Assembly, and Jacques-Pierre Brissot (1754–1793), publisher, were tireless in their efforts to promote these concepts.[2]

The increasing support for antislavery sentiment led to the creation of the Société des amis des noirs (Society of the Friends of Blacks). Founded in February, 1788, by Brissot, the Society supported political rights for *affranchis* and sought to abolish the slave trade and slavery in the colonies. By the end of the year, the Society had over 140 members. In addition to Condorcet and the Abbé Grégoire, supporters of the Society included some of the most important persons of the period: Marquis de Lafayette (1757–1834), the formidable commander of French forces who fought alongside the Americans against the British in the American Revolution; Bernardin de Saint-Pierre; *l'Abbé* Raynal the *philosophe*, and Maximilien-François-Marie-Isidore de Robespierre (1758–1794), lawyer and advocate of rights for the poor.

In response to concepts promoted by the Société des amis des noirs, anti-abolitionists convened at the Hôtel Massiac in Paris. (Thereafter, this assembly was referred to as the Club Massiac.) With rare exceptions, the membership consisted of *planteurs* (rich and powerful plantation owners, or *grand blancs*) in the colonies, as well as those who resided in France (but still held onto plantations and other properties on the islands). The most influential member was Moreau de Saint-Méry. He was not a *planteur*, but his experience and legal mind seem to have been immeasurably helpful to the colonists. Moreau, "with his dossiers of laws and his cartons of colonial history, was the living code, the historian and, almost, the legislator of the colony."[3]

The Club Massiac was a very strong adversary of the Société des amis des noirs, not only because of their opposing goals, but also because of the manner in which each group tackled the issues. The Society engaged in a "paper war," based on moral grounds, and relied on the print media (newspapers, pamphlets, essays, etc.) to promote its call for political rights for *affranchis*, and the abolition of the slave trade and slavery. For the club, however, members were more concerned with economic prosperity, and thus vigorously supported the slave trade and the institution of slavery on economic grounds, for how else could they sustain their lavish lifestyle without the forced free labor of the enslaved? Thus, they vigorously opposed concepts of equality and freedom for *affranchis* and slaves.

In addition, *planteurs* were plagued by the *Exclusif*, a maritime system instituted over a century ago by Jean-Baptiste Colbert (1619–1683), minister of finance for Louis XIV. Under the *Exclusif*, colonies could not trade with neighboring islands or with the United States; they were compelled to trade only with France, and to use French ships to transport their goods. Further, it seems that colonies were forbidden to circulate French currency, "except the very lowest . . . lest the colonists use it to purchase foreign goods."[4] The *Exclusif* had been widely accepted in France and in the colonies in the early days of colonization, for it was strictly understood that France was the "protector" of the colonies and, as such, must be the primary benefactor of their commerce. However, the *planteurs*, after decades of a lifestyle of unlimited luxury that, to them, was rightfully theirs, vigorously opposed the *Exclusif*. They steadfastly maintained that the *Exclusif* was a hardship on the colonies, requested a larger share in maritime commercial interests in the colonies, and demanded that they be released from this old economic burden.[5]

After decades of miscegenation throughout the colonies, the number of *affranchis*, as well as their economic progress, had increased dramatically. These were major concerns for alarm for the *colons*. How ironic, for such widespread miscegenation could not have occurred without the full participation of the same men who were now challenging the rights of the offspring of such unions. The *planteurs* vehemently opposed granting *affranchis* any political representation in the National Assembly, even though *La Déclaration des droits de l'Homme et du citoyen* (Declaration of the Rights of Man and Citizen), adopted by the National Assembly on August 29, 1789, clearly so states in Article 1:

> Men are born and remain free and equal in rights. Social distinctions may only be founded upon the general good.

and in Article 6:

> All citizens, being equal in the eyes of the law, are equally eligible for all dignities and for all public positions and occupations, according to their abilities, and without distinction except that of their virtues and talents.

The Declaration primarily represented one of the first official steps in the destruction of the absolute monarchy of the Old Regime, and in the establishment of a representative government. The emphasis on individual liberties in the Declaration, however, caused much apprehension among the *planteurs*. Despite the promulgation of numerous laws granting and upholding rights for all citizens, they steadfastly refused to accept colored people as equals in any sense. *Colons* retained their standing as "masters" of the Colonial Assembly, and continued the persecution of *affranchis* through stringent enforcement of older laws that impacted all facets of their lives. The adaptation of such actions proved to be vast miscalculations by the *planteurs*; for, as history has shown us, they grossly overestimated the extent of their control over the minds of *affranchis* (their descendants) and the enslaved masses.

Concurrently, France was undergoing tremendous dissension at home. The nation was plagued by huge financial debts, immense food shortages due to failing crops and bad weather, endless struggles between the royal family and factions of government, social unrest among the impoverished rural masses, and demands of the rich and expanding bourgeoisie for political power. The high level of discontent reached a climax on July 14, 1789. An armed mass of Parisians stormed the Bastille, a French state prison that symbolized the tyrannical rule of absolute monarchism. This marked the onset of the French Revolution. Events leading up to this tumultuous event, the Revolution itself, and its effects have been studied by numerous scholars and need not be repeated here. For our purposes, it is more important to explore the ways in which the Revolution and actions of the *planteurs* affected theatre activities in the colonies.

Theatres: Patriotism

The time is late evening, September 1789. The place is the Saint-Pierre Comédie, Martinique, "crowded as usual."[6] A spectator is wearing the national cockade (blue, white, and orange knot of ribbon) pinned to his hat. His repeated whisperings become rather distracting to the audience, but not, however, to the extent that they would allow it to disrupt their evening at the theatre. At the conclusion of the performance, several people follow the man out onto the gallery, where he tells them about the fall of the Bastille and events that had occurred subsequently in France. The stranger is very surprised at the indifference shown by his audience. I cannot, of course, state with any degree of certainty why patrons of the theatre seemed to show little concern for this tumultuous event. However, a closer look at the mindset of this elite sector of society, and at the colony itself, can shed some light on reasons for their lack of concern. First of all, we must keep in mind that the primary functions of the theatre were to provide its patrons with an escape from reality and an opportunity to "taste the fruits of peace," thereby lessening the tension of their daily lives. Besides, there was the customary grand ball to attend, where they could dance until the wee hours of the morning, and any discussion of an angry mob thousands of miles away was hardly worth spoiling their evening of pleasure. After all, the uproar at the Bastille had to be a momentary event, because France, with all its military power, would surely prevail.

It is also important to note that conditions in Martinique had been somewhat less volatile than in Saint-Domingue, due in part to several actions taken by the government. In 1783, the king had granted colored slave owners the right to command "the same obedience and respect" from other *affranchis* and the enslaved as that of their white counterparts.[7] Further, in order to increase the ranks of the military for the protection of the colony from foreign invasion, slave rebellions, and other problems in areas inhabited or frequented by blacks, heads of military divisions not only enlisted *affranchis*, they also promised freedom to slaves in exchange for military service. Four years later, the colony also obtained the right to establish a colonial assembly. Since Guadeloupe was under the administration of the two heads of state quartered in Martinique, the same conditions also applied to *affranchis* and slaves on that island. This was in stark contrast to conditions in Saint-Domingue, where one of the primary goals seems to have been to create, strengthen, and maintain division and tension between sectors of the nonwhite population. Even in the militia—composed only of whites, free coloreds, and free blacks—the governor of Saint-Domingue made it quite clear that there would be no mixing among the three classes.[8]

Colons in Martinique and Guadeloupe, like their counterparts in Saint-Domingue, also misjudged the desire for equality and freedom by all sectors of the lower social hierarchy. In small parishes, villages, and communes, where most *affranchis* and slaves lived, the people held numerous fêtes in support of the *patriotes* (opponents of the *planteurs*). Priests and wives of patriots organized religious services. Generally, these were followed by balls and other festivities that featured military music and popular songs and dances. The first of these seems to have occurred in Martinique on September 26–27, 1789[9]—approximately during the same period that spectators at the Saint-Pierre Comédie reflected very little concern about the attack on the Bastille, its causes and effects. Patriotic fêtes were very popular events and soon spread to other small rural communities.

On the other hand, *colons* maintained control in the large cities, for this is also where most of the military was stationed. In Saint-Pierre, the theatre became the main political venue for meetings between *planteurs*, government officials, and mercantile businessmen. In fact, the Comédies in all colonies were transformed into "patriotic" or "national" theatres. It became customary for singers to perform airs between two pieces (operas or plays) or between acts, extolling the virtues of the king and of France, and the evening generally concluded with patriotic hymns. Directors and patrons also organized special programs to honor the "paternal views of a king who used all his glory to bring happiness to his subjects."[10] Strange though this may sound, the reader must keep in mind that gazettes and theatres were financed and controlled by the government. There was no freedom of the press, not even in the *Spectacles* (theatre) section. In sum, these two entities were mouthpieces of the monarchy.

The grandest celebration occurred in Port-au-Prince, the seat of the two heads of state. Festivities lasted for eight days: Sunday, September 27, through Sunday, October 4, 1789. Reasons for such an elaborate event were based on a "mélange of satisfaction and of fear."[11] According to colonial administrators, citizens were joyful at news of the return of Louis XVI to Paris, and, thus, at the "perspective of the regeneration of the kingdom."[12] Nonetheless, people feared for Paris because "a crowd of odious people had fomented disorder [with] their false and insidious actions." There was also much anxiety for the provinces, where, they deemed, it would be much more difficult to restore calm because of their distance from the king and the National Assembly. In order to illustrate their loyalty to the nation and support for the king, colonial authorities spared no expense in their quest to maintain the peace, to ensure respect for the social hierarchy, and to promote French music. In this regard, it is worth pointing out a few highlights of festivities that involved the Port-au-Prince Comédie.[13]

Day 1 (Sunday, September 27): The national cockade, which few citizens had carried at first, was universally adopted. At the theatre, it was presented to the commander of the military amid repeated cries of the spectators: *Vive le Roi! Vive la Nation!* The Comédie performed *La Partie de chasse de Henry IV*, a *comédie* in three acts. At the conclusion of the program, "the public presented the national cockade to the actors who played the roles of this good king and [the Duke of] Sully, [the king's minister of finance]."[14]

Day 2 (Monday, September 28): The commander of the military, accompanied by "a great number of persons," went to the home of the governor-general and presented the national cockade to him, who "received [it] with pride, sincerity, and loyalty." That afternoon, around 150 people gathered and presented the cockade to the intendant, "who received it with a sensibility that was observed by everyone [as was also] his response: *Amour du Roi, tout pour le Public, & pour notre Pays.* (Love from the king, for all the public and for our country)." Mr. and Madame Marbois, organizers of the fête, invited the assembly to drink to the health of the king and of the nation. Everyone then went into the garden, where "they drank successively to the health of the king, the nation, the governor, the Intendant, and the Conseil Supérieur" (the highest-ranking court).

Day 3 (Tuesday, September 29): The national cockade was presented to the commander of the naval forces of His Majesty, who received it in "the most affable manner." The ceremony concluded with military music.

Day 4 (Wednesday, September 30): The Comédie held a benefit for a soldier injured the previous Saturday during the performance of *Gaston & Bayard*, *tragédie*, when the gunpowder in his right hand exploded. The governor attended and was universally welcomed with applause and military music. A citizen in the parterre addressed the governor, complimenting him on the joy that he always brought to the people when they saw him. The *comédiens* then gave a repeat performance of *Gaston & Bayard.*

Day 5 (Thursday, October 1): A public meeting of the Conseil took place in the morning. Members of the court and officers of the *sénéchaussée* and the Admiralty received cockades. A representative for the *procureur général* of the king made a discourse on the vigilance necessary in all divisions, and particularly by the magistrates. Everyone renewed their vows of service to France. A ball was held that evening for the injured soldier.

Day 8 (Sunday, October 4): The governor reviewed the battalion of militia. Everyone remarked on the good deportment of the troops, which were three ranks deep and occupied the entire government plaza. Everyone wore the national cockade. The day ended with a representation of *La Répétition interrompue*, "a little *divertissement* . . . composed rapidly by a local citizen." The piece was very successful; everyone applauded the zeal of the actors and musicians as well as evolutions of the military executed by grenadiers of the Regiment of

Port-au-Prince. Colonial documents do not provide the name of the composer (or librettist), identifying him only as the "author." Here, again, we observe the French propensity for inconsistent terminology, for contemporaries frequently applied the terms "author" and "composer" to both librettists and composers. Fouchard maintains the author was Charles Mozard, "journalist, dramatic author, and theatre critic"[15] However, it is rather unlikely that someone with no known musical background actually composed an entire work (music and text) in a few days for such an important occasion. I find it more plausible that the piece, originally, was an *opéra comique* (one act, same name) that had premiered at the Foire Saint Laurent in 1735, composed by Jean Claude Gillier (1667–1737) on a libretto by Charles-Simon Favart (1710–1792), an extremely popular and prolific librettist and composer.[16] Further, it is more likely that "the author" made a few revisions of the Gillier-Favart piece to make it more suitable for the occasion (for example, the inclusion of elaborate military participation).

As we can see, colonial authorities went to great lengths to promote the glorious power of France and the "culturally uplifting" character of French theatre. The critic's closing remarks remind us again of the deeply embedded bonds between politics and culture in French colonial society:

> Such is the account of what occurred here on the occasion of the national news. The particular joy of the public has not been troubled by the lightest circumstance. One owes this satisfaction to the wisdom of the heads of state. One owes this calm to the liberty that allowed wise and peaceful citizens to follow the impulses of their hearts, which could only be deeply affected upon learning that Paris had been exposed to huge evils and atrocious betrayals.

Theatres: The Performers after July 14, 1789

Minette was one of several singers applauded in the gala performance of *La Répétition interrompue* on October 4, 1789—but not, however, as a soloist. Notices and analyses of the event do not provide any information regarding her participation other than merely the insertion of her name in the list of performers. Unfortunately, this is the last mention in the sources of any performances by her—or by Lise after the latter's successful Léogane performance in January, 1788 (*Le Faux-Lord, ou le Pacotilleur*). The sisters seem to have disappeared without a trace. There have been several assumptions and speculations regarding their lives after 1789, but none have been substantiated. Several writers assumed that the sisters, like hundreds of other persons, perished in the bloody revolts of 1791.[17]

In an excellent study on French theatre in New Orleans, Louisiana, René Gardeur poses some interesting hypotheses regarding life for the sisters after 1789.[18] Under the directorship of a Mme Durosier, possibly from Saint-Domingue, the cast of the New Orleans theatre included colored actresses as early as 1793 and were received very well by audiences.

> As the theatre was thereby enabled to remain open at a time when it appeared to be on the verge of collapse, the implication is strong that the new actresses were favorably received by the public and that their engagement brought about an improvement in the quality of the performances.[19]

Gardeur questions whether Minette and Lise could have been part of this group. Further, the author opines, colored performers undoubtedly would not be accepted by New Orleans audiences unless they were exceptionally talented and experienced artists, and these performers could hardly have acquired such experience in New Orleans by the early 1790s. Thus, it is more conceivable that they came from Port-au-Prince, Saint-Marc, Léogane, or Les Cayes, where, as I have illustrated above, colored artists had performed several times for white audiences.

A few years later, the New Orleans theatre announced that a benefit would be held on November 25, 1806, for Mlle Minette Ferrand, "an artist who has had a long career, who is burdened with the support of a numerous family, and whose debut has been and still is delayed by the state of illness from which she has been suffering for a long time."[20] The performance was postponed twice, probably due to her illness; she died shortly thereafter (January 2, 1807). Gardeur provides some very interesting facts about Mlle Ferrand. Born in Port-au-Prince, she was about thirty-eight years old at the time of her death—approximately two years younger than our Minette. A year later, the theatre announced that "*une jeune personne*, niece of Mr. Ferrand," would make her debut on January 27, 1808.[21] Gardeur suggests that this singer possibly could have been Mlle Ferrand's sister (or, that is, Lise). Although she performed again anonymously, her real name remains unknown. Unfortunately, there seems to be no further trace of these two singers beyond this two-year period (1806–1808). Gardeur concludes that "more positive evidence," rather than a hypothesis, is required before any definite conclusions regarding Minette and Lise can be drawn.

The quest for "more positive evidence" regarding the last years of Minette and Lise continues. An interesting but rather perplexing attempt in this direction was made recently by Bernard Camier, who has taken Gardeur's "hypothesis" as proof that Mlle Minette Ferrand was, indeed, the famous Minette of Port-au-Prince. Mlle Minette Ferrand was baptized as Elisabeth Alexandrine Louise, father unknown, at Port-au-Prince on August 11, 1767.[22] However, Camier seems to have had problems deciding on the identity of her father. At first, he suggested it was Saint-Martin, director of the Port-au-Prince Theatre;[23] later, he provided a "plausible hypothesis" that Joseph Sartre was her father.[24] Then, two years later, he said her father was Marin Ferrand, an influential government official.[25] Camier attempts to prove the true identity of Minette as Elisabeth Alexandrine Louise, simply by stating that "Minette" was a "stage name" (*nom de scène*),[26] or describing her as a "mythical character" (*Minette est un personnage mythique*).[27] Unfortunately, he provides no basis for these assumptions. Further, the author claims "the verified existence of a brother of Minette."[28] Verified by whom or what, Camier does not say. He merely states that Marin Ferrand and Elisabeth Daguin (Minette's parents, according to Camier) had a son; therefore, he had to be Minette's brother. Strangely, however, Camier never really accounts for Lise in his two genealogical essays.[29] There is plenty of documented evidence that Minette and Lise were sisters, but none has surfaced that indicates they had a brother. It is also curious that when chronicling the career of Minette, Camier never mentions Madame Acquaire.[30] In fact, such an array of inconsistencies tends to lend more weight to the probability that Minette Ferrand (Elisabeth Alexandrine Louise) was *not* the famous Minette of the Port-au-Prince Comédie.

Thus, while we cannot state with any certainty that Minette and Lise actually escaped to New Orleans (or anywhere else, for that matter), it is documented fact that amidst the mounting onslaught of slave revolts and other atrocities in Saint-Domingue, several white actresses, singers, musicians, and other artists returned to France or fled to Martinique, where the theatre still flourished.[31] Several others fled to New Orleans and to Charleston, South Carolina, where the French Antilles passion for opera found other homes for the same kind of repertoire that had been so popular in the colonies. New Orleans and Charleston were the first two cities to house permanent French theatres in the United States. Théâtre St.-Pierre in New Orleans opened on October 4, 1792, and the Charleston French Theatre opened on April 12, 1794.[32] The New Orleans theatre was built by Jean-Marie and Louis-Alexandre Henry, two brothers from Paris, who settled in New Orleans around the end of 1788. In Charleston, patrons of the arts and other citizens sympathetic to Saint-Domingue refugees who had escaped the "frightful massacre that almost depopulated one of the gems of the Antilles" provided the *comédiens* with their own building within a few months after their arrival in Charleston.[33]

Two of the most prominent members of the Cap Français theatre, Mme Marsan and Jean-Baptiste Le Sueur Fontaine (1742–1814), settled in New Orleans in the early 1790s. The last mention of Mme Marsan in Saint-Domingue occurred in the Cap Français *Gazette du Jour* on December 18, 1790. A few years later (around 1794), she was performing in the New Orleans theatre. The Madame garnered the highest praises from New Orleans audiences, just as she had experienced in Saint-Pierre and in Cap Français. Fontaine served as director of the Cap Français Comédie (1780–1791) during its finest years. The date of his departure from the colony is unknown. However, after immigrating to the United States, he continued to make a solid imprint on French colonial opera, and after settling in New Orleans, he assumed several important positions—actor, theatre director, and editor of *Le Moniteur de la Louisiane*.

One of the most prominent figures in the Charleston French Theatre was Alexander Placide, dancer and actor. Born in France, Placide had achieved success throughout France and was also heralded in London, Holland, and other European theatres as one of the best dancers during the 1770s and 1780s. He arrived in Cap Français in 1788 and continued a successful career, performing in cities throughout the colony until September 1791, at which time he departed the colony. He stopped in Charleston for a short time, then traveled north to New York and to Boston, making dancing appearances in both cities. He then returned to Charleston and, in 1794, became manager of the French Theatre.

While there is documented proof that performers from the Saint-Domingue theatres migrated to Baltimore, New York, and other cities in the United States,[34] New Orleans and Charleston were the only two cities that actually provided the Saint-Domingue artists with a physical structure for a theatre.

Lastly, we have seen that, against the backdrop of the dehumanizing slave trade, the support of the horrid institution of slavery, and the inequalities suffered by *affranchis*, the French Antilles showcased some of the most fascinating events of the period. Several talented black and colored musicians, singers, and an ambitious colored entrepreneur displayed remarkable talent, strength, and determination, and became prominent in the theatre. Their phenomenal accomplishments under the harsh conditions of colonial rule, coupled with the unprecedented and daring support of white benefactors, are truly culturally uplifting.

EPILOGUE

> Emancipation of blacks, such is our first vow. Prosperity of the colonies, such is our second vow. We ask for one in the name of humanity, the other in the name of nationality, [and] both in the name of justice.
>
> —Victor Schoelcher, *Des Colonies françaises: Abolition immédiate de l'esclavage*[1]

P*aradise*? That cruelly provocative institution was dismantled, mentally as well as physically, by the same group of people for which it was created. It engendered hostilities between all sectors of the population. In Cap Français, mothers, *négresses libres* (free black women), were pitted against their daughters when they sought to be seated in the same boxes with them. In the South Province, many free coloreds were legitimate children of mixed-race marriages and enjoyed special seating privileges in the *Paradis*, which caused more dissension within the free colored population. Colonial authorities continuously passed laws restricting freedoms previously enjoyed by free coloreds, particularly in the south, regardless of their material possessions; and by the late 1770s, this frontier society was transformed into a social hierarchy based on race, like the remainder of Saint-Domingue and the other colonies.

Colons had badly misjudged the desire for equality and freedom by all sectors of the lower social hierarchy. After the outbreak of the French Revolution, France and her colonies continued to be in a state of utter confusion and disruption. The English invaded Guadeloupe and Martinique, and slave rebellions were rampant in all colonies, particularly in Saint-Domingue. France, occupied with the Revolution, was unable to send troops to quell slave revolts or to aid the colonies in their fight against the British. In Saint-Domingue, *affranchis* were denied equality on all levels and, later, joined slaves in the rebellion, totally disarming the *planteurs*, who had always depended on the loyalty of their descendants *(affranchis)* as a guarantee against revolts, runaways, and other disturbances by the enslaved masses. Their cries for equality were far stronger than bloodlines to their white parents and ancestors. In fact, the incessant appeals of *affranchis* for equality, granted to them over a century ago in the *Code Noir*, grew louder and louder. Simultaneously, the enslaved were becoming more aggressive and disruptive in their quest for freedom. These cries were heard on both sides of the Atlantic. In Paris, their supporters were influenced by abolitionist movements in England and in the United States, as well as by the incessant attempts of the *philosophes* to promote concepts of equality and liberty.

However, throughout the colonies, regardless of the increasing turmoil, authorities kept their focus on the theatre as a means of maintaining control, ensuring respect for the established hierarchy, and promoting French culture. Comédies in all colonies were transformed into "patriotic" or "national" theatres. They became the main political venue for meetings between *planteurs*, government officials, and mercantile businessmen. The two major mouthpieces of the monarchy, the theatre and the press, were major supporters of productions in which patrons organized special programs to honor the king. These included some of the best singers, performing airs between two pieces (operas or plays) or between acts, extolling the virtues of the king and of France. The evening generally concluded with patriotic hymns.

In the midst of all the turmoil in the colonies, some very talented young black musicians rose to prominence in the theatre. It seems that there were no schools or studios set up to train slave musicians. My research does indicate, however, that parish priests and other members of the Catholic clergy were very successful in training young slaves in various musical techniques, and also taught them to play European orchestral instruments, especially the violin and other strings. As I indicated above, the Jesuits possessed and used their unique pedagogical skills to train the enslaved masses on their plantations in several areas of musical performance; and since the Jesuits were not forced out of the colonies until 1763, it is quite reasonable to assume that they were largely responsible for several young blacks being able to play in concert and opera orchestras. While I cannot say with any degree of certainty that Jesuits were teachers of any of the musicians mentioned above (chapter 4), it is quite possible, however, because they were performing in Cap Français orchestras as early as 1762.

Nevertheless, regardless of how well, and under what circumstances, these musicians were trained and performed, the demeaning titles of slave status always accompanied both *affranchis* and the enslaved. Further, it is rather curious that Moreau de Saint-Méry never mentions any slave musicians in his glowing description of Saint-Domingue during that glorious decade of the 1780s. It seems that for this author of several thousand pages devoted to lifestyles, laws, and other conditions in his adopted home, these musicians were not important and, therefore, did not exist. In fact, despite the significant contributions that young slave musicians made to colonial musical theatre, nowhere in the numerous newspapers, travel narratives, *mémoires*, letters, etc., I examined during the subject period did I find any mention, analysis, or description of their performances. To the authors of these documents, the young musicians were invisible. Nevertheless, their presence in concert and opera orchestras as early as the 1760s helped to prepare the way for the debut of Minette and, later, her sister, Lise.

This concept of invisibility also reared its ugly head in opera productions with African elements. Two of the most notable examples occur in *La Négresse, ou le pouvoir de la reconnaissance*. Frontin disguises himself *en Nègre* and "besmears his face to not be recognized as a white man." The concept is reinforced in scenes 10 and 11 when, still disguised *en Nègre*, his white friends "treat [him] like a Negro": they ignore him.

A sort of invisibility of Minette and Lise occurred in the Northern Province. The sisters did not perform in Cap Français; nor were they mentioned in discussions about productions at that theatre—except when critics attempted to compare the "incapabilities" of Minette to the "superb" qualities of Madame Marsan. In order to devalue Minette, however, while lauding Madame Marsan, they had to mention Minette, thereby elevating her stature.

When one looks at the types of operas, the frequency of appearances, and the lead roles performed by the sisters, it is obvious that their talents were highly regarded by the public. The sisters appear to have been consummate professional artists, always critiquing and honing their craft, for throughout their short careers, they acquired and maintained a formidable stature in colonial opera. The public also looked forward anxiously to seeing Minette in Easter and Christmas concerts, events produced in the same tradition as those in France—with much pomp and grandeur. After the death of Saint-Martin, Minette's appearance in these concerts came to an abrupt halt.

Critics constantly reminded the sisters of *their place* in colonial society. To underscore Minette's *inferior* social status, newspapers continued for several years to refer to Minette as "*la jeune personne*," and her last name is never mentioned in any of the numerous sources examined for the present study. However, despite her subordinate rank on the ever-present ladder of colonial hierarchy, the Port-au-Prince Comédie continued to give benefits in her honor; for, undoubtedly, such occasions meant additional money in the Comédie treasury (or in the pockets of the *Commissaires*). The customary grand balls and elaborate buffets that concluded an evening at the theatre were strictly off-limits to the sisters—even for benefits in their honor. Nor is there evidence that they received any funds from these events or for their performances. However, from all outward appearances, these situations seem to have had a minor effect on Minette and Lise, for they continued to perform exceedingly well under the unwavering guidance and support of two of the most important persons in colonial theatre activity—Madame Acquaire and Saint-Martin.

It may seem curious, at first glance, that the same conditions applied to Lise when she performed at the Léogane Comédie. Although financed and directed by a colored man, the theatre was required to have that special section (*Paradis pour les gens de couleur*) reserved for *affranchis*, as in all colonial theatres. Further, Labbé and his militia of colored men, charged with guarding the Comédie, were under the command of a white military officer, and the Comédie was under the supervision of *Commissaires*. In other words, even though Labbé was rich, an owner of several slaves, financier and director of a theatre, he was still only a *nommé*, controlled by and subservient to white colonial authorities.

In the midst of all the turmoil of the 1780s, colonial authorities continued to mount lavish productions of operas while simultaneously ignoring pleas of the *affranchis* for equality, and continuing to support the deplorable institution of human bondage. Under such inhumane conditions, it is no wonder that the Cap Français and Port-au-Prince theatres, the major showplaces of the richest colony, built on the backs of the enslaved, were among the first monuments to be completely burned to the ground during the first days of that bloody rebellion.

Through the present study, however, we can now see that despite being surrounded by immense hatred, violence, and turmoil, a significant amount of pure, natural talent continued to blossom under the decadence of French colonial rule. It was in the theatres in the frontier society where the two sisters excelled, where a *quarteron* purchased a theatre, and where communities thrived on the strengths and successes of racially mixed families. These artists and their accomplishments are the personification of the strong bonds between music, society, and the French concept of the sub-Saharan African Other. With the publication of this book, Minette, Lise, the young black musicians, and their magnificent achievements can now, deservedly, occupy their own space in the annals of opera, of black history, and of French Caribbean studies.

GLOSSARY

Affranchis: free black and free colored persons who acquired their freedom from slavery in accordance with specific conditions as set forth in *Le Code Noir* (the Black Code).

Air: The French operatic *air* is a short strophic song in syllabic style and binary form that dates from the late sixteenth century. At that time, popular *airs* were usually based on love poems. In the early seventeenth century, the *air* became more serious (*air de cour*), was nurtured in the court ballet (*ballet de cour*) and the *comédie-ballet*, and became the standard type of *air* in French opera, usually in the form of dialogue, monologue, or dance. The accompaniment was light (harpsichord, bass or bassoon, and violoncello).

Ariette: a virtuoso solo piece accompanied by full orchestra. In breadth, the *ariette* is like the Italian *da capo* aria. However, unlike the Italian form, the *ariette* carried little dramatic significance and was used primarily in the *divertissement*. Examples of the *ariette* composed by two successors of Lully are provided in appendix 6, discography (*Mondonville, Titon et l'Aurore* and Grétry's *Grétry, Zémire et Azor* and *La Caravane du Caire*). A music score of *Zémire et Azor* is provided in appendix 2.

Ballet de cour (court ballet): The *ballet de cour* was an extremely popular type of court entertainment in France for over a century, dating from 1681 until the first quarter of the eighteenth century. The genre consists of a series of *entrées*, each of which is preceded by a *récit*, narrative solo sections positioned at the beginning of each act that present and explain the subject. The work concludes with a *grand ballet*—called *grand ballet* because the number of dancers is always greater than that in any of the other *entrées*, and a larger number of passages and figures are found there. Ordinarily, everyone who has danced in the ballet is reassembled for this *entrée*.

Bourrée: a *galant* dance in duple or quadruple meter; fast tempo

Chaconne: a *galant* dance in triple meter; moderate tempo

Colon: owner of one or several plantations

Courante: a *galant* dance in triple meter; slow tempo

Créole: In the first half of the seventeenth century, the term "*créole*" designated a white person born in the French Antilles. By the middle of the century, the terms "black *créole*," "white *créole*," and "Indian *créole*" were frequently used to make the distinction between the races and also to identify those blacks and Indians born in the French Antilles. By the second half of the eighteenth century, "*créole*" generally applied to all people born in the colonies, regardless of race. See also "*Créole* language."

***Créole* language**: a language spoken primarily by blacks (enslaved and free). It seems that most whites viewed *créole* as a "corrupted" version of the French language mingled with African words, and therefore, because of its close association with African culture, they considered *créole* to be an inferior language.

Divertissement: a period of relaxation in the drama consisting of songs and dances that emanated from the subject and functioned as a participant in the overall plan of action. Such involvement usually followed one of two distinct paths. First, it operated as a purely decorative entity, such as accompanying festivities, particularly those that underscored virtuous love and the pleasures of life. Second, the *divertissement* could assume a dramatic function, where the librettist would skillfully tie dances and songs to the action in a manner that set the stage for the ensuing climactic (or other highly dramatic) event, such as the fate of a rival or an enemy being exposed through an oracle or some other divine presence. Irrespective of which role the *divertissement* assumed, it seems to have been generally accepted that the responsibility of maintaining a solid liaison between repose and action remained that of the librettist. Unless indicated otherwise, it is the first path that the works discussed in the present study followed.

Engagés: See "indentured servants."

Engagés forcés: less fortunate groups of vagabonds, smugglers, troubled youth, and others on the low rungs of French society dispatched to the colonies by the government

Engagés volontaires: unemployed domestics and other skilled workers who willingly contracted their services

***Galant* dances**: very popular entertainment pieces in the court of Louis XIV (1643–1715) and also in French opera, up until the last quarter of the eighteenth century. These were graceful dances such as the *bourrée*, *chaconne*, *courante*, *gigue*, *menuet*, and *sarabande*. The texture was light, employing only a few instruments, e.g., violins 1 and 2, cello, and harpsichord, rather than the thick, heavy texture of full orchestral accompaniment used for other types of pieces. *Galant* dances were set in a variety of simple meters: duple, triple, or quadruple, with a mood that could be gay and quick, or slow and tender.

Gavotte: a *galant* dance in duple or quadruple meter; usually a fast tempo, or sometimes rather slow and tender

Gens de couleur: offspring of mixed unions of white French men and black African women

Gigue: a *galant* dance in duple or quadruple meter; fast tempo

Grand blancs: white owners of large plantations, and other white, rich, and influential businessmen

Griffe: offspring of a mixed union of a black and a mulatto person, or an Indian and a black person

Indentured servants (*les engagés*): white people who, generally, could not earn a living in France and were drawn to the island by fantastic stories of opportunities to enrich oneself in a relatively short period. All classes of indentured servants were contracted for three years of service to the plantation owner who paid for their passage. Contract terms were reduced to eighteen months in 1670, and then raised back to three years in 1699. At the end of the contract, an indentured servant received his pay in several pounds of sugar, tobacco, and/or cash and could then return to France.

Lament: a vocal melody usually set in *récitatif* style. The lament occupied a special dramatic position in operas from the seventeenth century onward, reinforcing exceptional emotional situations. Its intense expression is accomplished through a slow pace and the use of short dissonant melodic phrases, repetition of words or phrases in a melodic sequence, and descending dissonant **tetrachords**.

Marrons: runaway slaves

Mestive/métive (fem.); *mestif/métif* (masc.): offspring of the mixed union of a white male and a *quarteronne*

Menuet: a *galant* dance in triple meter; quick tempo

Monologue scene: In the monologue scene, the vocal piece (*air*, *ariette*, or *récitatif*) focuses on the concerns of one character, and reflects one or several contrasting affections—solitude, anxiety, sadness, joy, tenderness, etc. The scene is presented in a variety of forms—an air, a *récitatif accompagné*, or a combination of these. These forms are frequently mixed with instrumental pieces, preludes, interludes, and postludes, in order to complement and enhance a particular dramatic effect. Lully established a particular format for monologue scenes in *Acis et Galathée*, a *pastorale héroïque* (1686). The first act commences with a motto prelude of ten measures. Acis, a shepherd, waits for his beloved, Galathée, a sea nymph, by the seashore. He is confused and sad, however, because in spite of the constant praises that he has showered on Galathée, she still ignores him, and her absence causes him to sink lower into the abyss of despair. The first scene sets the tone for the entire opera, for it presents the three emotions upon which the opera is based, love, sadness, and agitation: love for the serenity of nature, frequently coupled with tenderness for the character's beloved; sadness or confused state of the character; and that person's agitation and growing despair over a seemingly hopeless situation. These three sentiments were expressed in a similar manner in opening monologues for the next several decades.

Mulâtre (male); ***mulâtresse*** (female): offspring of the mixed union of a white man and a black woman

Nègres nouveaux (new or newly arrived Negroes): slaves not born in the colonies

Nommé (masc.); ***nommée*** (fem.): "called" or "named," applied to all slaves regardless of whether they were recent imports from Africa or born in the colonies. The term *le nommé* preceded the name of the slave, which was the surname of the slave owner or a forename given to the slave by the owner, as in *le nommé* Rousseau, *le nommé* Pierre, or *la nommée* Giselle.

Ouverture (overture): Solemn and brilliant, the French overture was designed to command the attention of the audience and to prepare them for the magnificence to follow. It commences with a moderately paced section in duple or quadruple meter with dotted rhythms and is followed by a sharply contrasting section, slightly fugal, in a faster tempo. The *ouverture* has been described in a countless number of contemporary and modern-day sources as pompous, stately, kingly, and majestic, adjectives all of which were used to personify and extol the glorious stature of Louis XIV. The subject is, therefore, generally spectacular and full of praises.

Petits blancs ("little whites"): carpenters, plantation managers, goldsmiths, masons, merchants, and other small-business entrepreneurs; on the lowest rung of the social ladder for whites, a distinction between them and the rich, powerful plantation owners (*grand blancs*)

***Poissard* opera**: the portrayal of a very low class of people notorious for their foul language and gross manners

Quarteron (masc.); ***quarteronne*** (fem.): offspring of the mixed union of a white male and a mulatto female

Récitatif accompagné: Lully created the French recitative (*récitatif*), a declamatory style with fluctuating meters that were designed to accommodate the inflections of the French language. The *récitatif accompagné* received full orchestral treatment and was used to heighten certain dramatic situations or moods of a main character. The *récitatif simple* was accompanied by the basso continuo (or thoroughbass), a bass line with figures inserted below individual notes to indicate to the organist, harpsichordist (or other keyboard player), and other instrumentalists which notes are to be played above the bass line in order to complete the harmony. While the organ was the designated basso continuo instrument for church music, composers of secular music used a variety of instruments: harpsichord, harp, lute, guitar, bassoons, theorbo, violoncello, etc.

Sarabande: a *galant* dance in triple meter; slow tempo; serious mood

Scène lyrique: a spoken monodrama (also known as *mélodrame*) with instrumental interjections

Sub-Saharan Africa: countries located south of the Sahara Desert. For the present study, this specifically includes coastal areas in West Africa from as far north as Senegal, inland to Mali, and back down the coast to the southern tip of Angola.

Symphonies: instrumental music of French concert and theatre music of the seventeenth and eighteenth centuries. In opera, a "dramatic *symphonie*" is an instrumental section (e.g., *prélude* or *ritournelle*) that is connected to the action.

Tetrachord: a series of four notes contained within the interval of a perfect fourth, e.g., c-d-e-f.

APPENDIX 2

"LA FAUVETTE" (THE WARBLER)

Source: *Zémire et Azor (1771). Comédie-ballet mêlée d'ariettes et de danses*, André-Ernest-Modeste Grétry (1741–1813), composer. Paris: Ches Houbaut, ca. 1772.

Corni in D. la Re
2.d Cors ad libitum
solo
Flauto 1 solo
V.V.
unis
Viola
col b.
Zemire
Allegro moderato
Basse.

tutti
unis
La Fauvet-te a vec ses petits se croit la

reine du boccage se croit la rei-ne du boccage de leur re--veil
par son ramage, tous les echos sont a-ver--
col 1r v.
col 2d v.
unis

tis de leur reveil par son ra-ma-
unis
ge de leur re--veil par

unis
col b.
son ra mage, tous les e--chos sont aver tis, tous les echos sont
F
col 1º v.
col 1º v.
unis
col b.
aver. tis .

Andantino
Sa nais san - te fa
mille autour d'elle sautille voltige et prend l'essor; rassemblés sous son

coll b.
ai-le de leur amour pour elle, elle jou-it en---com- mais par mal-
unis
heur vient l'oiseleur qui lui ravit son esperance, la pauvre me re'elle ne

col b.
pense elle ne pense qu'à son malheur . tout retentit de sa dou - leur .
F
tout retentit de sa dou leur de sa douleur.
F

col.b.
La Fauvette a-vec ses petits secroitla reine du boc-
cage se croit la reine duboccage: de leur re-veil, par son ra-mage,

P
tous les echos sont aver tis de leur reveil par son ra-
P
ma-

unis
-ge de leur re-veil par
unis
son ramage tous les echos sont aver tis. tous les echos tous les echos

cres.
F
cres
F
cres
F
tous les echos sont a - - - ver - - - - tis
cres
F

MOREAU: EFFECTS OF MISCEGENATION

The first part of Moreau's listing contains several categories of descendants of mixed unions between a white man (*un blanc*) and a colored female. He then illustrates mathematical calculations of the proportions of white and black blood produced after seven generations of miscegenation. A few examples:

					PARTS	
					WHITE	BLACK
un blanc	+	*une sacatra*	=	*quarteron[né]*	72	56
blanc	+	*négresse*	=	*mulâtre[sse]*	64	64
blanc	+	*mulâtresse*	=	*quarteron[né]*	96	32
blanc	+	*quarteronné*	=	*métis [métive]*	112	16
blanc	+	*métive*	=	*mamelouque*	120	8
blanc	+	*mamelouque*	=	*quarteron[né]*	124	4
blanc	+	*quarteronné*	=	*sang-mêlé[e]*	126	2
blanc	+	*sang-mêlée*	=	*sang-mêlé[e]*	127	1

Moreau then continues his calculations with several pages of subdivisions within the colored sector. A few examples:

					PARTS	
					WHITE	BLACK
un sang-mêlé	+	*une sang-mêlée*	=	*sang-mêlé[e]*	126	2
quarteron	+	*sang-mêlée*	=	*sang-mêlé[e]*	125	3
métis	+	*sang-mêlée*	=	*mamelouque*	119	9
sang-mêlé	+	*mulâtresse*	=	*quarteron[né]*	95	33
mulâtre	+	*métive*	=	*quarteron[né]*	95	33
sang-mêlé	+	*griffe*	=	*quarteron[né]*	79	49
nègre	+	*sang-mêlée*	=	*mulâtre[sse]*	63	65
quarteron	+	*négresse*	=	*marabou*	48	80
mulâtre	+	*marabou*	=	*mulâtre[sse]*	56	72
nègre	+	*mulâtresse*	=	*griffe*	32	96
griffe	+	*négresse*	=	*sacatra*	16	112

By contrast, classifications in Martinique and Guadeloupe differed greatly with categories limited to:

un blanc	+	*une négresse*	=	*mulâtre[sse]*
blanc	+	*mulâtresse*	=	*métif [métive]*
blanc	+	*métive*	=	*carteron*
blanc	+	*carteronné*	=	*mamelouque*
noir	+	*mulâtresse*	=	*câpre [câpresse]*
mulâtre	+	*métive*	=	*mulâtre[sse] ou métif [metive]*
métis	+	*carteronné*	=	*métif [metive] ou carteron[né]*

Further, it appears that the term "*sang-mêlé*" was not used in Martinique and Guadeloupe until the early part of the nineteenth century.[1]

DESCRIPTIONS OF COLONIAL THEATRES

Cap Français Comédie (1766)

On représenta Dimanche dernier pour la premiere fois à la Salle de Spectacle nouvellement construite. Cette Salle, de 120 pieds de longueur sur 40 de largeur, remplit à bien des égards l'idée que l'on peut se former d'une Salle de Spectacle bien entendue. Elle est partagée en trois parties égales: le Théâtre, le Parterre, y compris l'Orchestre; l'Amphithéâtre & les derrieres. Son plan est ovale, & rapproche les auditeurs. Au moyen d'une avant-scene, l'Acteur se trouve avancé; ce qui empêche sa voix de se perdre dans les coulisses. Il y a dix premieres & dix secondes loges de chaque côté; à droite est celle du Roi, qui est double, peinte en or aux Armes de France & de Navarre, & ornée de deux tapis brodés en or & semés de fleurs-de-lis; à gauche est une loge de six pieds pour M. l'Intendant, ornée des attributs de la Marine; les autres loges du premier rang sont aussi ornées de différens hiérogliphes aussi bien adaptés que bien exécutés; les secondes loges sont peintés également en mosaïque jaune de Naples sur un fond bleu de Roi. Les décorations théatricales ont été remarquées par les gens de goût: deux Satyres gigantesques en buste, que l'on voit à l'avant-scene, semblent soutenir tout l'édifice: au frontispice, on voit les armes du Roi. Le rideau est fond bleu, sur lequel sont peints quatre Génies, symboles de la Tragédie & de la Comédie, & deux autres planant dans les airs, qui soutiennent une légende où on lit ces termes en lettres d'or: CASTIGAT RIDENDO MORES. Les Décorations & Peintures sont de la composition du Sieur Gervais, Peintre & Sculpteur en cette Ville, & font honneur à cet Artiste. On a observé en général qu'on n'avoit pas réussi dans la maniere d'éclairer, tant du côté de la scene que du côté des Spectateurs: il faut avouer que c'est là principalement qu'échoue l'art. Cette Salle exige un plus grand nombre de lumieres que celles qui l'éclairoient à cette premiere représentation. L'obscurité que ce défaut occasionne, assoiblit le charme du Spectacle & la beauté des décorations. On pense que quelques bras placés de distance en distance le long des premieres loges, produiroient tout l'effet que l'on pourroit desirer. . . . L'Arrière-Amphithéâtre ne sera uniquement que pour les mulâtres & mulâtresses.

Source: *Affiches Américaines* [April 23, 1766], 145–46.

Cap Français Comédie (1784)

Au mois d'Avril 1784, on a ajouté un troisième rang de loges aux deux formées en 1766. Il y a vingt loges au premier rang & vingt & une autres, à cause de celle qui répond à l'entrée de l'amphithéâtre. Ces loges contiennent, à l'aise, six personnes, trois sur le devant & trois sur le derrière, mais on entasse huit.

Les deux premières loges du premier rang vers le théâtre, n'en forment qu'une de chaque côté; celle de la droite est pour le gouverneur-général, ceux qu'il y invite, ou les officiers de la garnison; celle de la gauche appartient à l'intendant et les officiers d'administration s'y placent. Un factionnaire garde l'une, et quelquefois un hoqueton de l'intendance, l'autre.

En avant de ces deux loges honorifiques, sont deux balcons qui se trouvent sur l'avant-scène et qui ont six places sur le devant. Après ces balcons se trouve une demi-loge de chaque côté; elles sont suivies des coulisses.

Des 10 loges qui sont le plus au fond du troisième rang, sept reçoivent les mulâtresses et trois, les négresses. Il y a le long du parterre trois loges grillées de chaque côté. En arrière de l'orchestre, on a pris sur le parterre de quoi former un banc de toute la largeur, c'est là que se met l'état-major de la place et des corps militaires. Le Spectacle peut contenir 1500 personnes. La salle qui était peinte en mosaïque jaune de Naples sur un fond bleu de roi, a été mis en 1784 en blanc cendré avec des panaux et des filets bleus, et l'on a ôté de deux en deux loges les piliers de bois & de forme carrée qui gênaient la vue.

Deux satyres gigantesques en buste, placés à l'avant-scene, semblent soutenir l'édifice. Au frontispice, sont les armes de France. Le rideau peint en bleu a quatre génies, dont deux sont les symboles de la tragédie & de la comédie, & deux autres planant dans les airs, qui soutiennent une légende avec ces mots en lettres d'or: CASTIGAT RIDENDO MORES. La salle est éclairée par les lampions du théâtre, mais comme le fond était dans l'obscurité, on a placé, entre chaque rang, des bras portant des bougies, dont la nuance blanchâtre de la salle augmente l'effet. Les deux loges des Administrateurs ont sur le devant un tapis peint avec des attributs militaires ou de marine.

En entrant dans le Spectacle, où l'on arrive par quatre marches, on a devant soi un intervalle au fond duquel est le corps-de-garde, c'est le dessous de l'amphithéâtre. Des deux côtés est un escalier qui mène aux loges. A côté de celui de la gauche, est un passage qui conduit au parterre, & en face de ce passage un escalier séparé, par lequel les gens de couleur se rendent à leurs loges.

Source: Moreau de St.-Méry, *Description topographique*, 1:361–62.

Port-au-Prince Comédie (1776)

Le 30 Novembre 1755, un officier de l'état-major voulut contraindre tous les vendeurs à former le marché au devant de la maison du gouvernement, mais les pacotilleurs & les matelots y opposèrent une résistance à laquelle on céda, & le ministre maintint le marché dans ce local, par une lettre du 6 Avril 1759.

En 1765, le marché ayant été transféré sur la place de l'Intendance, l'îlet dont je parle resta sans destination jusqu'en 1773, qu'on y planta des arbres, qu'on en ferma l'enceinte par des balustrades, qu'on projetta de placer une fontaine à son milieu & qu'on l'appela *place Vallière*, du nom du gouverneur-général de cette époque.

MM. d'Ennery & de Vaivre [governor and intendant, respectively] accordèrent le 26 Septembre 1776, la concession de toute la partie méridionale de cette place, sur 19 toises, du Nord au Sud, à MM. Mesplès, négocians du Port-au-Prince, à la charge de faire construire avant tout sur ce terrain, à leurs frais, une salle de spectacle de 100 pieds de long sur 40 de large & 24 d'élévation. . . .

On désirait voir une sale absolument consacrée au spectacle, lorsque MM. Mesplés frères adressèrent aux Administrateurs, à cet égard, des propositions qui furent agréées. Ceux-ci leur accordèrent en consequence le 26 Septembre 1776, 117 pieds du Nord au Sud, sur 140 pieds Est & Ouest du côté Méridional de la place de Vallière, & les assujettirent, comme je l'ai dit, à faire une salle de spectacle d'après un plan déjà dressé par M. de Boisforest, ingénieur en chef; & quant au surplus du terrain concédé, MM. Mesplés en furent déclarés propriétaires irrévocables. . . .

Cette salle, dont j'ai déjà indiqué les dimensions, a sur la Grande-rue son entrée, qui ne diffère point de celle d'une maison ordinaire; elle est seulement précédée d'une petite avant-cour. A droite en entrant, est une buvette, en face de laquelle est le bureau pour la distribution des billets. On a alors devant soi un espace à chaque bout duquel est un escalier menant aux loges. On contourne ces escaliers & l'on suit un corridor par lequel on parvient au parterre.

Il y a de chaque côté 9 loges, dont une fait face au theatre. Elles contiennent en général trois personnes sur le devant & quatre sur le derrière, parce qu'on a cherché à leur donner, en les divisant, une direction plus tournée vers le theatre qu'elles ne l'auraient eue en suivant celle du carré long de la salle. La loge du gouverneur-général qui répond à l'orchestre à droite, &

celle de l'intendant qui lui correspond à gauche, sont plus grandes. Plus près du théâtre, il y a sur chaque côté un balcon où se mettent les membres des divers tribunaux de justice. Au dessous d'un amphithéâtre assez spacieux, on a mis depuis peu, cinq loges grillés regardant le théâtre, & l'on a supprimé la loge où se mettaient MM. les officiers de la Sénéchaussée & de l'Amirauté, & qui formait au même point un retranchement dans le parterre. Au devant de celui-ci & à toucher l'orchestre, est un espace de toute la largeur de la salle pour MM. les officiers de la garnison.

Sous les deux balcons & les loges les plus voisines du théâtre, sont trois loges grillées de chaque côté.

La division des secondes loges est semblable à celle des premières, mais avec de simples loges au dessus des deux balcons. On y trouve cependant une loge de plus, formé de l'espace qui aux premières sert à aller à l'amphithéâtre.

Des 21 loges, 15, savoir: celle de fond & 7 de chaque coté, sont destinées aux gens de couleur, qui s'y mêlent sans distinction.

Les 6 autres loges, qui sont plus près du théâtre & où l'on peut arriver aussi par les corridors de celui-ci, ont été divisées en loges de 4, de 6 & de 8 places, qu'on loue à l'année de 3 à 500 liv. au delà du prix de l'abonnement, ainsi que toutes les autres loges grillées. Elles ont des chassis en treillage qu'on peut ouvrir & fermer à volonté.

Cette salle est fort chaude, assez mesquinement décorée, & l'on conçoit que son peu de solidité n'a pas dû exciter à y faire des dépenses. Elle peut contenir en tout environ 750 spectateurs.

Source: Moreau de St.-Méry, *Description topographique*, 2:322, 324–25, 326–27.

Léogane Comédie (1786)

La salle de spectacle est dans une maison ordinaire & a conservé la forme d'un carré long. Elle est petite & basse; aussi a-t-on été forcé de renoncer à l'usage d'éclairer le théâtre avec des lampions dont l'odeur & la fumée étaient insupportables. On a pratiqué, de chaque côte, un balcon qui forme les loges. On y entre par l'extrémité opposée au théâtre, de manière que ceux qui se placent jusqu'au fond ont de la peine à en sortir avant la fin du spectacle, quand le reste s'est rempli. Au bout & sur l'orchestre, est, à droite, la loge du commandant pour le roi, à gauche, celle de l'officier d'administration. On les distingue l'une et l'autre à une petite claire-voie & à un morceau de maroquin rouge qui couvre l'appui rembouré du devant de la loge. Les premières loges peuvent recevoir environ 50 personnes de chaque côté. L'amphithéâtre, qui peut en contenir à peu près 70, est destiné aux gens de couleur, qui s'y placent en confondant les nuances, mais de manière que les femmes soient sur le devant. La partie inférieure forme le parterre & l'orchestre. Quatre violons, un clairon & un basson composent celui-ci. Le parterre, où peuvent être 180 personnes, a dix bancs de chaque côté, à partir de l'orchestre; on est debout dans le reste de l'espace. Sous la loge de l'officier d'administration, en est une grillée, c'est celle du directeur.

Le spectacle peut donc contenir environ 400 personnes. Il est éclairé par les bougies du théâtre & par quatre lustres de bois placés aux quatre angles et formés d'une queue clouée au plancher, & dans laquelle sont emmortoisées deux traverses de bois garnies d'une bougie à chaque bout. Le théâtre est petit, comme tout le reste, mais les décorations sont gaies et fraîches.

On joue pour la direction le jeudi, le dimanche et les fêtes et les abonnements suspendus sont pour le mardi et le samedi. Toutes les places sont indistinctement à une gourde. La garde consiste en un brigadier & trois hommes de maréchaussée & en 10 hommes de milice, gens de couleur, à la tête desquels est le directeur Labbé lui-même, comme sergent de milices.

L'entrée du spectacle est petite; c'est la porte d'une maison. La galerie de quatre pieds qu'elle a en avant sert à abriter le receveur, dont une chandelle éclaire les opérations.

Si l'on pouvait apporter dans un pareil lieu l'idée de la comédie enchanteresse qui fait les délices de la capitale de la France, on serait bientôt puni de son injustice. Mais il n'est pas vrai que les autres spectacles de la Colonie ne doivent pas souffrir de parallèle avec celui de Léogane, & il est peut-être tel jour où ce serait à celui-ci à en rougir. On a dit dans *les Affiches Américaines*, du 2 août 1787, qu'on avait pratiqué avec art dans la couverture de cette salle des trous, qui montrant quelquefois la pluie, les éclairs & le tonnerre, rendaient dans certaines pièces à tempête l'illusion parfaite. Pour moi, qui n'y ai pas rencontré ces effets du hasard, je me rappelle d'avoir assisté avec plaisir à quelques représentations & d'y avoir applaudi en 1788 une jeune actrice [Lise], qui, d'après ce qu'elle avait acquis depuis son début aux Cayes en 1784, promettait d'ajouter aux annales théatrales de la Colonie un exemple aussi heureux que celui de sa sœur [Minette], que j'ai louée à l'article du spectacle du Port-au-Prince.

D'ailleurs, si la perfection engendrait seule le plaisir, il faudrait la croire bannie de plusieurs lieux de la terre, & presque toujours des Colonies. Les spectacles dans ces dernières, entretiennent la sociabilité, ils adoucissent les mœurs, ils enseignent la langue; enfin, ils peignent & des vices & des vertus, dont la leçon n'est pas toujours perdue. C'est un amusement pour les habitans de la ville, & une récréation pour ceux de la plaine. . . . Je fais donc des voeux pour la durée du spectacle de Léogane, surtout quand je considère que son directeur n'y cherche pas de gain; & son motif est trop généreux pour que je ne m'empresse pas de le louer.

Source: Moreau de St.-Méry, *Description topographique*, 2:461–62.

Les Cayes Comédie (1786)

La salle . . . est formée d'un clissonnage extérieur. Sa longueur totale est de 118 pieds, sa largeur totale de 64. Le parterre a 32 pieds de long, l'orchestre 8, le théâtre 42. On y voit deux rangs de loges de chaque côté; chaque rang a 7 loges. Elles sont disposées de manière que rien n'y gêne la vue.

La décoration intérieure est assez gaie, mais les peintures du plafond sont très-mauvaises. On voit au haut de l'avant-scène un Apollon et des Muses dont les proportions & les traits annoncent que le climat a défiguré le Dieu du Permesse [*sic*] & les Noeuf-Soeurs. Dans l'avant-scène même sont deux caryatides qui paraissent la porter. Pour mieux exprimer leurs efforts, le peintre leur a fait rentrer le cou dans la poitrine et le menton se trouve au bas de l'estomac.

On regrette avec raison que cette salle n'ait pas été construite sur la place, où elle aurait été plus aërée, avec des abords plus faciles, & l'on aurait pu y faire arriver par un large perron, qui aurait donné de la grace et de la noblesse à l'entrée. Au lieu de cela, on a été obligé de prendre le repose des quatre marches du perron actuel dans le terrain de la salle même, de sorte que ce perron a l'air d'un grand marche-pied mis contre le mur dans la rue.

Pour rendre cette entrée plus ridicule encore, on en a ceintré le haut en forme d'alcove, & au moyen d'une croisée mise sur le toit, le bâtiment a l'air d'un pignon où serait une fenêtre pour remplir des greniers.

Source: Moreau de St.-Méry, *Description topographique*, 2:699–700.

Saint-Marc Comédie (1772)

La salle, qui est la même qu'on a construite en 1772, a 90 pieds de l'Est à l'Ouest sur 50 pieds du Nord au Sud. Elle est garnie de deux rangs de loges, d'un amphithéâtre qui peut contenir 70 personnes & d'un parterre où l'on est assis, au fond duquel se placent les gens de couleur, sans distinction de nuances. Le théâtre a 40 pieds de profondeur à partir de l'avant-scène, sur les côtés de laquelle sont de petites loges louées à l'année. Dans le contour du théâtre sont les loges des acteurs. La salle qui peut contenir environ 500 personnes, est bien distribuée & le point de vue y est bien ménagé. . . . L'ouverture de la salle eut lieu le 28 Avril 1773.

Source: Moreau de St.-Méry, *Description topographique*, 2:202.

Saint-Pierre Comédie (1787)

Le principal divertissement des Français dans ces contrées, est le spectacle. Il y'a un magnifique théâtre à Saint-Pierre, qui surpasse pour le grandeur & le goût les bâtimens en ce genre les plus renommés en Europe. Il a une vaste cour, & devant le portail une place (d'arrivée), où les porteurs de litiere prennant le haut quand ils arrivent & le bas quand ils s'en retournent. Il a quatre rangs de loges, dont le premier a tout à l'entour une galerie en dehors, où l'on s'amuse en attendant que le spectacle commence; on y vient aussi prendre le frais dans les entr'actes, sans perdre pour cela sa place à la loge. Il n'y a aucune séparation dans les rangs de loges, & chacun peut y prendre la place qui lui plaît le mieux. Le quatrième rang s'appelle *le Paradis pour les Gens de couleurs*. Là sont relégués tous ceux qui ne peuvent pas prouver leur descendance de Parens Européens. On voit souvent ici des Christises (1), dont la peau est incomparablement plus blanche que celle de nos habitans du Nord de l'Europe.

On donna pendant mon séjour ici, uniquement des opéras ou des pièces mêlées de chant. J'assistai à Orphée & Euridice, qui fut assez bien rendu. Mais le Public me parut beaucoup plus content que Je ne l'étois moi-même, car avant que le pièce fut finie, on jetta à Orphée une couronne de myrthe, des loges sur le théâtre, à quoi le Parterre applaudit extraordinairement.
(1): Issus à la quatrieme génération d'un Pere Européen & d'une Négresse.

C'est un grand inconvénient pour nous autres Européens du Nord, que d'être suffoqués dans ces grandes assemblées par l'odeur du musc, dont le beau monde est parfumé.

Encore si l'on s'en tenoit là; mais pour mieux empoisonner l'air tout à l'entour de soi, chacun a son éventail, avec lequel il agite la vapeur désolante, comme un ouragan soulève la poussiere. Il seroit contre la décence qu'un Créole (2) parût au spectacle sans son éventail.
(2) Américains, nés d'Européens.

Source: Paul Erdman Isert, *Voyage en Guinée et dans les Îles Caraïbes en Amerique* [Paris: Chez Maradan, 1793], 339–41.

Guadeloupe Comédies (1787)

La Guadeloupe a une compagnie de comédiens, & un théâtre à Basse-Terre, & à Pointe-à-Pitre. Le dernier n'est point proportionné au nombre des spectateurs. La troupe est présentement ici. Elle ne donne guères que des opérettes comme le fête de *la Rosiere*, *la Mélomanie*, *la belle Arsenne*, *Zémire & Azor*. Ils ont ajouté à cette dernier un prologue pantomime relatif à l'intrigue de la pièce. Ils donnent d'ordinaire pour conclusion des ballets toujours très spirituels. On n'aime ici que les opéras, les autres pieces sont pour ainsi dire bannies du spectacle. Parmi les acteurs se distingue M. Fleury (j'entens dans le comique). Mademoiselle Martin enchante autant par la délicatesse de sa voix, qu'elle gagne d'adorateurs, par la beauté de sa personne. La compagnie est pensionnée par le Roi. Le directeur qui ordonne les pieces que l'on doit jouer, & a inspection sur le théâtre, est décoré du titre de major de la place.

Source: Paul Erdman Isert, *Voyage en Guinée et dans les Îles Caraïbes en Amerique* [Paris: Chez Maradan, 1793], 326.

PREMIERES OF PLAYS BY MOLIÈRE AND VOLTAIRE

IN FRANCE	IN THE COLONIES
Molière	
Amphytrion *comédie*, three acts Théâtre du Palais-Royal, January 13, 1668	Cap Français: 16 March 1769 Port-au-Prince: March 31, 1778
Avare, l' *comédie*, five acts Palais-Royal, September 9, 1668	Cap Français: February 28, 1765
Bourgeois gentilhomme, le *comédie-ballet*, five acts Chambord, October 4, 1670 Palais-Royal, November 23, 1670	Cap Français: January 3, 1783 Port-au-Prince, March 2, 1777
Ecole des femmes, l' *comédie*, five acts (1662) Palais-Royal, December 26, 1662	Cap Français: October 31, 1765
Ecole des maris, l' *comédie*, three acts Palais-Royal, June 24, 1661	Cap Français: September 19, 1765

IN FRANCE	IN THE COLONIES
Fourberies de Scapin, les *comédie*, three acts Palais-Royal, May 24, 1671	Cap Français: July 4, 1765
George Dandin, ou le mari confondu *comédie-ballet*, three acts Versailles, July 19, 1668 Palais-Royal, November 9, 1668	Cap Français: June 30, 1765
Malade imaginaire, le *comédie-ballet*, prologue, three acts, and three *intermèdes* Palais-Royal, February 10, 1673	Cap Français: February 12, 1767 Port-au-Prince: February 8, 1780
Mariage forcé, le *comédie-ballet*, three acts The Louvre, January 29, 1664 Palais-Royal, February 15, 1664	Cap Français: July 4, 1765
Médecin malgré lui, le *comédie*, three acts Palais-Royal, August 6, 1666	Cap Français: February 6, 1766
Misanthrope, le *comédie*, five acts Palais-Royal, June 4, 1666	Cap Français: 1783
Monsieur de Pourceaugnac *comédie-ballet*, three acts Chambord, October 6, 1669 Palais-Royal, November 15, 1669	Cap Français: January 8, 1767 Port-au-Prince: March 27, 1779 Saint-Marc: January 9, 1786
Précieuses ridicules, les *comédie*, 17 scenes Petit-Bourbon, November 15, 1659	Cap Français: January 3, 1765
Sganarelle ou le Cocu imaginaire *comédie*, 24 scenes (1660) Petit-Théâtre Bourbon, May 28, 1660	Cap Français: June 9, 1768
Tartuffe, le *comédie*, five acts (1669 version) Palais-Royal, February 5, 1669	Cap Français: June 16, 1765 Port-au-Prince: October 12, 1779

IN FRANCE	IN THE COLONIES
Voltaire	
Adélaide du Guesclin *tragédie*, five acts Comédie-Française, January 18, 1734	Cap Français: September 13, 1774
Alzire, ou les américains *tragédie*, five acts Comédie-Française, January 27, 1736	Cap Français: June 20, 1765 Port-au-Prince: February 2, 1779
Droit du Seigneur, ou l'écueil du sage, le *comédie*, three acts Comédie-Française, January 18, 1762 (five acts) Comédie-Française, June 12, 1779 (three acts)	Cap Français: December 15, 1778
Ecossaise, l' *comédie*, five acts Comédie-Française, July 26, 1760	Cap Français: November 3, 1765
Enfant prodigue, l' *comédie*, five acts Comédie-Française, October 10, 1736	Cap Français: January 3, 1765 Saint-Marc: October 8, 1768
Fanatisme, ou Mahomet le prophète *tragédie*, five acts Lille, France, April 1741 Comédie-Française, August 29, 1742	Cap Français: January 13, 1765 Port-au-Prince: February 10, 1784
Mérope *tragédie*, five acts Comédie-Française, February 20, 1743	Cap Français: October 17, 1773 Port-au-Prince: November 11, 1783 Saint-Marc: March 18, 1784
Nanine, ou le préjugé vaincu *comédie*, three acts Comédie-Française, June 16, 1749	Cap Français: October 28, 1764
Œdipe *tragédie*, five acts Comédie-Française, November 18, 1718	Cap Français: December 13, 1774
Olympie *tragédie*, five acts Comédie-Française, March 17, 1764	Cap Français: March 26, 1772 Port-au-Prince: January 27, 1784

IN FRANCE	IN THE COLONIES
Sémiramis *tragédie*, five acts Comédie-Française, August 29, 1748	Cap Français: September 8, 1771 Port-au-Prince: January 20, 1784
Tancrède *tragédie*, five acts Comédie-Française, September 3, 1760	Cap Français: January 28, 1772
Zaïre *tragédie*, five acts Comédie-Française, August 13, 1732	Cap Français: April 18, 1769 Saint-Marc: December 3, 1768 Port-au-Prince: November 8, 1778

APPENDIX 6

DISCOGRAPHY

Seventeenth Century

Lully, Jean-Baptiste. *Acis et Galatée, pastorale héroïque*. Les Musiciens du Louvre, Marc Munkowski, conductor. Archiv Produktion. Deutsche Grammophon GmbH, Hamburg, 1998.

- *Ouverture*
- Monologue (Acis): "C'est en vain" (I, 1)
- Dialogue air, "Que tardons-nous?" (Polyphème and Galatée), (I, 8)
- *Récitatifs simples* (simple recitatives): "Les voici, ces tendres amants" (The Priest); "Que vois-je?" (Polyphème and chorus), and "Fuyons sa violence extrême" (Galatée and Acis), (III, 2–4)
- *Récitatif accompagné* (accompanied recitative): "Quel chemin ont-ils pris?" (Polyphème), (III, 5)
- Solo-choral ensemble: "Je sors de mes grottes profondes" (Neptune and chorus), and "Que votre sang se change" (Neptune, Galatée, and Acis), (III, 8–9)
- *Finale*: Dance (*passacaille*) and chorus of water divinities (III, 9)

Eighteenth Century

Gluck, Christoph Willibald. *Orphée et Euridice* (1774 Paris Version). Opera Lafayette Orchestra and Chorus. Ryan Brown, conductor.

- *Récitatif accompagné*, "Quel est l'audacieux?" (Chorus and Orphée), (II, 1)
- Dialogue scene in *Récitatif accompagné*: "Ah, puisse ma douleur finir!" (Orphée), and "Arrête, Orphée!" (L'Amour, Orphée, and Euridice), (III, 1)

Grétry, André-Ernest-Modeste. *Grétry, Zémire et Azor*, Choeurs & Orchestre de Chambre de la RTB, EMI Classics, EMI Music France, 2002.

- *Ouverture*
- *Ariette*, "La Fauvette" (III, 5)
- Ballet, *Entrée des Génies qui rendent homage à Zémire* (Entrée of genies who pay homage to Zémire), (III, 4).
- *Récitatif accompagné* (accompanied recitative), "Ah!, mon père, ah! Cruel!" (Zémire and Azor), (III, 7)
- *Finale*: "Amour, Amour" (chorus of genies), (IV, 6)

Grétry, André-Ernest-Modeste. *La Caravane du Caire*. Ricercar Academy, Marc Minkowski, conductor.

- *Ariette*, "Ne suis-je pas aussi captive?" (I)
- *Récitatif simple*, "Me voici de retour" (II)
- *Divertissement*: Air, "Du Pacha qu'on révère"; Dance, *Tambourin*; *Récitatif*; *Air*, "Almaïde, de votre zèle"; *Récitatif* (II)
- *Récitatif accompagné*, "Vous brulez de revoir les riens" (III)
- *Récitatif accompagné*, "Tu me condamnes donc" (III)

Mondonville, Jean-Joseph Cassanéa. *Titon et l'Aurore*, Les Musiciens du Louvre, Marc Munkowski, conductor. Musifrance, Erato/Radio France, 1992.

- *Ouverture*
- Monologue air, "Que vois-je?" (Titon), (III, 2)
- *Ariette*, "Du Dieu des cœurs," (Titon), (III, 5)
- Dance, *Contredanse* (III, 5)
- Solo choral ensemble, "Vents furieux, sortez de la grotte profonde" (Eole and chorus of winds), (II, 4).

Philidor, François-André Danican. Tom Jones, opéra-comique. Opéra de Lausanne. La Sinfonette de Lausanne. Jean-Claude Malgoire, conductor.

- Chorus, "Et nos chasseurs chantent tous à l'envie" (I)
- *Ariette*, "Amour, quelle est donc ta puissance" (II)
- *Récitatif accompagné*, "Où suis-je?" (III)

APPENDIX 7

COLONIAL PRODUCTIONS WITH SUB-SAHARAN AFRICAN ELEMENTS

TITLE COMPOSER/ AUTHOR LIBRETTIST	PREMIERES IN PARIS ACADEMY ROYALE DE MUSIQUE	 COMÉDIE-ITALIENNE/ OPÉRA-COMIQUE	 OTHER THEATRES	PREMIERES IN COLONIES
Acajou, *opera comique*, three acts Charles-Simon Favart (1710–1792) (music and text)	October 1744	July 19, 1773	Foire Saint-Germain, March 18, 1744	Port-au-Prince, December 7, 1784 Saint-Marc, January 12, 1784 Cap Français, January 30, 1786
Adélaide du Guesclin, *tragédie*, five acts Voltaire (1694–1778)			Comédie-Française, January 18, 1734	Cap Français, September 13, 1774

TITLE COMPOSER/ AUTHOR LIBRETTIST	PREMIERES IN PARIS ACADEMY ROYALE DE MUSIQUE	 COMÉDIE-ITALIENNE/ OPÉRA-COMIQUE	 OTHER THEATRES	PREMIERES IN COLONIES
Alexis & Justine, comédie lyrique mêlée d'ariettes, two acts Nicolas Dezède (1740?–1792) Jacques-Marie Boutet de Monvel (1745–1812)	Versailles, January 14, 1785	January 17, 1785		Cap Français, January 22, 1786 Port-au-Prince, January 24, 1786
Alzire, ou les américains, tragédie, five acts Voltaire (1694–1778)			Comédie-Française, January 27, 1736	Cap Français, June 20, 1765 Port-au-Prince, February 2, 1779
Amant statue, comédie mêlée d'ariettes, L', one act Nicolas-Marie Daleyrac (1753–1809) François F. D. Desfontaines (1733–1825)		February 20, 1781		Port-au-Prince, October 10, 1786 Saint-Marc, January 8, 1787 Léogane, January 22, 1788

TITLE COMPOSER/ AUTHOR LIBRETTIST	PREMIERES IN PARIS ACADEMY ROYALE DE MUSIQUE	 COMÉDIE-ITALIENNE/ OPÉRA-COMIQUE	 OTHER THEATRES	PREMIERES IN COLONIES
Amitié à l'Epreuve, comédie mêlée d'ariettes, L', two acts André Ernest Modeste Grétry (1741–1813) Charles-Simon Favart (1723–1799); Claude-H. F. de Voisenon (1708–75)	Fontainebleau, November 13, 1770	January 24, 1771		Cap Français, February 25, 1772 Saint-Marc, February 27, 1775 Port-au-Prince, February 14, 1778
Amoureux de quinze ans, ou le double fête, comédie mêlée d'ariettes, L', three acts Johann Paul Aegidius Martini (1741–1816) Pierre Laujon (1727–1811)	1777	April 18, 1771		Cap Français, February 16, 1773 Saint-Marc, December 1, 1780 Port-au-Prince, October 2, 1781
Amours de Mirabalais, parodie Nègre du Devin du village, Les (author unknown)			Variétés-Amusantes, c.1782	Saint-Marc, February 6, 1786
Amours de Montmartre, comédie, Les (author unknown)			Variétés-Amusantes, c.1785	Port-au-Prince, July 25, 1786

TITLE COMPOSER/ AUTHOR LIBRETTIST	PREMIERES IN PARIS ACADEMY ROYALE DE MUSIQUE	 COMÉDIE-ITALIENNE/ OPÉRA-COMIQUE	 OTHER THEATRES	PREMIERES IN COLONIES
Anglais à Paris, ou le fou raisonnable, comédie, L', two acts (author unknown)			Variétés-Amusantes, c.1782	Cap Français, October 25, 1783 Port-au-Prince, February 2, 1785
Aristote amoureux, ou le philosophe bridé, opéra comique, one act Augustin de Piis (1755–1832) P.Y. Barré (1749–1809)		August 11, 1780		Cap Français, November 26, 1782
Arlequin mûlatresse protégée par Macanda, grand pantomime, two acts Mr. Acquaire (music and text)				Port-au-Prince, March 21, 1786
Arlequin sauvage, comédie, three acts Louis François Delisle de la Drevetière (1682–1756)		June 17, 1721		Cap Français, September 29, 1765 Port-au-Prince, April 1, 1783

TITLE COMPOSER/ AUTHOR LIBRETTIST	PREMIERES IN PARIS ACADEMY ROYALE DE MUSIQUE	COMÉDIE-ITALIENNE/ OPÉRA-COMIQUE	OTHER THEATRES	PREMIERES IN COLONIES
Aucassin & Nicolette, ou les moeurs du bon vieux temps, comédie mêlée d'ariettes, three acts André Ernest Modeste Grétry (1741–1813) Michel-Jean Sedaine (1719–1797)		Versailles, December 30, 1779		Cap Français, July 22, 1783 Port-au-Prince, November 25, 1783
Avocat chansonnier, comédie, L' (author unknown)			Variétés-Amusantes	Léogane, February 19, 1787
Azémia, ou les sauvages, comédie mêlée d'ariettes, three acts Nicolas-Marie Dalayrac (1753–1809) A.E.X. de La Chabeaussière (1752–1820)		Fontainebleau, October 17, 1786 Paris, May 3, 1787		Cap Français, August 21, 1788

TITLE COMPOSER/ AUTHOR LIBRETTIST	PREMIERES IN PARIS ACADEMY ROYALE DE MUSIQUE	COMÉDIE- ITALIENNE/ OPÉRA-COMIQUE	OTHER THEATRES	PREMIERES IN COLONIES
Belle Arsène, comédie-féerie mêlée d'ariettes, La, four acts Pierre Alexandre Monsigny (1729–1817) Charles-Simon Favart (1710–1792)		Fontainebleau, November 2, 1773 Paris, August 14, 1775		Port-au-Prince, October 25, 1778 Cap Français, January 16, 1779 Les Cayes, March 30, 1784 Guadeloupe, 1787 Martinique, 1787
Belle esclave, ou Valcour et Zeila, comédie mêlée d'ariettes, La, one act François-André Danican Philidor (1726–1795) Antoine-Jean Dumaniant (1752–1828)			Théâtre du Comte de Beaujolais, September 18, 1787	Cap Français, January 24, 1789
Blaise & Babet, ou la suite des trois fermiers, comédie mêlée d'ariettes, two acts Nicolas Dezède (?1740–1812) Jacques-Marie Boutet de Monvel (1745–1812)		Versailles, April 4, 1783		Port-au-Prince, November 9, 1784 Cap Français, January 22, 1785

TITLE COMPOSER/ AUTHOR LIBRETTIST	PREMIERES IN PARIS ACADEMY ROYALE DE MUSIQUE	COMÉDIE-ITALIENNE/ OPÉRA-COMIQUE	OTHER THEATRES	PREMIERES IN COLONIES
Cacophonie, ou le procureur changé en âne, comédie, Le (author unknown)			Variétés-Amusantes	Port-au-Prince, November 21, 1786 Cap Français, January 8, 1785
Caravane du Caire, opéra-ballet, La, three acts André Ernest Modeste Grétry (1741–1813); Etienne Morel de Chédeville	January 15, 1784			Port-au-Prince, January 1787
Cartouche, ou les voleurs, comédie, three acts LeGrand (1737–?1800)				Léogane, January 29, 1788
Colonie, opéra comique, La, two acts Antonio Sacchini (1730–1786) Nicolas E. Framery (1745–1810)		August 16, 1775		Port-au-Prince, January 29, 1782 Saint-Marc, February 8, 1782 Cap Français, July 26, 1787

TITLE COMPOSER/ AUTHOR LIBRETTIST	PREMIERES IN PARIS ACADEMY ROYALE DE MUSIQUE	COMÉDIE-ITALIENNE/ OPÉRA-COMIQUE	OTHER THEATRES	PREMIERES IN COLONIES
Corsaire, comédie mêlée d'ariettes, Le, three acts Nicolas-M. Dalayrac (1753–1809) A.E.X. de La Chabeaussière (1752–1820)		Versailles, March 7, 1783		Martinique, July 30, 1788 Cap Français, 1788
Créoles africaines, ou les effets de l'amour, comédie mêlée de divertissements [and] *vaudevilles,* one act Jean-Baptiste Radet (1752–1830) P.Y. Barré (1749–1809)		June 15, 1787 (titled *La Négresse, ou le pouvoir de la reconnaissance*)		Port-au-Prince, January 26, 1788
Démocrite amoureux, comédie, five acts Jean François Regnard (1655–1709)				Port-au-Prince, May 1, 1781
Deux billets, ou Arlequin Roi, dame, & valet, comédie, Les one act (author unknown)				Port-au-Prince, September 3, 1782

TITLE	PREMIERES IN PARIS			
COMPOSER/ AUTHOR LIBRETTIST	ACADEMY ROYALE DE MUSIQUE	COMÉDIE-ITALIENNE/ OPÉRA-COMIQUE	OTHER THEATRES	PREMIERES IN COLONIES
Deux tuteurs, comédie mêlée d'ariettes, Les, two acts Nicolas-Marie Dalayrac (1753–1809) A.E.X. de La Chabeaussière (1752–1820)		May 8, 1784		Cap Français, December 3, 1785 Port-au-Prince, July 25, 1786 Léogane, January 22, 1788
Devin du village, intermède, Le, one act Jean-Jacques Rousseau (1712–1778) (music and text)		Fontainebleau, October 18, 1752 Paris, March 1, 1753		Cap Français, May 26, 1764 Saint-Marc, November 25, 1769
Diable à quatre, ou la double métamorphose, opéra comique, Le, three acts François-André Danican Philidor (1726–1795) Michel-Jean Sedaine (1719–1797)		January 30, 1764	Foire Saint Laurent, August 19, 1756	Cap Français, February 9, 1766
Enfants trouvés, ou le Sultan poli par l'Amour, Les, parody of Voltaire's *Zaïre* (1732), one act (author unknown)				Cap Français, April 18, 1769

TITLE COMPOSER/ AUTHOR LIBRETTIST	PREMIERES IN PARIS ACADEMY ROYALE DE MUSIQUE	 COMÉDIE- ITALIENNE/ OPÉRA-COMIQUE	 OTHER THEATRES	PREMIERES IN COLONIES
Enrôlement supposé, comédie, L', one act (author unknown)			Variétés-Amusantes	Cap Français, October 22, 1783 Port-au-Prince, January 27, 1784 Saint-Marc, January 8, 1787
Épreuve villageoise, opéra bouffon, L', two acts André Ernest Modeste Grétry (1741–1813) Pierre-Jean-Baptiste Desforges (1746–1806)		June 24, 1784		Cap Français, August 19, 1785 Port-au-Prince, October 11, 1785 Léogane, February 19, 1787
Événemens imprévus, comédie mêlée d'ariettes, Les, three acts André Ernest Modeste Grétry (1741–1813) Thomas D'Hèle (?1740–1780)		Versailles, November 11, 1779 Paris, November 13, 1779		Cap Français, December 29, 1781 Port-au-Prince, January 15, 1782
Fanatisme, ou Mahomet le prophète, tragédie, Le, five acts Voltaire (1694–1778)			Lille, April 1741 Comédie-Française, August 9, 1742	Cap Français, January 13, 1765 Port-au-Prince, February 10, 1784

TITLE COMPOSER/ AUTHOR LIBRETTIST	PREMIERES IN PARIS ACADEMY ROYALE DE MUSIQUE	COMÉDIE-ITALIENNE/ OPÉRA-COMIQUE	OTHER THEATRES	PREMIERES IN COLONIES
Fausses consultations, comédie, Les, one act Dorvigny (?1742–1812)			Variétés-Amusantes, c.1782	Port-au-Prince, March 24, 1783
Faux lord, ou le pacotilleur, opéra comique, Le, two acts Niccolò Piccinni, *père* (1728–1800) G. M. Piccinni, *fils* (1758–1826)		Versailles, December 5, 1783		Cap Français, January 15, 1785 Port-au-Prince, September 20, 1785 Léogane, January 29, 1788
Fée Urgelle, ou ce qui plaît les dames, comédie mêlée d'ariettes, La, three acts Egidio Duni (1708–1775) Charles-Simon Favart (1710–1792)	?1766	Fontainebleau, October 26, 1765		Cap Français, February 11, 1768 Saint-Marc, January 25, 1776 Port-au-Prince, July 19, 1778
Félix, ou l'enfant-trouvé, opéra, three acts Pierre-Alexandre Monsigny (1729–1817) Michel-Jean Sedaine (1719–1797)		Fontainebleau, November 1777		Cap Français, January 31, 1784 Port-au-Prince, November 16, 1784

TITLE COMPOSER/ AUTHOR LIBRETTIST	PREMIERES IN PARIS ACADEMY ROYALE DE MUSIQUE	 COMÉDIE-ITALIENNE/ OPÉRA-COMIQUE	 OTHER THEATRES	PREMIERES IN COLONIES
Femmes vengées, opéra-bouffon, Les, one act François-André Danican Philidor (1726–1795) Michel-Jean Sedaine (1719–1797)		March 20, 1775		Cap Français, November 26, 1776 Port-au-Prince, September 8, 1778
Fille mal gardée, ou le pendant amoureux, comédie mêlée d'ariettes, La, one act Egidio Duni (1708–1775) Charles-Simon Favart (1710–1792), Marie-Justine-Benôite Favart (1727–1772), and Jean-Baptiste Lourdet de Santerre (1723–1815)		March 4, 1758		Cap Français, May 2, 1765 Saint-Marc, December 14, 1781 Port-au-Prince, November 5, 1783
Folle journée, ou le mariage de Figaro, comédie, La, five acts Pierre-Augustin Caron de Beaumarchais (1732–1799)			Comédie-Française, April 27, 1784	Cap Français, June 11, 1785 Port-au-Prince, August 30, 1785 Saint-Marc, January 23, 1786

TITLE COMPOSER/ AUTHOR LIBRETTIST	PREMIERES IN PARIS ACADEMY ROYALE DE MUSIQUE	 COMÉDIE-ITALIENNE/ OPÉRA-COMIQUE	 OTHER THEATRES	PREMIERES IN COLONIES
Gilles, garçon peintre, s'amoureux-t-et-rival (*parodie du peintre amoureux de son modèle, opéra-ballet* [E. Duni]), *opéra-bouffon*, one act Jean-Benjamin-François de La Borde (1734 1794) Antoine Alexandre Henri Poinsinet (1735–1769)		February 26, 1767		Port-au-Prince, December 28, 1779 Cap Français, February 5, 1780
Gilles ravisseur, ou le commerce de l'horlogerie, comédie-parade, one act (author unknown)				Cap Français, July 30, 1782 Port-au-Prince, December 7, 1784
Grand ballet des Sauvages, pantomime sérieuse (author unknown)		November 10, 1763		Cap Français, January 20, 1776

TITLE COMPOSER/ AUTHOR LIBRETTIST	PREMIERES IN PARIS ACADEMY ROYALE DE MUSIQUE	COMÉDIE-ITALIENNE/ OPÉRA-COMIQUE	OTHER THEATRES	PREMIERES IN COLONIES
Héroine Américaine, pantomime, L', three acts Louis-François Ribié (1758–c.1830)		1784	Ambigu-Comique, 1786	Cap Français, July 26, 1787 Martinique, 1788
Héros africain, ou la traité des noirs, Le, pantomime (author unknown)				Martinique, August 11, 1788 Cap Français, May 28, 1797
Huron, comédie mêlée d'ariettes, Le, two acts A.E.M. Grétry (1741–1813) J.F. Marmontel (1723–1799)		August 20, 1768		Cap Français, May 14, 1769 Saint-Marc, February 27, 1774 Port-au-Prince, November 24, 1778
Île des fous, comédie mêlée d'ariettes, L', two acts Egidio Duni (1708–1775) Louis Anseaume (1721–1784)		December 29, 1760		Cap Français, October 26, 1773 Port-au-Prince, November 26, 1782
Impatient, comédie, L', one act (author unknown)				Cap Français, October 16, 1781 Port-au-Prince, November 20, 1781

TITLE COMPOSER/ AUTHOR LIBRETTIST	PREMIERES IN PARIS ACADEMY ROYALE DE MUSIQUE	COMÉDIE-ITALIENNE/ OPÉRA-COMIQUE	OTHER THEATRES	PREMIERES IN COLONIES
Infante de Zamora, opéra-féerie, L', three acts Giovanni Paisiello (1740–1816) Nicolas Etienne Framery (1745–1810)	Versailles, 1781			Port-au-Prince, February 4, 1783 Cap Français, November 29, 1783 Les Cayes, October 1, 1785
Isabelle et Gertrude, ou les sylphes supposes, comédie mêlée d'ariettes, one act Adolphe Benoît Blaise (d.1772) Charles-Simon Favart (1710–1792)		August 14, 1765		Cap Français, July 5, 1767 Port-au-Prince, October 8, 1775
Jérome Pointu, comédie, one act (author unknown)				Port-au-Prince, November 26, 1782
Jugement de Midas, opéra-comique, Le, three acts A.E.M. Grétry (1741–1813) Thomas d'Hèle (?1740–1780)		June 27, 1778		Cap Français, November 20, 1781 Port-au-Prince, December 18, 1781

TITLE COMPOSER/ AUTHOR LIBRETTIST	PREMIERES IN PARIS ACADEMY ROYALE DE MUSIQUE	COMÉDIE-ITALIENNE/ OPÉRA-COMIQUE	OTHER THEATRES	PREMIERES IN COLONIES
Juliet et Susette, comédie locale, traduction nègre de Blaise et Babet, comédie mise en musique, two acts Claude Clément (music and text)				Cap Français, February 7, 1788
Julien et Zila, comédie locale, traduction nègre de Blaise et Babet, comédie mise en musique, two acts ?Clément				Cap Français, January 8, 1791
Loi de Jatab, ou le Turc à Paris, comédie, La, one act Antoine-Jean Dumaniant (1752–1828)				Port-au-Prince, September 12, 1789
Maître en droit, ou le tuteur dupe, opéra bouffon, two acts Pierre Alexandre Monsigny (1729–1817) Pierre R. Lemonnier (1731–1796)		February 8, 1762	Foire Saint Laurent, August 22, 1761	Cap Français, December 20, 1768 Port-au-Prince, March 20, 1781

TITLE COMPOSER/ AUTHOR LIBRETTIST	PREMIERES IN PARIS ACADEMY ROYALE DE MUSIQUE	 COMÉDIE-ITALIENNE/ OPÉRA-COMIQUE	 OTHER THEATRES	PREMIERES IN COLONIES
Malborough, drame burlesque, two acts (author unknown)				Port-au-Prince, December 9, 1783 Léogane, January 22, 1788
Maréchal-ferrant, opéra comique, Le, two acts François-André Danican Philidor (1726–1795) Antoine-François Quétant (1733–1823)				Port-au-Prince, May 20, 1781
Maréchal de Logis, pantomime, Le (author unknown)				Port-au-Prince, January 31, 1786 Saint-Marc, January 8, 1787 Cap Français, July 21, 1787
Mariage d'Antonio, ou la suite de Richard Coeur de Lion, comédie mêlée d'ariettes, one act A.E.M. Grétry, Lucile Grétry (1772–1790), and Mme de Beaunoir		July 29, 1786		Port-au-Prince, May 10, 1787

TITLE COMPOSER/ AUTHOR LIBRETTIST	PREMIERES IN PARIS ACADEMY ROYALE DE MUSIQUE	 COMÉDIE-ITALIENNE/ OPÉRA-COMIQUE	 OTHER THEATRES	PREMIERES IN COLONIES
Mariage par lettres de change, ou du Négociant du Cap, Le, comédie avec un divertissement et des couplets créoles (author unknown)				Port-au-Prince, May 7, 1785
Matinée et la veillée villageoise, ou le Sabot perdu, opéra comique, two acts Augustin de Piis (1755–1832) P.Y. Barré (1749–1809)		March 27, 1781		Cap Français, January 5, 1782 Port-au-Prince, September 3, 1782
Mélomanie, opéra comique mêlée d'ariettes, La, one act Stanislas Champein (1753–1830) E. Grenier (?)	January 23, 1781, Versailles	January 29, 1781		Cap Français, December 21, 1783 Port-au-Prince, March 30, 1784 Guadeloupe, 1787 Martinique, 1787
Mercure et les ombres, pièce épisodique, mêlée de musique, one act (author unknown)				Port-au-Prince, January 31, 1789

TITLE COMPOSER/ AUTHOR LIBRETTIST	PREMIERES IN PARIS ACADEMY ROYALE DE MUSIQUE	 COMÉDIE-ITALIENNE/ OPÉRA-COMIQUE	 OTHER THEATRES	PREMIERES IN COLONIES
Nègre blanc, comédie, Le, one act Dorvigny (?1742–1812)		Versailles, June 1780	Variétés-Amusantes, June 28, 1780	Port-au-Prince, February 1, 1785
Nègres de place ou les commerçants de nuit, comédie locale, two acts (author unknown)				Saint-Marc, January 9, 1786 Port-au-Prince, November 14, 1786
Nina, ou la folle par amour, comédie mêlée d'ariettes, one act N.-M. Dalayrac (1753–1809) B.-J. Marsollier des Vivetières (1750–1817)		May 15, 1786		Port-au-Prince, March 6, 1787
Nouvelle école des femmes, opéra comique, La, three acts François-André Danican Philidor (1726–1795) Alexandre-Guillaume Mouslier de Moissy (1712–1777)		January 22, 1770		Port-au-Prince, November 3, 1778 Cap Français, December 16, 1780

TITLE COMPOSER/ AUTHOR LIBRETTIST	PREMIERES IN PARIS ACADEMY ROYALE DE MUSIQUE	 COMÉDIE-ITALIENNE/ OPÉRA-COMIQUE	 OTHER THEATRES	PREMIERES IN COLONIES
On fait ce qu'on peut et non pas ce qu'on veut, proverbe dramatique, one act Dorvigny (?1742–1812)				Cap Français, January 26, 1782 Port-au-Prince, March 24, 1783 Jacmel, August 14, 1785
On ne s'avise jamais de tout, opéra bouffon, one act Pierre A. Monsigny (1729–1817) Michel-Jean Sedaine (1719–1797)	Versailles, December 2, 1761	February 3, 1762	Foire Saint Laurent, September 14, 1761	Cap Français, May 29, 1766 Léogane, December 6, 1772 Port-au-Prince, May 21, 1775
Orphée et Eurydice, tragédie opéra, three acts Christoph Willibald Ritter von Gluck (1714–1787) Ranieri de Calzabigi (1714–1795), Vienna production (1762); Pierre-Louise Moline (1739–1820), Paris production (1774)	August 2, 1774			Port-au-Prince, March 19, 1782 Cap Français, November 13, 1784 Martinique, 1787

TITLE COMPOSER/ AUTHOR LIBRETTIST	PREMIERES IN PARIS: ACADEMY ROYALE DE MUSIQUE	PREMIERES IN PARIS: COMÉDIE-ITALIENNE/ OPÉRA-COMIQUE	PREMIERES IN PARIS: OTHER THEATRES	PREMIERES IN COLONIES
Oui ou non, comédie, one act (author unknown)			Variétés-Amusantes	Cap Français, September 22, 1783 Port-au-Prince, July 25, 1786
Partie de chasse d'Henri IV, comédie mêlée de vaudevilles, La, three acts Charles Collé (1709–1783)			Comédie-Française, 1764	Cap Français, December 16, 1766 Saint-Marc, February 27, 1775 Port-au-Prince, May 18, 1784
Peintre amoureux de son modèle, opéra-ballet, Le, two acts Egidio Duni (1708–1775) Louis Anseaume (1721–1784)		February 6, 1762	Foire Saint Laurent, September 26, 1757	Port-au-Prince, December 28, 1779 Cap Français, January 3, 1786
Plaideurs, comédie, Les, three acts Jean Racine (1639–1699)			Hôtel de Bourgogne, 1668 Comédie-Française, 1680	Port-au-Prince, March 6, 1781
Prométhée, pantomime, five scenes (author unknown)				Port-au-Prince, November 26, 1782

TITLE COMPOSER/ AUTHOR LIBRETTIST	PREMIERES IN PARIS ACADEMY ROYALE DE MUSIQUE	COMÉDIE-ITALIENNE/ OPÉRA-COMIQUE	OTHER THEATRES	PREMIERES IN COLONIES
Pygmalion, scène-lyrique Jean-Jacques Rousseau (1712–1778) Rousseau and Horace Coignet (1735–1818)			Hotel de ville, Lyons, France, 1770	Saint-Marc, August 23, 1769 Cap Français, February10, 1776 Port-au-Prince, February 13, 1781
Raccoleurs, opéra comique, Les Jean-Joseph Vadé (1719–1757)		August 1, 1762	Foire Saint Germain, March 11, 1756,	Cap Français, February 28, 1765 Saint-Marc, March 4, 1769 Port-au-Prince, November 18, 1783
Ramir, comédie-héroïque, five acts (author unknown)				Cap Français, November 5, 1776 Port-au-Prince, October 23, 1781 Saint-Marc, September 9, 1782
Renaud d'Ast, comédie mêlée d'ariettes, two acts Nicolas Dalayrac (1753–1809) Jean Baptiste Radet (1752–1830) and P.Y. Barré (1749–1809)		July 19, 1787		Port-au-Prince, September 12, 1789

TITLE COMPOSER/ AUTHOR LIBRETTIST	PREMIERES IN PARIS ACADEMY ROYALE DE MUSIQUE	COMÉDIE-ITALIENNE/ OPÉRA-COMIQUE	OTHER THEATRES	PREMIERES IN COLONIES
Répétition interrompue, opéra comique, La, one act Jean-Claude Gillier (1667–1737) Charles-Simon Favart (1710–1792)			Foire Saint Laurent, August 6, 1735 Foire Saint Laurent, March 14, 1757 (titled *La Répétition interrompue, ou le petit-maître malgré lui)*	Port-au-Prince, September 27, 1789 (probably an arrangement by "a citizen" of the Gillier-Favart work)
Richard, Coeur de lion, comédie mise en musique, three acts A.E.M. Grétry (1741–1813) Michel-Jean Sedaine (1719–1797)		October 21, 1784		Port-au-Prince, December 5, 1786 (version by A.E.M. Grétry and M. d'Hêle [1740?–1780])
Sara, ou la fermière ecossaise, opéra, two acts Pierre Vachon (1731–1803) Jean-Baptiste Collet de Messine (d.1787)		May 8, 1773		Port-au-Prince, November 20, 1781

TITLE COMPOSER/ AUTHOR LIBRETTIST	PREMIERES IN PARIS ACADEMY ROYALE DE MUSIQUE	 COMÉDIE-ITALIENNE/ OPÉRA-COMIQUE	 OTHER THEATRES	PREMIERES IN COLONIES
Sauvages, ou le pouvoir de la danse, Divertissement, Les Pierre Gabriel Gardel (1758–1840) and Maximilien Léopold Philippe Joseph Gardel (1741–1787) (music and choreography)	October 31, 1786			Martinique, 1788
Servante maîtresse, La, parody of *La Serva padrona, intermède italien,* two acts Pierre Baurans, translator (1710–1764)	October 4, 1746 (original title, *la Serva padrona,* intermezzo, composed by G.B. Pergolesi (1710–1736)	August 17, 1754		Cap Français, December 26, 1765 Port-au-Prince May 4, 1778
Silvain, comédie mêlée d'ariettes, one act A.E.M. Grétry (1741–1813) J.F. Marmontel (1723–1799)		February 19, 1770		Cap Français, October 28, 1770 Port-au-Prince, June 25, 1775

TITLE COMPOSER/ AUTHOR LIBRETTIST	PREMIERES IN PARIS ACADEMY ROYALE DE MUSIQUE	COMÉDIE-ITALIENNE/ OPÉRA-COMIQUE	OTHER THEATRES	PREMIERES IN COLONIES
Soliman second, ou les trois sultanes, opéra comique, three acts Paul César Gibert (1717–1787) Charles-Simon Favart (1710–1792)	December 19, 1761	April 9, 1761		Cap Français, September 30, 1766 Saint-Marc, November 28, 1774
Souliers mordorés, ou le cordonnière allemande, comédie-lyrique, Les, two acts Alessandro Maria Antonio Fridzéri (1741–1825) Ferrières, Alexandre, Marquis de (?) Michel-Jean Sedaine (1719–1797) (librettist, February 15, 1784, version)	February 15, 1784	January 11, 1776		Cap Français, October 15, 1776 Port-au-Prince, June 2, 1778 Martinique, August 11, 1788

TITLE COMPOSER/ AUTHOR LIBRETTIST	PREMIERES IN PARIS ACADEMY ROYALE DE MUSIQUE	 COMÉDIE-ITALIENNE/ OPÉRA-COMIQUE	 OTHER THEATRES	PREMIERES IN COLONIES
Thérèse et Jeannot, nègre parodie du Devin du village, one act Claude Clément (music and text)				Cap Français, 1758 Léogane, January 3, 1773 Port-au-Prince, February 13, 1781 Les Cayes, March 30, 1784
Toinon et Toinette, opéra comique, two acts François Gossec (1734–1829) Jean-Auguste-Julien Desboulmiers (1731–1771)		June 20, 1767		Cap Français, January 13, 1777 Port-au-Prince, October 23, 1781
Tonnelier, opéra comique, Le, one act François-Joseph Gossec (1734–1829); Nicolas-Médard Audinot (1732–1801) and Antoine-François Quétant (1733–1823)		March 16, 1765	Prince of Condé, Chantilly, July 26, 1767,	Cap Français, November 25, 1766 Port-au-Prince, December 29, 1778 Saint-Marc, February 6, 1786

TITLE COMPOSER/ AUTHOR LIBRETTIST	PREMIERES IN PARIS ACADEMY ROYALE DE MUSIQUE	COMÉDIE-ITALIENNE/ OPÉRA-COMIQUE	OTHER THEATRES	PREMIERES IN COLONIES
Trois fermiers, comédie mêlée d'ariettes, Les, two acts Nicolas Dezède (1740?–1792) Jacques-Marie Boutet de Monvel (1745–1812)	May 16, 1777	May 24, 1777		Cap Français, March 31, 1778 Port-au-Prince, November 3, 1778 Saint-Marc, December 25, 1780
Turcaret, comédie, five acts Alain-René LeSage (1668–1747)			Foire Saint Laurent, 1709 Comédie-Française, 1732	Cap Français, March 24, 1765 Port-au-Prince, November 5, 1783
Vendangeurs, ou les deux baillis, Les, one act Augustin de Piis (1755–1832) P.Y. Barré (1749–1809)		November 7, 1780		Cap Français, May 18, 1782 Port-au-Prince, January 17, 1786
Voyages de Rosine, Les, opéra-comique, two acts Augustin de Piis (1755–1832) P.Y. Barré (1749–1809)		May 30, 1783		Port-au-Prince, December 21, 1784

TITLE COMPOSER/ AUTHOR LIBRETTIST	PREMIERES IN PARIS: ACADEMY ROYALE DE MUSIQUE	PREMIERES IN PARIS: COMÉDIE-ITALIENNE/ OPÉRA-COMIQUE	PREMIERES IN PARIS: OTHER THEATRES	PREMIERES IN COLONIES
Zémire et Azor, comédie-ballet mêlée de chants & de danses, four acts A.E.M. Grétry (1741–1813) J.F. Marmontel (1723–1799)		Fontainebleau, November 9, 1771 Paris, December 16, 1771		Cap Français, August 30, 1772 Port-au-Prince, February 17, 1778 Guadeloupe, 1787 Martinique, 1787

Total Productions with Sub-Saharan African Elements, 1764–1789

Operas 65
Divertissements/ballets 7
Plays 29
Total. 101

NOTES

Preface

1. In the present study, the terms "Africans" and "nonwhites" apply only to sub-Saharan Africans and their descendants, unless specifically indicated otherwise. Further, French authorities attached to these persons several subcategories, many of which are discussed in chapter 1.
2. In accordance with French tradition dating back to the seventeenth century, usage of the term "opera" refers to any staged musical production that consists of a continuous dramatic action throughout the work, as well as those pieces in which each act (or *entrée*) has a different subject, all of which are tied together by an overall theme expressed by a title such as *Les Arts* (The Arts) or *Les Saisons* (The Seasons). By the beginning of the eighteenth century, it was also customary for librettists and composers to indicate the kind of action and the rank of characters in an opera by giving the work a descriptive subtitle. Subsequently, they applied to their works a wide variety of epithets, such as *ballet*, *ballet héroïque*, *comédie lyrique*, *comédie mêlée d'ariettes*, *comédie mise en musique*, *intermède*, *opéra-ballet*, *opéra comique*, *opéra-féerie*, *pastorale*, *pastorale-héroïque*, *scène lyrique*, and *tragédie lyrique*. While several of these types are discussed during the course of this study, specific subtitles will be mentioned only when deemed necessary to clarify certain events. Those ballets in which there is no text are indicated by the subtitle *ballet-pantomime*.
3. *Artistes et repertoire des scènes de Saint-Domingue* (Port-au-Prince: Imprimerie de l'État, 1955); *Le théâtre à Saint-Domingue* (Port-au-Prince: Imprimerie de l'État, 1955); *Les plaisirs de Saint-Domingue* (Port-au-Prince: Imprimerie de l'État, 1955); and *Les marrons du syllabaire* (1953; reprint,

Port-au-Prince, Haiti: Éditions Henri Deschamps, 1988).

4. *La musique dans la société antillaise, 1635–1902: Martinique, Guadeloupe* (Paris, 1986); and *Jazz et biguine: Les musiques noires du Nouveau-Monde* (Paris: Éditions l'Harmattan, 1993). For an excellent review of the first work (*La musique*) by Jacqueline Guibault, see *Latin American Music Review* 9, no. 2 (Autumn–Winter, 1988): 272–74.
5. "Le théâtre de Saint-Pierre au XVIIIe siècle: Les années difficiles," *Annales des Antilles* 1 (1955): 53–64; *St.-Pierre, Martinique* (Fort-de-France, Martinique: Bezaudin, 1971); *La Martinique au fil de son histoire* (Fort-de-France, Martinique: Bezaudin, 1972); and *Les Grandes heures du théâtre de Saint-Pierre* (N.p.: Berger Bellepage, S.A., 1974).
6. *Loix et Constitutions des colonies françaises de l'Amérique sous le vent*, 6 vols. (Paris, 1784–1790); *Description topographique, politique, physique, civile, et historique de la partie française de l'isle Saint-Dominique, avec des observations générales sur sa population, sur le caractère & les moeurs de ses divers habitans; sur son climat, sa culture, ses productions, son administration, etc., etc.* (Philadelphia, 1797–1798); and *Description topographique et politique de la partie espagnole de l'isle Saint-Dominique, avec des observations générales sur le climat, la population, les productions, le caractère & les moeurs des habitans de cette colonie & un tableau raisonné des différentes parties de son administration* (Philadelphia, 1798).

Introduction

1. The *philosophes*, a group of French thinkers, flourished in the middle of the eighteenth century and were largely responsible for the development of the *siècle des lumières* (the Enlightenment). United by a common dedication to dispelling certain erroneous thought processes of man, they were concerned primarily with laws of nature, improvement of humanity, and religious institutions. The most influential *philosophes* were Jean-Jacques Rousseau (1712–1778), François Marie Arouet (Voltaire, 1694–1778), Denis Diderot (1713–1784), and Baron de Montesquieu (1689–1755). These great thinkers expounded their concepts and philosophies in several treatises, plays, essays, operas, and other literary and musical works—many of which are discussed in the present study. The embodiment of the spirit of the *siècle des lumières* was captured in the monumental *Encyclopédie, ou dictionnaire raisonné des sciences, des arts et des métiers*, 35 vols. (Paris, 1751–80). Organized and coordinated by Diderot and Jean le Rond d'Alembert (1717–1783), the *Encyclopédie* is considered the greatest achievement of the *philosophes*. The work included contributions from over one hundred French thinkers. Diderot, himself a prolific writer, wrote several essays on art, music, philosophy, and science, and D'Alembert, a mathematician and scientist, wrote the preface that presents their views toward various categories of human knowledge.
2. The last event did not, of course, include Saint-Domingue, for in 1804 the colony claimed its independence and its pre-Columbian name, *Haïti* (Arawak origin, meaning "hilly country").
3. "Arawaks et Caraïbes dans quelques chroniques des petites Antilles," *Parallèles* 24 (1967): 17–19. For

more information on the pre-Columbian era, see Thibault de Chanvalon, *Voyage à la Martinique, contenant diverses Observations sur la Physique, l'histoire naturelle, l'Agriculture, les moeurs & les usages de cette Isle, faites en 1751 & dans les années suivantes* (Paris, 1763), 38; and *Antilles d'hier et d'aujourd'hui: Tout l'univers antillais du début de la colonisation à nos jours* (Fort-de-France, Martinique: Emile Désormeaux, 1978), 1, 65.

4. For a detailed account of the various tribal groups in the colonies, see Gaston Martin, *Nantes au XVIII*[e] *. . . L'Ère des négriers (1714–1774) d'après des documents inédits avec 7 planches hors-texte* (1931); Nicole Vanony-Frisch, "Les Esclaves de la Guadeloupe à la fin de l'ancien régime d'après les sources notariales (1770–1789)," *Bulletin de la Société d'histoire de la Guadeloupe* (1985): 32–36; and Lucien Abenon, Jacques Cauna, and Liliane Chauleau, *La Révolution aux Caraïbes* (Paris: Éditions Nathan, 1989), 68–71.
5. C.L.R. James, *The Black Jacobins: Toussaint L'Ouverture and the San Domingo Revolution*, 2nd ed. (New York: Vintage Books, 1989), 6.
6. Unless specifically indicated otherwise, usage of the term "Indian" refers only to the original inhabitants of the Americas.
7. John W. Yolton, Roy Porter, Pat Rogers, and Barbara Maria Stafford, "Race," *The Blackwell Companion to the Enlightenment*, intro. Lester G. Crocker (Cambridge, MA: Blackwell Publishers, 1992).
8. *Nous et les autres: La Réflexion française sur la diversité humaine (Paris, 1989)*, translated by Catherine Porter as *On Human Diversity: Nationalism, Racism, and Exoticism in French Thought* (Cambridge, MA: Harvard University Press, 1993).
9. Ibid., 264–66. Emphasis added.
10. The reference to "the fruits of peace" is drawn from a statement by the regent of France in 1716, which is discussed in chapter 1.
11. The Code and its ramifications are detailed in chapters 1 and 2.
12. Instituted in 1598 during the reign of Henry IV; revoked in October 1685.
13. Jean-Jacques Rousseau (1712–1778): Born in Geneva, Switzerland, Rousseau was raised in a Calvinist environment. He spent most of his adult life in France while writing several essays, novels, and works for the musical theatre. Rousseau was greatly influenced by Denis Diderot, who encouraged him to write the first of several famous essays, *Discours sur les sciences et les arts*, 1750.
14. *Discours sur l'origine et les fondements de l'inégalité parmi les hommes* (1755), *Discours sur l'économie politique* (1755), and *Du Contrat social* (1762), in *Oeuvres complètes*, vol. 3 (Paris: Éditions Gallimard, 1964).
15. *Du Contrat social*, 4.
16. *Candide* (1759), in *Oeuvres complètes de Voltaire* (Paris, 1823), 1:279–80. François Marie Arouet (Voltaire, 1694–1778) was born of middle-class parents and educated by the Jesuits in Paris. Voltaire studied law, then abandoned it to become a writer. One of the greatest eighteenth-century writers,

he is noted for his classical tragedies and several philosophical works. He spoke out against established religious and political systems (*Lettres philosophiques*, 1734) and chronicled historical events (*Charles XII*, 1731; and *Le Siècle de Louis XIV*, 1751). *Candide* is regarded by most scholars as his masterpiece.

17. Ibid.
18. Denis Diderot (1713–1784): Diderot's philosophical works cover a wide variety of subjects ranging from anti-Christian ideas (*Pensées philosophiques*, 1746 [Philosophical Thoughts]), to new experimental methods in the sciences (*Pensées sur l'interprétation de la nature*, 1754 [Thoughts on the Interpretation of Nature] and *Eléments de physiologie*, 1774–1780 [Elements of Physiology]). He wrote several novels, dialogues, plays, and various literary and musical reviews and critiques that were published posthumously in Friedrich Melchior Grimm, *Correspondance littéraire, philosophique et critique* (1754–1813).
19. Bougainville (1729–1811), French mathematician and fleet commander, was the first Frenchman to make a trip around the world. He was commissioned by the French government to establish a colony in the Falkland Islands (ceded to the Spanish government in 1767), and then to continue his exploratory voyage. Departing from Nantes, France, on November 15, 1766, his route took him to South America, south to Cape Horn, across the Pacific Ocean, through the South Sea Islands and the Philippines, around the Cape of Good Hope, and northward, arriving in St. Malo, Brittany, on March 16, 1769, "having lost only seven men, during the two years and four months that had expired since his departure from Nantes." In 1772 Bougainville became secretary to Louis XV and commanded a French fleet off the coast of North America in support of the American Revolution. After the French Revolution, Napoleon I made him a senator, count, and member of the Legion of Honor. *Voyage autour du monde par la frégate du roi La Boudeuse, et la flûte l'Etoile* (Paris, 1771), *Voyage Round the World*, translated from the French by John Reinhold Forster (London, 1772).
20. *Supplément au voyage de Bougainville* (1796), in *Oeuvres complètes de Diderot*, ed. J. Assézat (Nendeln, Liechtenstein: Kraus Reprint, 1966), 2:193–250. See also *Supplément au voyage de Bougainville*, ed. Herbert Dieckmann (Geneva, 1955).
21. *Supplément au voyage de Bougainville*, in *Oeuvres complètes*, 2:223, 245.
22. Charles-Louis de Secondat, baron de la Brède et de Montesquieu (1689–1755): Born into a prominent family in Bordeaux, Montesquieu was well educated. After completing his study of law at the University of Bordeaux, he moved to Paris for further study and practice in law. By 1720 he was back in Bordeaux and shortly thereafter published his *Lettres persanes*, 1722 (*Persian Letters*), a satirical portrait of French, and particularly Parisian, society as supposedly seen through the eyes of two Persian travelers. His most notable work, *L'Esprit des loix*, 1750 (*The Spirit of Laws*), was a major contribution to political theory. In 1728 he was elected to the Académie Française. Of all the *philosophes*, he was probably the most widely traveled, visiting in two years (1729–1731) Vienna, Hungary, Italy (Venice, Florence, Rome, Naples), Germany, Holland, and England.

23. For knowledge of Persia, Montesquieu relied primarily on travel narratives of Jean Chardin, *Voyages de Monsieur le Chevalier Charden en Perse et autres lieux de l'Orient* (1711) and Jean-Baptiste Tavernier, *Les six voyages en Turquie, en Perse et aux Indes pendant l'espace de quarante ans . . . accompagnez d'observations particuliers sur la qualité, la religion, le gouvernement, les coutumes & le commerce de chaque pais, avec les figures, le poids, & la valeur des monnoyes qui y ont cours* (1676).
24. For more information on the theories of Montesquieu, see Charles de Secondat, Baron de Montesquieu, *Persian Letters* (Paris, 1721), trans. John Ozell, intro. William Graves, 2 vols. (New York: Garland Publishing, 1972); Melvin Richter, *The Political Theory of Montesquieu* (Cambridge: Cambridge University Press, 1977); and *Montesquieu, The Spirit of the Laws*, trans. and ed. Anne M. Cohler, Basia Carolyn Miller, and Harold Samuel Stone (Cambridge: Cambridge University Press, 1989).
25. Guillaume Thomas Raynal, *Histoire philosophique et politique des établissements et du commerce des Européens dans les deux Indes* (Geneva, 1780), 3:178. This work first appeared in 1770 in twenty volumes and was revised several times during Raynal's lifetime (1713–96). It is a compendium of historical and contemporary concepts and includes extensive discourses regarding European colonial practices. Several people contributed to the various editions, particularly Diderot. For those portions credited specifically to Diderot, I have relied upon Herbert Dieckmann, *Inventaire du Fonds Vandeul et textes inédits* (Paris, 1951); Hans Wolpe, *Raynal et sa machine de guerre: "l'Histoire des Deux Indes" et ses perfectionnements* (1957; reprint, New York: AMS Press, 1967); and Yves Benot, *Diderot de l'athéisme à l'anticolonialisme* (Paris, 1970).
26. Raynal, *Histoire philosophique et politique,* 3:178.
27. Voltaire, *Alzire, ou les Américains, tragédie*, IV, 3 (1736). In *Théâtre de Voltaire* (Paris, 1860).
28. "Lettre LXXVIII," *Lettres persanes*, ed. Laurent Versini (1721; reprint, Paris: Imprimerie nationale, 1986).
29. In *Oeuvres complètes de Diderot*, 5:359–489.
30. The *intermède* was a small musical theatre piece and a favorite entertainment of the French court. Members of the royal family and the court participated. Because of the French penchant for dancing, the ballet had a prominent role. There were two ways in which the *intermède* was performed. Like its sixteenth-century predecessor, the Italian *intermezzo*, the *intermède* was generally performed between acts of a play or of a larger musical drama. In the eighteenth century, the *intermède* was also performed independently. This form generally consisted of one act originally written in French. *Le Devin du village* is set in the latter type.
31. For a thorough examination of the debate, see Denise Launay, ed., *La Querelle des Bouffons, Paris (1752–54), texte des pamphlets avec introduction, commentaires et index*, 3 vols. (Geneva: Menkoff Reprints, 1973).
32. Jean-Baptiste Lully [Giovanni Battista Lulli] (1632–1687) was born in Florence, Italy, and went to Paris at age fourteen as a *valet de chambre* and teacher of Italian to a member of the royal family. Also a good dancer, violinist, and composer of ballets, Lully was able to ingratiate himself

with Louis XIV, an ardent supporter of court ballet. Lully was appointed as a court composer at age twenty-one. Eight years later (1661), Louis XIV appointed him to the coveted position of *surintendant de la musique de la chambre.* Lully also received his naturalization papers later that same year, and officially, Giovanni Battista Lulli became Jean-Baptiste Lully. With his unrelenting demands for high standards of performance, Lully created French national opera, the *tragédie lyrique*, as an institution of the court.

33. "On te croit vaillant sur ta foy; / Mais la couleur de ton visage, / Répond mal à ta valeur" (III, 1).
34. "Est-ce par la couleur / Que l'on doit juger du courage?"

    See tables 1 and 2 for more examples of the various ways in which cultural and political themes regarding the sub-Saharan African Other were dramatized in operas produced in France. Opera performances staged by the Académie are reflected chronologically in table 1, and performance records of public theatres are in table 2. The works cited in the two tables are not intended to be an exhaustive listing of musical dramas that included references to the sub-Saharan African Other or to the monarchy's *cultural* political campaign. Rather, the two tables represent various examples of *how* the concept of the sub-Saharan African Other was dramatized on the French stage.
35. Annual fairs had been held in France since the Middle Ages. They were the favorite places of entertainment for the public, with their carnival atmosphere of fireworks, marionettes, plays, cabarets, restaurants, and boutiques. Merchants not only sold food, beverages, and household goods, they also offered a variety of stalls for gambling and other vices within their establishments. The two most important fairs were Saint-Germain (Foire Saint-Germain) and Saint-Laurent (Foire Saint-Laurent) and, in the early part of the eighteenth century, became the most important venues for musical dramas presented for and financed by the public.
36. The *commedia dell'arte*, a semi-improvised stage work, was developed in Italy in the early sixteenth century and maintained its popularity until the middle of the eighteenth century. "From the Italians the [Opéra] Comique appropriated Arlequin, Scaramouche, Colombine, the gentle Isabelle, and the handsome Léandre. Arlequin was the great favorite of the crown. Costumed in his traditional checkered outfit with a baton at his side, he was transformed in the French theatre from the foolish, rough valet from Bergamo [Italy] to a sly, impudent rogue. He was industrious, usually amorous, often cynical, very giddy, and full of pranks. . . . Always engaged in intrigues, usually cast as a servant though appearing in many disguises, Arlequin was the consummate burlesque character." Robert M. Isherwood, *Farce and Fantasy: Popular Entertainment in Eighteenth Century Paris* (New York: Oxford University Press, 1986), 73. See also M. D'Origny, *Annales du Théâtre Italien, depuis son origine jusqu'a ce jour* (Paris, 1788), 1:4–5.
37. The genre they developed was also called *opéra comique*, but without the hyphen and initial capital letters. For more information on the various types of entertainment at the fairs, see Isherwood, *Farce and Fantasy*, 22–80.
38. Contemporary usage of the term *comédie* applies to the physical theatre as well as to a light drama (as opposed to the serious *tragédie*). A *comédien* was an individual performer and/or a member

of a *troupe de comédiens* (actor, actress, singer, dancer, instrumentalist, director, technician, etc.).

39. To name a few composers: François-André Danican Philidor (1726–1795), André-Ernest-Modeste Grétry (1741–1813), Nicolas-Marie Dalayrac (1753–1809), and Pierre-Alexandre Monsigny (1729–1817). A few librettists: Michel-Jean Sedaine (1719–1797), François Marmontel (1723–1799), and Louis Anseaume (1721–1784). Charles-Simon Favart (1710–1792) composed the music and supplied texts for several works. These artists produced works for both theatres.
40. In French concert and theatre music of the seventeenth and eighteenth centuries, the term *symphonie* refers to all instrumental music. In opera, a "dramatic *symphonie*" is an instrumental section (e.g., *prélude* or *ritournelle*) that is connected to the action.
41. For a detailed study on their contributions to the new operatic style, see Isherwood, *Farce and Fantasy*, 101–23.
42. For a recording of this piece, see appendix 6, discography.
43. A declamatory style, with fluctuating meters and full orchestral treatment in order to heighten certain dramatic situations.
44. Mondonville dedicated this work to Charles de Rohan, prince of Soubise (1715–1787), a close friend of Louis XV and his mistress, Madame de Pompadour.

    Mondonville was a very successful violinist, conductor, and composer. He arrived in Paris around 1733, during which year he published his first violin sonatas. His skill as a virtuoso violinist earned him many successful appearances at the Concert Spirituel, a concert series founded in 1725 by Anne Danican Philidor (1681–1728) to provide musical entertainment during the period when the Opéra was closed for religious considerations. By 1739, Mondonville had established himself as one of the finest musicians in France. He composed several motets, harpsichord pieces, and trio sonatas, many of which were performed at the Concert Spirituel. Mondonille entered the service of the king in 1739 as violinist in the royal chapel and chamber. His later court appointments included *maître de musique* and *surintendant de la chapelle de Versailles*. In 1755, he assumed directorship of the Concert Spirituel, a position he held until 1762. Mondonville composed the two most successful *pastorales-héroïques*: *Le Carnaval du Parnasse* (1749) and *Titon et l'Aurore* (1753). His operatic output also includes *Isbé, pastorale-héroïque* (1742); *Venus et Adonis, ballet-héroïque* (1752); *Daphnis et Alcimadure, pastorale languedocienne* (1754); *Les Fêtes de Paphos, ballet-héroïque* (1758); and *Les Projets de l'Amour, ballet-héroïque* (1771). For an exhaustive study on the composer's life, see Roberte Machard, *Jean-Joseph Cassanéa de Mondonville, virtuose, compositeur et chef d'orchestre* (Paris: Société de Musicologie du Languedoc, 1980).
45. For a recording of this piece, see appendix 6, discography.
46. New *entrées* were added October 9, 1714 ("La critique des fêtes de Thalie"), March 12, 1715 ("La veuve coquette"), and September 17, 1722 ("La Provençale"). After 1720, this opera was known under the revised title *Les Fêtes de Thalie*.
47. See *La Caravane du Caire* (table 1), *Amitié à l'épreuve*; *Zémire et Azor*; *Azémia, ou les sauvages*; and *La Belle esclave* (table 2).

48. "Pas un seul Français dans ces lieux / Ne veut me réconnoître. / Et le meilleur de mes amis / Me traite comme un Nègre."
49. This work premiered in Port-au-Prince six months later under the title *Les Créoles africaines, ou les effets de l'amour*. See chapter 6.
50. Jean Bernabé, Patrick Chamoiseau, and Raphaël Confiant, *Éloge de la Créolité*, édition bilingue français/anglais, trans. M. B. Taleb-Khyar (Baltimore: Johns Hopkins University Press, 1990), 92–94. The authors created the movement about 30 years ago. The *Éloge* is the seminal essay on *créolité*. For more information, see Carolyn J. Mooney, "On Martinique, Elevating the Status of Creole," *Chronicle of Higher Education* (June 9, 2000); and Julian Gerstin, "Musical Revivals and Social Movements in Contemporary Martinique: Ideology, Identity, Ambivalence," in *The African Diaspora: A Musical Perspective*, ed. Ingrid Monson (New York: Garland Publishing, 2000), 205–327.
51. Although the list of travel narratives is somewhat endless, the most informative and detailed sources include R.P.J.B. Du Tertre, *Histoire générale des Antilles, habitées par les François, contenant l'histoire naturelle, enrichy de cartes & de figures* (Paris, 1667); Jean-Baptiste Labat, *Nouveau voyage aux isles de l'Amerique, contenant l'histoire naturelle de ces pays, l'origine, les moeurs, la religion & le gouvernement des habitans anciens & modernes* (Paris, 1722); Thibault de Chanvalon, *Voyage à la Martinique, contenant diverses Observations sur la Physique, l'histoire naturelle, l'Agriculture, les moeurs & les usages de cette Isle, faites en 1751 & dans les années suivantes* (Paris, 1761); and Paul Erdman Isert, *Voyage en Guinée et dans les Iles Caraïbes en Amerique* (Paris, 1793).
52. Berlioz, a prolific French composer, was noted for his extremely skillful and innovative approach to orchestration. His *Grande messe des morts* (1837) is scored for as many as 10 cymbals.
53. Christoph W. Gluck (1714–1787), Bohemian-Austrian composer, seems to have been the first one to use the tambourine in the orchestra (*Echo et Narcisse*, opera, performed in Paris 1779). A few years later, Wolfgang A. Mozart (1756–1791) used the tambourine in a dance suite (German Dances, K.571, 1789). Berlioz used three tambourines in a symphony, *Harold en Italie* (1834), and two in an opera, *Benvenuto Cellini* (1838).

Chapter 1. Establishment of Colonial Hierarchy

1. Jacques Petitjean Roget, *Le gaoulé: La révolte de la Martinique en 1717* (Fort-de-France, Martinique: Société d'histoire de la Martinique, 1966), 113; and Maurice Nicolas, *St.-Pierre, Martinique* (Fort-de-France, Martinique: Bezaudin, 1971), 8. In 1635 Pierre Belain d'Esnambuc, French explorer, landed at Saint-Pierre and took possession of the island in the name of the king (Louis XIII).
2. For more information on the duties and responsibilities of governors, *intendants*, the judiciary, and other officials in colonial and provincial governments, see Roland E. Mousnier, *The Institutions of France under the Absolute Monarchy, 1598–1789: The Organs of State and Society*, trans. Arthur Goldhammer (Chicago: University of Chicago Press, 1984), 2:469–80, 502–65; Médéric-Louis-Elie

Moreau de Saint-Méry, *Description topographique, physique, civile, politique et historique de la partie française de l'isle Saint-Domingue, avec des observations générales sur sa population, sur le caractère & les moeurs de ses divers habitans; sur son climat, sa culture, ses productions, son administration* (Philadelphia, 1797–1798), 1:493–97, 2:376–80; "Instructions données à l'intendant des îles françaises du vent, le 25 août 1716," and "Mémoire du Roi pour server d'instruction au S. de Ricouart, intendant des îles françoises du vent," *Revue de l'histoire des colonies françaises* 17 (1924): 67–92; Louis E. Elie, *Histoire d'Haïti: Les origines du people haïtien* (Port-au-Prince: n.p., 1945), 2:66–88, 216–24; Jacques Petitjean Roget, *Le gaoulé: La révolte de la Martinique en 1717* (Fort-de-France, Martinique: Société d'histoire de la Martinique, 1966), 112–63; Thomas Madiou, *Histoire d'Haïti* (Port-au-Prince: A. A. Héraux, 1923), 2:21–75; and Jonathan Brown, *The History and Present Condition of St. Domingo* (London: Frank Cass, 1971), 57–180.

3. Moreau de Saint-Méry, *Description topographique . . . partie française*, 1:490–93. The author devotes more than 300 pages to various aspects of government, accomplishments of citizenry, and lifestyles in Cap Français. Other sources consulted for this section include J. Tramond, "Saint-Domingue en 1756 and 1757 d'après la correspondance de l'Ordonnateur Lambert," *Revue de l'histoire des colonies françaises* 20 (1927): 161–200; Mercier, "La vie au Cap Français en 1789," *Revue d'histoire des colonies françaises* 26 (1933): 101–30; Fouchard, *Le théâtre*, 1–7; and numerous issues of colonial gazettes.
4. "Provisions pour M. le Comte de Blénac, le Gouverneur-Lieutenant-Général des Isles sous le vent, dont le Gouvernement est declaré independant de celui des îsles du vent, du 1er Janvier, 1714," in Moreau de Saint-Méry, *Loix et constitutions*, 2:408–9. See also "Instructions données à l'Intendant des îles françaises du vent (25 August 1716)," *Revue de l'histoire des colonies françaises* 7 (1924): 67–91; and "Port-au-Prince (1749–1750)," *Revue de l'histoire des colonies françaises* 36 (1927): 225–37.
5. "Le Code Noir, ou, Édit servant de réglement pour le gouvernement et l'administration de la justice, et de la police des Isles Françoises de la Amérique et pour la discipline & le commerce des Nègres et esclaves dans ledit pays" (Versailles, 1685).
6. "Louis, par la grâce de Dieu roi de France et de Navarre: à tous, présents et à venir, salut. Comme nous devons également nos soins à tous les peuples que la divine providence a mis sous notre obéissance, nous avons bien voulu faire examiner en notre présence les mémoires qui nous ont été informés du besoin qu'ils ont de notre autorité et de notre justice pour y maintenir la discipline de l'Eglise catholique, apostolique et romaine, pour y régler ce qui concerne l'état et la qualité des esclaves dans nos dites iles, et désirant y pouvoir et leur faire connaitre qu'encore qu'ils habitent des climats infiniment éloignés de notre séjour ordinaire, nous leur sommes toujours présent, non seulement par l'étendue de notre puissance, mais encore par la promptitude de notre application à les secourir dans leurs nécessités." Ibid. All translations are mine except where otherwise indicated.
7. Louis Sala-Moulins, *Le Code Noir, ou la calvaire de Canaan* (Paris: Presses Universitaires de France, 1987), 90.

8. J. Teilhard de Chardin, *La Guinée supérieure et ses missions, étude géographique, sociale et religieuse des contrées évangélisées par les missionaires de la Société des Missions Africaines de Lyon* (1889), 35–36. See also Liliane Chauleau, ed., *La Société à la Martinique au XVIIe siècle, 1635–1713* (Caen: Comité d'études historiques et juridiques, 1966), 144–49; Jacqueline Rosemain, *La musique dans la société antillaise, 1635–1902: Martinique, Guadeloupe* (Paris: Éditions L'Harmattan, 1986), 29; and Sala-Moulins, *Le Code Noir, ou la calvaire de Canaan*, 90–91.
9. "Lettres-patentes concernant les juifs," signed April 23, 1615; published May 18, 1615. In Moreau de Saint-Méry, *Loix et constitutions*, 1:13–14.
10. "Ordonnance de M. de Baas, touchant les religionnaires, les juifs, les cabaretiers et les femmes de mauvaise vie," August 1, 1669, Moreau de Saint-Méry, *Loix et constitutions* 1:180–82.
11. Ibid.
12. "Lettre du Roi à M. de Baas, pour lui dire de laisser entière liberté de conscience au juifs des Isles, et de les faire jouer des même privileges que les autres habitants," May 23, 1671, *Loix et constitutions*, 1:225–26.
13. The French ell (*aune*) is about 48 inches.
14. "Arrêt du Conseil d'Etat, sur l'exécution de l'Article quarante-quatrième de la Déclaration du mois de Mars 1685, touchant les Esclaves des Isles de l'Amérique, qui déclare les nègres meubles," August 22, 1687, *Loix et constitutions*, 1:460.
15. "Extrait de la lettre du Ministre à M. Ducasse, concernant les nègres amenés en France, et la liberté à donner aux mulâtres," February 5, 1698, *Loix et constitutions*, 1:579.
16. Ibid. Médéric-Louis-Elie Moreau de Saint-Méry (1750–1819) was born in Fort-Royal, Martinique, studied law in Paris, and in the late 1770s moved to the most thriving city in the French Antilles: Cap Français, Saint-Domingue. In 1780 he was appointed member of the Conseil Supérieur, the colony's highest judicial body. He returned to Paris in 1784, where he wrote the monumental *Loix et constitutions des colonies françaises de l'Amérique sous le vent*, 6 vols. (Paris, 1784–1790). While in Paris, he also became one of the most important leaders of the French Revolution. Unfortunately, caught up in the increasing unrest and violence that had overtaken France, he was forced to leave Paris abruptly in November 1793, in order to avoid an order for his arrest. He sought refuge in Philadelphia, where he published *Description topographique et politique de la partie espagnole de l'isle Saint-Dominique, avec des observations générales sur le climat, la population, les productions, le caractère & les moeurs des habitans de cette colonie & un tableau raisonné des differentes parties de son administration* (1796), and *Description topographique, politique, physique, civile, et historique de la partie française de l'isle Saint-Dominique, avec des observations générales sur sa population, sur le caractère & les moeurs de ses divers habitans; sur son climat, sa culture, ses productions, son administration, etc., etc.* (1797–1798). The latter work alone is a massive two-volume set of more than 1,700 pages. He died in Paris in January 1819.
17. "Ordonnance du Roi concernant l'affranchissement des esclaves," October 24, 1713, in *Loix et constitutions*, 2:398–99.

18. "Ordonnance du Roi concernant les esclaves des îsles françoises de l'Amérique," June 15, 1736, *Le Code Noir, ou Recueill des reglemens rendu, jusqu'à present*, 476.
19. "Edit du Roy, concernant les esclaves nègres des colonies," October 1716, *Le Code Noir, ou Recueill des reglemens rendu, jusqu'à present*, 192–206.
20. Ibid.
21. "Extrait de la lettre du Ministre à M. Ducasse, concernant les nègres amenés en France, et la liberté à donner aux mulâtres," February 5, 1698, *Loix et constitutions*, 1:579.
22. "Déclaration du Roi, concernant les nègres-esclaves des colonies amenés en France, du Décembre 1738" (13 articles), *Le Code Noir, ou Recueill des reglemens rendu, jusqu'à present,* 481–85; and *Loix et constitutions*, 3:547–50.
23. "Déclarations du Roi, concernant les nègres-esclaves des colonies amenés en France," December 15, 1738, in Moreau de Saint-Méry, *Loix et constitutions*, 3:547–50; and "La Police des noirs sous Louis XVI en France," *Revue de l'histoire des colonies françaises* 21 (1928): 433–46.
24. "La Police des noirs sous Louis XVI," 433–45.
25. "Déclaration du Roi pour la police des noirs, donnée à Versailles le 9 août 1777, registrée en Parlement le vingt-sept août 1777," *Revue de l'histoire des colonies françaises* 21 (1928): 436–41. See also "Arrêt du Conseil d'État du Roi concernant le retour des noirs, mûlatres ou autres gens de couleur aux colonies," September 7, 1777; "Arrêt du Conseil d'État du Roi pour la police des noirs, mûlatres ou autres gens de couleur qui sont dans la ville de Paris," January 11, 1778; and "Ordonnance du Roi portant defenses aux capitaines de navires de laisser débarquer aucun noir, mûlatre ou autres gens de couleur, avant d'avoir fait leur rapport à l'Amirauté," February 23, 1778, *Revue de l'histoire des colonies françaises* 21 (1928): 441–45.
26. "Déclaration du Roi, touchant les libres qui recèlent des esclaves, et les donations faites aux gens de couleur par les blancs," February 8, 1726, in *Loix et constitutions*, 3:159–60.
27. Total population figures for Guadeloupe and Martinique during this period are rather sparse and inexact.
28. These figures are not absolute, as no one knows the exact number of slaves in the colonies. Nevertheless, the numbers are staggering (as several studies on the Atlantic slave trade clearly reveal), as is also the perpetuation of horrendous monstrosities of the system. See René Cottrel and Théodore Baude, *Tricentenaire des Antilles: Guadeloupe-Martinique, 1635–1935* (Fort-de-France, Martinique: 1935), 149–60; Antoine Gisler, *L'esclavage aux antilles françaises (XVIIe–XIXe siècles)* (Fribourg, Switzerland: Éditions Universitaires, 1965); Yvan Debbasch, *Couleur et liberté* (Paris: Librairie Dalloz, 1967), 79–81; Philip D. Curtin, *The Atlantic Slave Trade: A Census* (Madison: University of Wisconsin Press, 1969), 51–94, 163–203; Émile Hayot, *Les gens de couleur libres du Fort-Royal, 1679–1823* (Paris: Société française d'histoire d'outre-mer et Librairie orientaliste Paul Geuthner S.A., 1971), 6–8; Léo Elisabeth, "The French Antilles," and Gwendolyn Midlo Hall, "Saint-Domingue," in *Neither Slave Nor Free*, ed. David W. Cohen and Jack P. Greene (Baltimore: Johns Hopkins University Press, 1972), 134–92; Nicole Vanony-Frisch, "Les esclaves

de la Guadeloupe à la fin de l'ancien régime d'après les sources notariales, 1770–1789," *Bulletin de la Société d'histoire de la Guadeloupe* 63–64 (1985): 19–40; Louis Sala-Moulins, *Le Code Noir, ou la calvaire de Canaan*, 14–16; and Clarence J. Munford, *The Black Ordeal of Slavery and Slave Trading in the French West Indies, 1625–1715*, 3 vols. (Lewiston, NY: Edwin Mellen Press, 1991).

29. Jacques Henri Bernardin de Saint-Pierre (1737–1814), French writer and army engineer, spent part of his youth in Martinique and the majority of his army service in Île de France (now Mauritius), a French colony in the Indian Ocean. These experiences undoubtedly touched him very deeply, for they became the bases for two of his most important works, *Voyage à l'Île de France* (1773), a chronicle of his stay in that colony, and *Paul et Virginie* (1788), a novel of blooming love between two young innocents in a natural setting that ends tragically when French civilization intrudes on their virtuous lifestyle.
30. "Lettre XII, Des Noirs, 25 Avril 1760, *Voyage à l'Ile de France*," in *Oeuvres de Jacques-Henri-Bernadin de Saint-Pierre* (Paris, 1840).
31. Ibid.
32. Ibid. The massacre of Huguenots (Protestants) began in Paris on Saint Bartholomew's Day, August 24, 1572. For a similar condemnation of the *philosophes*, see Michel-René Hilliard d'Auberteuil, *Considérations sur l'état present de la colonie française de Saint-Domingue* (Paris, 1776), 1:130–31. Hilliard d'Auberteuil (ca. 1740–1789), a solicitor and *colon*, resided in Cap Français, Saint-Domingue.
33. *Contrat social*, 1:4.
34. See "Esclaves," *Dictionnaire philosophique par Voltaire*, vol. 5 (Paris: J.N. Barba, 1828). Each of the three terms, *mortaillables*, *mainmortables*, and *serfs de glèbe*, represent a form of enslavement, as the landowner maintains a right to perpetual ownership of everything and everyone residing on his property—including serfs and all other persons who work for him, their families, and all their belongings.
35. *Essai sur les moeurs et l'esprit des nations* (1756), in *Oeuvres complètes de Voltaire* (1820), 15:7.
36. Ibid., 15:27–28, 31.
37. *L'Esprit des loix* (1750; Paris: Société des Belles Lettres, 1955), 15:18.
38. Ibid.
39. Raynal, *Histoire philosophique et politique*, 3:182.
40. Ibid., 1:544–45.
41. Ibid., 3:193.
42. Thibault de Chanvalon, *Voyage à la Martinique, contenant diverses observations sur la physique, l'histoire naturelle, l'agriculture, les moeurs & les usages de cette Isle, faites en 1751 & dans les années suivantes* (Paris, 1761), 42.
43. Ibid., 45.
44. Ibid., 60.
45. Ibid., 62–63.
46. Emphasis added. Some of the theories are explored in G. S. Rousseau, "Le Cat and the Physiology

of Negroes," *Studies in Eighteenth Century Culture*, vol. 3, *Racism in the Eighteenth Century*, ed. Harold E. Pagliaro (Cleveland: Case Western Reserve University Press, 1973), 369–86.

47. Bufffon's greatest achievement was *Histoire naturelle, générale et particulière* (1749–1804), a 44-volume account of natural history, geology, and anthropology. Thirty-six volumes were published during his lifetime, and the remaining eight volumes were completed after Buffon's death by Étienne de La Ville-sur-Illon, Count de Lacépède (1756–1825), a naturalist and Buffon's close associate. Buffon was a friend of Diderot and Rousseau and a frequent visitor to literary and philosophical salons in Paris. Formal education of Buffon included studies in law, medicine, botany, and mathematics. In 1732, he visited London and gained membership in the Royal Society of London. Buffon returned to France in 1733 and settled on the family estate in Montbard. He served as treasurer of the Académie de Sciences and was elected to the Académie Française in 1753. Buffon enjoyed the patronage of J.F.P. de Maurepas, minister of marine, and in 1739 was appointed keeper of Jardin du Roi (the royal botanical garden) and its museum. Maurepas instructed him to prepare a catalog of royal collections in natural history. Buffon transformed this task into his greatest achievement, *Histoire naturelle, générale et particulière*. For more information on the life of Buffon and his theories, see Otis E. Fellows and Stephen F. Milliken, *Buffon* (New York: Twayne Publishers, 1972).

48. *Histoire naturelle, générale et particulière. Servant de suite à l'histoire naturelle de l'homme*, Supplément 4 (1777): 454.

49. Rousseau, *Discours sur l'origine et les fondements de l'inégalité* (1755), in *Oeuvres complètes* (Paris: Éditions Gallimard, 1964), 3:212.

50. "L'Histoire naturelle de l'homme, variétés dans l'espèce humaine," 3:371–530.

51. Ibid., 3:524.

52. Ibid.

53. Ibid., 3:522.

54. *L'Esprit des loix*, 17:2.

55. Voltaire, François-Marie Arouet, *Essai sur les moeurs*, in *Oeuvres complètes de Voltaire* (1820), 15:7 and 17:318.

56. Ibid.

57. It seems that, originally, blacks conferred the name on poor whites to make the distinction between them and the rich, powerful plantation owners (*grand blancs*). See Jonathan Brown, *The History and Present Condition of St. Domingo*(1837; reprint, London: Frank Cass, 1971), 1:112.

58. Louis E. Elie, *Histoire d'Haïti* (Port-au-Prince, 1945) 2:56–58.

59. See "Arrêt du Conseil de la Martinique, qui condamne des Vagabonds à server comme engagés," February 16, 1671; "Ordre du Roi pour porter des engagés aux îles," February 19, 1698; "Ordonnance du Roy contre les vagabonds et les gens sans aveu," November 1718; "Déclaration du Roi, qui permet d'envoyer les condamnés aux galères, les bannis, les vagabonds & les gens sans aveu aux colonies, pour y server comme engages," January 8, 1719; "Déclaration du Roi, concernant les vagabonds & gens sans aveu," March 12, 1719; "Déclaration du Roi, qui ordonne que la Déclaration du 8 janvier

1719, au sujet des vagabonds gens sans aveu, etc., sera executé selon sa forme et teneur, par tout le Royaume," May 12, 1719; and "Arrêt du Conseil d'Etat du Roi, qui ordonne qu'il ne sera plus envoye de vagabonds, gens sans aveu, fraudeurs & criminals à la Loüisianne, que les ordres qui Sa Majesté auroit pû donner à ce sujet seront changez, et la destination desdits vagabonds faite pour les autres colonies Françaises," May 9, 1720.

60. Ibid. See also Liliane Chauleau, ed., *La Société à la Martinique au XVIIe siècle, 1635–1713* (Caen: Comité d'études historiques et juridiques, 1966), 179; and Roget, *Le gaoulé*, 37–40.

61. The English called natives of the Americas *Indians*, i.e., people of the Indies, following the usage of Columbus and the Spaniards (*indios*).

62. See "Sauvages," *Encyclopédie, ou dictionnaire raisonné des sciences, des arts et des métiers* (Paris, 1751–1780).

63. Moreau de Saint-Méry, *Description topographique . . . partie française*, 1:64–65.

64. Hayot, *Les gens de couleur libres du Fort-Royal*, 12–13.

65. Although the list of travel narratives is somewhat endless, the most informative and detailed sources include R.P.J.B. Du Tertre, *Histoire générale des Antilles, habitées par les François, contenant l'histoire naturelle, enrichy de cartes & de figures* (Paris, 1667); Jean-Baptiste Labat, *Nouveau voyage aux isles de l'Amerique, contenant l'histoire naturelle de ces pays, l'origine, les moeurs, la religion & le gouvernement des habitans anciens & modernes* (Paris, 1722); Thibault de Chanvalon, *Voyage à la Martinique, contenant diverses Observations sur la Physique, l'histoire naturelle, l'Agriculture, les moeurs & les usages de cette Isle, faites en 1751 & dans les années suivantes* (Paris, 1761); and Paul Erdman Isert, *Voyage en Guinée et dans les Iles Caraïbes en Amerique* (Paris, 1793).

66. Various attempts to resolve the issue from religious and musical bases are explored in chapter 2, "Religious Power."

67. See "Le Code Noir ou Edit du Roi, servant de reglement pour le gouvernement & l'administration de la justice, police, discipline & le commerce des esclaves negres, dans la Province & colonie de la Louisianne," March 1724; "Déclaration du Roi, concernant les Nègres-Esclaves des Colonies amenés en France," December 15, 1738, in *Loix et constitutions*, 3:547–50; "Lettre du Ministre aux Administrateurs, sur les Sangs-mêlés," May 27, 1771, in *Loix et constitutions*, 5:356; and "Arrêt du Conseil portant defense de célébrer mariage entre les blancs, noirs, mulâtres et autres gens de couleur, et à tous notaires de passer aucun contrat entre eux," April 5, 1778, *Recueil general des anciennes lois françaises, depuis l'an 420 jusqu'à la Révolution de 1789* (Paris, 1863), 25:257–58.

68. "Arrêt du Conseil portant defense de célébrer mariage entre les blancs, noirs, mulâtres et autres gens de couleur, et à tous notaires de passer aucun contrat entre eux," April 5, 1778, in *Recueil general des anciennes lois françaises, depuis l'an 420 jusqu'à la Révolution de 1789*, 25:257–58.

69. See "Lettre du Ministre aux Administrateurs, sur les sangs-mêlés," May 27, 1771, in *Loix et constitutions*, 5:356.

70. Antoine Gisler, *L'esclavage aux Antilles*, 35; Hayot, *Les gens de couleur*, 15–16, 49; and Cottrel, *Tricentenaire*, 149–50.

71. *Description topographique . . . partie française*, 1:68–99.
72. Ibid. For more information on Moreau's racial classification system, see the excellent article by Doris Lorraine Garraway, "Race, Reproduction and Family Romance in Moreau de Saint-Méry's *Description . . . de la partie française de l'Isle Saint-Domingue*," *Eighteenth-Century Studies* 38, no. 2 (2005): 227–46. See also David Lowenthal, "Free Colored West Indians: A Racial Dilemma," in *Studies in Eighteenth-Century Culture*, vol. 3, *Racism in the Eighteenth Century*, ed. Harold E. Pagliaro (Cleveland: Case Western Reserve University Press, 1937), 335–53.
73. See Jean Fouchard, *Les marrons du syllabaire* (1953; Port-au-Prince: Éditions Henri Deschamps, 1988), 46–59; Vanony-Frisch, "Les esclaves de la Guadeloupe," 91–115; and Hayot, *Les gens de couleur*, 23–59.
74. "Mémoire du 7 mars 1777 pour servir d'instructions aux Gouverneurs," in *Antilles d'hier et d'aujourd'hui: Tout l'univers antillais du début de la colonisation à nos jours* (Fort-de-France, Martinique: Emile Désormeaux, 1978), 6:66.
75. "Arrêt du conseil qui défend à tous curés, notaires, arpenteurs et autres officiers publics, de qualifier aucunes gens de couleur du titre de sieur et dame" (November 6, 1781), in *Recueil general des anciennes loix françaises depuis l'an 420 jusqu'à la Révolution de 1789*, 27:107. See also Léon Deschamps, *Histoire de la question coloniale en France* (Paris, 1891), 326; and Carl Ludwig Lokke, *France and the Colonial Question: A Study of Contemporary French Opinion, 1763–1801* (New York: Columbia University Press, 1932), 67.

Chapter 2. Politics and Power

1. Churches were established also in other Caribbean territories under French colonial rule (Saint-Christopher [now Saint Kitts], Saint-Martin, Saint-Barthélemy, Grenada, Marie-Galante, Saint-Croix, and Cayenne). However, these colonies did not produce any operatic or symphonic works and, therefore, are not included in the present study.
2. "Lettres-Patentes, portant Etablissement des Religieux de la Compagnie de Jésus dans l'Isle Saint-Domingue, du mois d'Octobre 1704. R. au Conseil du Cap, le 18 Mars 1705," in Mederic-Louis-Elie Moreau de Saint-Méry, *Loix et constitutions*, 2:18–20.
3. For more information regarding contractual arrangements between the monarchy and the four orders, see J. Teilhard de Chardin, *La Guinée supérieure et ses missions*; Cottrel and Baude, *Tricentenaire des Antilles*, 226–43; Jean Fouchard, *Les marrons du syllabaire* (Port-au-Prince: Éditions Henri Deschamps, 1953), 71–81; and Chauleau, *La Société à la Martinique*, 140–49.
4. "Rapport la Varenne, 10 Avril 1717, sur les biens des religieux," in Cottrel, *Tricentenaire des Antilles*, 274.
5. Cottrel, *Tricentenaire des Antilles*, 226–43. See also Fouchard, *Les marrons*, 71–81; Antoine Gisler, *L'esclavage*, 151–69; and J. Rennard, *Histoire religieuse des Antilles Françaises* (Paris: Société de

l'histoire des colonies françaises et Librairie Larose, 1954), 49–63, 177–295.

6. *Ordonnance*, 7 May 1745, cited in Fouchard, *Les marrons*, 71.
7. Fouchard, *Les marrons*, 79. See also Gisler, *L'esclavage*, 176–92; and Raynal, *Histoire philosophique et politique*, 3:200.
8. Cited in Gisler, *L'esclavage*, 180–81.
9. "La Fête-Dieu à la Martinique en 1753," *Revue de l'histoire des colonies françaises* 20 (1927): 600–603. Cited also in Rosemain, *La musique*, 57.
10. Corpus Christi (the Body of Christ) is celebrated on the Thursday after Trinity Sunday in honor of Christ in the Blessed Sacrament (the Eucharist).
11. Laws regulating the establishment, tenure, and expulsion of the Jesuits are reprinted in Moreau de Saint-Méry, *Loix et constitutions*, 2:18–20, 2:770–71, 4:613–15, and 5:162–63. In addition, copies of numerous laws on the subject are housed at the John Carter Brown Library, Brown University, and New York Public Library (Humanities-Research Division).
12. For more discussion regarding the "special catechism," see Fouchard, *Les marrons*, 43–46, and Gisler, *L'esclavage*, 185.
13. Marcel Chatillon, Camille Fabre, and Jacqueline Rosemain, "Messe en cantiques pour les esclaves (1763)," *Bulletin de la Société d'histoire de la Guadeloupe* 52 (1982): 49.
14. Traditionally, up until Vatican II (1962–1965), the Mass was sung in Latin. In February 1980, a trio of scholars (one musicologist and two historians) from Martinique and Guadeloupe discovered a collection of songs of the Mass with French texts ("Messe en cantiques à l'usage des Nègres") prepared by Jesuits for use in Cayenne (now the capital of French Guiana). This is a good example of the type of educational and missionary works performed by Jesuits, the only priests in that colony. The trio provided a transcription of the Mass in an excellent article: Chatillon, Fabre, and Rosemain, "Messe en cantiques pour les esclaves (1763)," *Bulletin de la Société d'histoire de la Guadeloupe* 52 (1982): 39–63.
15. *Relation du Père Pellerat de la Compagnie de Jésus dans les îles d'Amérique*. Cited in Jacqueline Rosemain, *La musique*, 30. See also Chatillon, Fabre, and Rosemain, "Messe en cantiques," 42–44, 49–50.
16. A teaching aid that uses syllables (do-re-mi-fa-sol-la-ti-do) to identify musical tones.
17. Rosemain, *La musique*, 30. See also Chatillon, Fabre, and Rosemain, "Messe en cantiques," 42–44, 50.
18. Letter, dated May 10, 1679, written by Father Mongin, a Jesuit priest in Martinique, cited in Chatillon, Fabre, and Rosemain, "Messe en cantiques," 42.
19. Jean-Baptiste Labat, *Nouveau voyage* (1742): 4:463.
20. Ibid. Believed to have come from Guinea, this dance was known also as the *chica* in Saint-Domingue, the *laguia* in Martinique, the *lewoz* in Guadeloupe, and the *congo* in other parts of the Caribbean.
21. Moreau de Saint-Méry, *Dance: An Article Drawn from the Work by M.L.E. St.-Méry Entitled:*

Repertory of Colonial Information, Compiled Alphabetically (1796), trans. and intro. Lily and Baird Hastings (Brooklyn, NY: Dance Horizons, 1975), 61–62.

22. Labat, *Nouveau voyage*, 4:464, 470.
23. See Labat, *Nouveau voyage*, 2:182–84; Thibault de Chanvalon, *Voyage à la Martinique*, 37, 61–62; and Raynal, *Histoire philosophique et politique*, 3:185–86.
24. Jean-Baptiste Du Tertre (1610–1687) and Jean-Baptiste Labat (1663–1738) examined a variety of issues (customs of Carib Indians and imported Africans, religion, music, politics and economics of the slave trade, etc.). Du Tertre spent several years in the French Antilles during the 1640s and 1650s, and Labat arrived in Martinique about forty years later (1694). Although both missionaries stayed primarily in Martinique and Guadeloupe, they also spent considerable time visiting other islands (Barbados, Dominica, Granada, Saint-Domingue, Saint Christopher [Saint Kitts], Saint Lucia, and Saint Vincent). See Jean-Baptiste Du Tertre, *Histoire générale des Antilles, habitées par les François, contenant l'histoire naturelle, enrichy de cartes & de figures* (1667); and Jean-Baptiste Labat, *Nouveau voyage aux isles de l'Amérique, contenant l'histoire naturelle de ces pays, l'origine, les moeurs, la religion & le gouvernement des habitans anciens & modernes* (1722).
25. Du Tertre, *Histoire générale des Antilles*, 2:526–27.
26. During his first ten years in Martinique, Labat transformed the Saint-Jacques property into an extremely prosperous plantation, with revenues doubling each year. During this period, he also held various important posts in the Dominican Order in Martinique (parish director, bursar, trustee, vicar-general, and papal prefect). Father Labat was also noted for meticulous observations of customs of the enslaved, and of various types of nonreligious events ranging from the minute details of a *cochon boucan* to a lengthy discourse on the division of slave labor on sugar-cane plantations. Father Labat describes a *cochon boucan* as an all-day feast that was held in the forest. Preparations usually began around 9:00 A.M. A pig (*cochon*) was roasted over a grill (*boucan*) constructed by guests and their slaves. The pig was laid on its back and its belly (split open) was filled with lime juice, salt, and crushed pimento. While the pig was cooking, a few guests ate breakfast while others went hunting. When the hunters returned with their game, the slaves cleaned and placed it in the belly of the pig or near the fire to be cooked. Labat, *Nouveau voyage*, 6:9–18, 7:232–36. Today, one of the most popular rums on the island still carries his name and picture on the bottle.
27. *Nouveau voyage*, 4:469–70.
28. Thibault de Chanvalon, *Voyage à la Martinique*, 66–67.
29. For detailed descriptions, functions, and origins of dances of the enslaved, see Moreau de Saint-Méry, *Dance*; Katherine Dunham, *Dances of Haiti* (Los Angeles: Center for Afro-American Studies, University of California, 1983); Jacqueline Rosemain, *La musique*; and Sully Cally, *Musiques et danses Afro-Caraïbes* (Martinique: Sully Cally, Lezin, 1990).
30. See Liliane Chauleau, ed., *La Société à la Martinique*, 29–31; and Labat, *Nouveau voyage*, 4:467–68.
31. John D. Garrigus, *Before Haiti: Race and Citizenship in French Saint-Domingue* (New York:

Palgrave Macmillan, 2006), 22.

32. The term "lower-echelon whites" refers to those at the bottom of the social ordering of whites (the poor, the uneducated, and those who did not own any slaves, land, or other property).

33. Maurice Nicolas, "Le théâtre de Saint-Pierre au XVIIIe siècle: Les années difficiles," *Annales des Antilles* 1 (1955): 54. See also Rosemain, *La musique*, 73–74.

34. See "Ordonnance du Roi, concernant la police des cabaretiers, 30 Septembre, 1766," in Moreau de Saint-Méry, *Loix et constitutions*, 5:60–61.

35. Ibid.

36. See *Série Colonies* C^{8A} 58, F° 249, April 15, 1749, Archives Nationales, Paris, France. See also in the same series of colonial documents C^{8A} 19, F° 388, June 23, 1713; C^{8A} 58, F° 24, January 12, 1718; C^{8A} 37, F° 307, April 17, 1727; C^{8A} 56, F° 289, January 30, 1746; C^{8A} 60, F° 123, March 1753; C^{8A} 60, F° 127, June 30, 1753; C^{8A} 60, F° 129, January 24, 1746; C^{8A} 60, F° 131, January 16, 1751; C^{8A} 85, F° 302–306, 1785; and C^{8A} 94, F° 31, January 20, 1790.

37. "Ordonnance du gouverneur-général, concernant des milices," June 30, 1762.

38. "Ordonnance générale des milices," January 15, 1765, in Moreau de Saint-Méry, *Loix et constitutions*, 4:822–23.

39. Jean-Joseph Vilaire, *4 Causeries sur "Boisrond Tonnerre: Nos Duels Historiques. Notre Créole. l'Esprit et les moeurs des Affranchis de St.-Domingue*," ed. Maurice Vilaire (n.p.: Imprimerie du Séminaire Adventiste, 1974), 78. For information on the makeup, function, and various sectors of the military, see Jonathan Brown, *The History and Present Condition of St. Domingo* (1837; reprint, London: Frank Cass and Co., 1972), 110–11; le R.P. Adolphe Cabon, *Histoire d'Haïti, cours professé au Petit-Seminaire-college, Saint-Martial* 1 (Port-au-Prince: Édition de La Petite Revue, 192_?–1937?), 1:247–50, 266–67, 287–89, 302–9, 315–16, and 2:347–49; Émile Hayot, *Les gens de couleur libres* (Paris: Société française d'histoire d'outre-mer et Librairie orientaliste Paul Geuthner, 1971), 15, 49; Léo Elisabeth, "The French Antilles," in *Neither Slave Nor Free*, ed. David W. Cohen and Jack P. Greene (Baltimore: Johns Hopkins University Press, 1972), 136; Gwendolyn Midlo Hall, "Saint Domingue," in *Neither Slave Nor Free*, 173–75; Stewart R. King, *Blue Coat or Powdered Wig* (Athens: University of Georgia Press, 2001), 52–57, 226–65, 269, 271–73; and John D. Garragus, *Before Haiti: Race and Citizenship in French Saint-Domingue* (New York: Palgrave Macmillan, 2006), 16–17, 42–43, 95–139.

40. John D. Garragus, *Before Haiti*, 100–108.

41. A. Martineau and Ph. May, *Trois siècles d'histoire antillaise Martinique Guadeloupe* (Paris: Société de l'histoire des colonies françaises, 1935), 51. Also cited in Rosemain, *La musique*, 34–35.

42. *Affiches Américaines* 11 (March 12, 1766): 97.

43. Numerous colonial newspapers and Rosemain, *La musique*, 14–15, discuss military reviews in each colony over a period of several decades. My description of the basic format of military reviews is a brief sketch drawn from these sources. See also "Ordonnance du Roi, au sujet des Places et Rangs dans les Eglises, Processions, Marches et autres Cérémonies publiques," September 30,

1713, in Moreau de Saint-Méry, *Loix et constitutions*, 2:392–95.

44. Emphasis added. *Supplément aux Affiches Américaines* 3 (January 19, 1774): 31.
45. For some of the most elaborate ceremonies in which military musicians participated, see *Avis divers et Petites, Affiches Américaines* 12 (March 20, 1765): 110–11; *Affiches Américaines* 48 (November 27, 1781): 49; and *Affiches Américaines* 7 (February 12, 1783).
46. See *Affiches Américaines* 3 (January 19, 1774): 31; 5 (February 2, 1774): 55; 10 (March 9, 1774): 115; 13 (March 30, 1779); *Supplément aux Affiches Américaines* 5 (February 1, 1780): 38; *Affiches Américaines* 8 (February 22, 1780); 55 (June 5, 1781): 219; and 48 (November 27, 1781): 470.
47. Composed by André-Ernest-Modeste Grétry (1741–1813) on a libretto by Michel-Jean Sedaine (1719–1797). The opera consisted of four acts, premiered in Versailles on December 30, 1779, and was repeated in Paris at the Comédie-Italienne on January 3, 1780. It was reduced to three acts and mounted again on January 7, 1782. *Aucassin et Nicolette* was also mounted three times with great success in Saint-Domingue at the Cap Français theatre: July 22, 1783; November 6, 1784; and May 14, 1785.
48. Premiered in Paris in May 1664, and performed in Port-au-Prince on August 13, 1782. Molière [Jean Baptiste Poquelin] (1661–1673), author.
49. Premiered in Paris in 1760 and performed in Port-au-Prince on December 14, 1782. Voltaire [François-Marie Arouet] (1694–1778), author.
50. Performed in Cap Français on January 24, 1765, and on February 7, 1765. In the first production, *Les Grenadiers* followed a performance of *Le Soldat magicien, ou le magnétisme animal*, a one-act opera by François-Danican Philidor (1726–1795), composer, and Michel-Jean Sedaine (1719–1797), librettist. The latter performance preceded a one-act play, *Les Trois Gascons* (Florent Carton Dancourt, 1661–1725, author).
51. May 11, 1785. For more information regarding such benefits, see *Affiches Américaines* 8 (February 22, 1780): 55; *Affiches Américaines* 23 (June 5, 1781): 213; and *Supplément aux Affiches Américaines* 19 (May 11, 1785): 213.
52. The number of studies on the lifestyle, status, and accomplishments of *affranchis* is endless. For more information on these issues, see Alfred de Laujon, *Souvenirs et voyages* (Bordeaux, 1835); François Alexandre Stanislaus, Baron de Wimpffen, *Saint-Domingue à la veille de la Révolution: Souvenirs du Baron de Wimpffen (1788–1790)*, ed. Albert Savine (Paris: Louis-Michaud, 1911); Louis E. Elie, *Histoire d'Haïti: Les origines du peuple haïtien*, 2 vols. (Port-au-Prince: n.p., 1945); Jean-Joseph Vilaire, *4 Causeries sur "Boisrond Tonnerre," "Nos Duels Historiques," "Notre Créole," "l'Esprit et les moeurs des Affranchis de St.-Domingue,"* ed. Maurice Vilaire (n.p.: Imprimerie du Séminaire Adventiste, 1974); le R.P. Adolphe Cabon, *Histoire d'Haïti, cours professé au Petit-Seminaire-college, Saint-Martial* (Port-au-Prince: Edition de La Petite Revue, 192_?–1937?); Émile Hayot, *Les gens de couleur libres du Fort-Royal, 1679–1823* (Paris: Société française d'histoire d'outre-mer et Librairie orientaliste Paul Geuthner, 1971); Jonathan Brown, *The History and Present Condition of St. Domingo*, 2 vols. (1837; reprint, London: Frank Cass and Co., 1972); Léo Elisabeth, "The

French Antilles," in *Neither Slave Nor Free*, ed. David W. Cohen and Jack P. Greene (Baltimore: Johns Hopkins University Press, 1972); Gwendolyn Midlo Hall, "Saint Domingue," in *Neither Slave Nor Free*; Stewart R. King, *Blue Coat or Powdered Wig* (Athens: University of Georgia Press, 2001); Doris Garraway, "Race, Reproduction and Family Romance in Moreau de Saint-Méry's *Description . . . de la partie française de l'isle Saint-Domingue*," *Eighteenth-Century Studies* 38, no. 2 (2005): 227–46; and John D. Garrigus, *Before Haiti*.

53. In chapter 3, I will take a closer look at this "Paradise" and the presumed "necessity" for maintaining a clear separation of races in theatres.
54. King, *Blue Coat or Powdered Wig*, 228. As indicated above, military service in the south was viewed rather negatively by free colored men, which negated the need for a "military leadership group."
55. Ibid., 228–29. King devotes considerable space to the makeup and accomplishments of the two groups of free colored people in Saint-Domingue (see pages 52–265). For similar developments in Martinique and Guadeloupe, see Hayot, *Les Gens de couleur libres*, 15–139, and Jacques Petitjean-Roget, *Le Gaoulé: La révolte de la Martinique en 1717* (Fort de France, Martinique: Société d'histoire de la Martinique, 1966), 67–111.
56. Physical layouts of theatres in each colony are discussed in chapter 3; and full descriptions are provided in appendix 4.
57. The lists of actors, dancers, musicians, and singers who traveled to the colonies are extremely long. Several artists who relate specifically to events covered in this study are mentioned in Chapters 3–5. For more detailed information, see Archives Ministres France d'Outre-mer, Régistre de catholicité du mouillage; Archives des affaires étrangères 5, 692, and 2, 107; Série Colonies A, Actes du pouvoir souverain, Ancien Régime; Série Colonies C^{8B} 15–80; Série Colonies F, Documents divers, Ancien Régime; Série F5B; and weekly periodicals published in each colony, 1764–1790.
58. "Mémoire concernant l'establissement d'un Spectacle à St. Pierre de la Martinique," August 5, 1780. Série Colonies $C8^{B}$ 15, Archives Nationales, Paris.
59. Moreau de Saint-Méry, *Description topographique . . . partie française*, 1:370–71.
60. Ibid., 1:371.
61. Moreau de Saint-Méry, *Dance*, 21–70, and *Description topographique . . . partie française*, 1:368–71. See also Fouchard, *Les plaisirs*, 127–41.
62. See Fouchard, *Les plaisirs*, 138–41; Moreau de Saint-Méry, *Dance*, 45–49; Rosemain, *La musique*, 44–47; Baron de Wimpffen, *Saint-Domingue à la veille de la Révolution*, 74–79; Vilaire, *4 Causeries*, 69–89; and Alfred Laujon, *Souvenirs de trente années de voyages à Saint-Domingue*, 1:266–302 (cited in Wimpffen, *Saint-Domingue*, 75).
63. "Ordonnance du Roi touchant la Police des Bals des Gens de couleur libres, et celle des Spectacles, du 11 Mars 1785," in Moreau de Saint-Méry, *Loix et constitutions*, 6:727–28.
64. Rosemain, *La musique*, 48. See also Moreau de Saint-Méry, *Dance*, 45–49.
65. See Moreau de St-Méry, *Dance*, 33–34.
66. See Alfred de Laujon, *Souvenirs et voyages* (Bordeaux, 1835), 267–69; Baron de Wimpffen,

Saint-Domingue à la veille de la Révolution, 120–21; Moreau de Saint-Méry, *Description topographique . . . partie française*, 1:92–97; "La Vie au Cap Français en 1789," *Revue d'histoire des colonies françaises* 36 (1927): 113, 120–21; and Rosemain, *La musique*, 47–48.

67. Ibid.

Chapter 3. Colonial Society at the Theatre

1. "Mémoire concernant l'établissement d'un Spectacle à Saint-Pierre de la Martinique," August 5, 1780, Colonies $C8^B$ 15, Archives Nationales, Paris, France.
2. *Affiches Américaines*, May 6, 1786. Cited also in Fouchard, *Le théâtre*, 66–67.
3. Contemporary writers also used the term "spectacle" to refer to entertainment in general, theatrical and nontheatrical (parades, acrobatic performances, fireworks, etc.).
4. In Paris, the court-sponsored opera and drama theatres (Académie Royale de Musique and Comédie Française, respectively) each had its own building, specifically designed for their particular genre.
5. Moreau de St-Méry, *Description topographique . . . partie française*, 1:359–71. See also Fouchard, *Le théâtre*, 6–9.
6. Descriptions of colonial theatres are provided in appendix 4. They are extracted from several documents, including but not limited to *Affiches Américaines* 17 (April 23, 1766): 145–46; Moreau de Saint-Méry, *Description topographique . . . partie française* 1:360–62, 2:202, 326, 461–62, 699–700; Paul Erdman Isert, *Voyage en Guinée et dans les Iles Caraïbes en Amérique* (Paris: Maradan, 1793); Fouchard, *Le théâtre*, 1–115; Jacqueline Rosemain, *La musique dans la société antillaise, 1635–1902* (Paris: Éditions l'Harmattan, 1986), 73–76; Maurice Nicolas, "Le théâtre de Saint-Pierre au XVIIIe siècle: Les années difficiles," *Annales des Antilles* 1 (1955): 53–64, and *Les Grandes heures du théâtre de Saint-Pierre* (n.p.: Berger Bellepage, n.d.); and Solange Contour, *Saint-Pierre, Martinique* (Paris: S. Contour, 1988) 1:122–27.
7. Archives Nationales, Paris, dossier T.210[3] (1771–1778); also printed in Fouchard, *Le théâtre*, 15–18.
8. In 1635 Pierre Belain d'Esnambuc, French explorer, landed at Saint-Pierre and took possession of the island in the name of the king (Louis XIII).
9. Maurice Nicolas, *Saint-Pierre, Martinique* (Fort-de-France: Imp. Bezaudin, 1971), 7.
10. See Rosemain, *La musique*, 40–44; and Maurice Nicolas, *Annales des Antilles* 1 (1955): 53–64, and *Les Grandes heures du théâtre*.
11. See "Ordonnance concernant l'établissement du Spectacle," April 1772, signed by Le Comte de Nozière, Governor, and Taskew, General Intendant, regarding an attempt to revive the theatre in Martinique. Conseil Supérieur (1771–1779), Martinique B^{13}, F° 41, Archives départementales de la Martinique; "Mémoire concernant l'établissement d'un Spectacle à St. Pierre de la Martinique," 1780, providing a financial plan and outlining advantages for all inhabitants (*Série* C^{8b} 15, 43 bis, Archives Nationales, Paris); and "Correspondence confirming that the above *Mémoire* was sent

to Mr. Tascher, President of the colony, on August 5th and hopes that he will sign his approval and forward it on to Monseigneur," 1780 (*Série* C8b 15, 53, Archives Nationales, Paris). See also Nicolas, *Annales des Antilles* 1 (1955): 53–64.

12. Program: *Le Pouvoir de Zèle* and *Le Jugement de Midas*. Nicolas, *Les Grandes heures du théâtre*, 12.
13. A copy of this photograph, taken prior to the volcanic eruption in 1902, is easily accessible for public view; it is enclosed in a weatherproof container on the sidewalk just left of the entrance to the theatre.
14. Paul Erdman Isert, "Lettre XII, de Saint-Pierre de la Martinique, du 10 juillet, 1787," *Voyage en Guinée et dans les Îles Caraïbes en Amérique* (Paris: Maradan, 1793), 339–40. The author defines *créoles* as "Americans, given birth by European parents," and *Christises* as "fourth-generation descendants of a European male and a black female."
15. Ibid., 340–41.
16. Maurice Nicolas, *St. Pierre, Martinique* (Fort-de-France, 1971), 37. Bordeaux, a flourishing city, slave port, and center of the wine trade on the western coast of France, was home to one of the most impressive (and the largest prerevolutionary) theatres in Europe. The Bordeaux Grand Théâtre, inaugurated in 1780, was the masterpiece of the architect Victor Louis (1731–1800), who was also the architect of Théâtre-Français, home of the Comédie-Française in Paris.
17. See "Saint-Pierre, ville d'art et d'histoire," *Guides Archéologiques de la Martinique* (Martinique: Ministère de la Culture et de la Communication sous direction de l'Archéologie, 1990), Archives d'outre-mer, Aix-en-Provence, B.6108; Henri Lagrave and Philippe Rouyer, *La Vie théâtrale à Bordeaux des origines à nos jours* (Paris: Éditions du centre national de la recherche scientifique, 1985), 167–255; Charles Marionneau, *Victor Louis, architecte du Théâtre de Bordeaux, sa vie, ses travaux et sa correspondance* (Bordeaux: Imprimerie G. Gounouilhou, 1881); and Maurice Nicolas, *St. Pierre, Martinique* (Fort-de-France, 1971), *Annales des Antilles* 1 (1955): 53–64, and *Les Grandes heures du théâtre*.
18. Each step in the six-year process of negotiations is outlined in "Ordonnance de Messeurs de Conflans et Maillard [governor and intendant, respectively] en date du 13 Juin 1749," in *Revue d'histoire des colonies françaises* 36 (1949): 231–37. See also Moreau de Saint-Méry, *Description topographique . . . partie française*, 2:315–21.
19. *Ordonnance* dated November 26, 1949. Moreau, *Description topographique . . . partie française*, 2:315–16. See also Fouchard, *Le théâtre*, 37–38.
20. Fouchard, *Le théâtre*, 40–41.
21. *Affiches Américaines* 7 (February 15, 1775): 78, and 52 (December 25, 1776): 617–18.
22. Mesplès provided a lengthy discussion regarding his background, experience, and negotiations for the construction of a theatre in Port-au-Prince. See *Revue d'histoire des colonies françaises* 36 (1949): 161–99. Also printed in Fouchard, *Le théâtre*, 48–64.
23. Moreau de Saint-Méry, *Description topographique . . . partie française*, 2:326. See also Fouchard, *Le théâtre*, 64–65.

24. Fouchard, *Le théâtre*, 64.
25. The program for the inauguration commenced with *Le Déserteur*, a play in five acts, by Louis-Sébastien Mercier (1740–1814), followed by a violoncello solo. The next piece was *La Nouvelle Annette*, an opera in one act by Jean-Benjamin-François de LaBorde (1734–1794), composer, and Jean-François Marmontel (1723–1799), librettist. The program concluded with a dance "by an amateur." *Affiches Américaines* 5 (February 3, 1778): 34–35.
26. See Rosemain, *La musique*, 42; and Paul Erdman Isert, "Lettre XII, De Saint-Pierre de la Martinique, 10 Juillet 1787," *Voyage en Guinée dans les Îles Caraïbes en Amérique* (Paris, 1793).
27. *Avis Divers* and *Petites Affiches Américaines* 21 (22 May 1765): 182.
28. See Moreau de Saint-Méry, *Description topographique . . . partie française*, 2:461–62.
29. Ibid., 2:200–201.
30. The program: *Cartouche, comédie*, and Rousseau's *Le Devin du village.*
31. Moreau de Saint-Méry, *Description topographique . . . partie française*, 2:202. See appendix 4 for a full description of the theatre.
32. Mercier, "La Vie au Cap Français en 1789," *Revue d'histoire des colonies françaises* 26 (1933): 124
33. Ibid., 126.
34. For information on controversies regarding parterres in French public and court theatres, see Jeffrey Scott Ravel, "The Police and the Parterre: Cultural Politics in the Paris Public Theater, 1680–1789," PhD diss. (University of California at Berkeley, 1991); Ravel, *The Contested Parterre: Public Theater and French Political Culture, 1680–1791* (Ithaca, NY: Cornell University Press, 1999); and Downing A. Thomas, *Aesthetics of Opera in the Ancien Régime, 1647–1785* (Cambridge: Cambridge University Press, 2002), 277, 291, 374.
35. Mercier, "La Vie au Cap Français en 1789," 126.
36. Ibid.
37. By the middle of the eighteenth century, the term "*négresses*" also referred to free black women (as well as to enslaved black females), a method to distinguish them from free colored women.
38. *Description topographique . . . partie française*, 1:365.
39. Molière and Voltaire were the favorite playwrights. Premieres of their works in Paris and in the colonies are provided in appendix 5.
40. *Supplément aux Affiches Américaines* 6 (February 8, 1783): 70.
41. Clarence D. Brenner, *The Theatre Italien: Its Repertory, 1716–1793* (Berkeley: University of California Press, 1961), 25.
42. The *intermède* is defined in Introduction, note 30.
43. Richard Semmens, *The "bals publics" at the Paris Opéra in the Eighteenth Century* (Hillsdale, NY: Pendragon Press, 2004), 163–64.

Chapter 4. Introducing the Stars

1. A few examples: *Gazette de Saint-Domingue*, February 15, 1764; *Avis Divers et Petites Affiches Américaines*, September 12, 1764; February 20, 1765; May 15, 1765; July 31, 1765; August 14 and 28, 1765; September 11, 1765; November 6, 1765; *Affiches Américaines*, January 28, 1766; October 7, 1767; April 25, 1768; June 13 and 20, 1768; *Supplément aux Affiches Américaines*, June 26, 1769, and October 25, 1769. See also Jean Fouchard, *Le théâtre à Saint-Domingue* (Port-au-Prince: Imprimerie de l'État, 1955), 345, and *Les marrons du syllabaire* (1953; reprint, Port-au-Prince: Éditions Henri Deschamps, 1988), 47–59.
2. *Gazette de Saint-Domingue*, February 15, 1764.
3. *Supplément aux Affiches Américaines*, December 14, 1779; December 21, 1779; October 31, 1781; July 5, 1783; July 12, 1783; July 19, 1783; February 1, 1786; *Affiches Américaines*, November 20, 1781; January 22, 1783; and *Feuille du Cap-François*, March 8, 1788.
4. Fouchard, *Le théâtre*, 346. The concerto was based on an *ariette* from the opera *La Belle Arsène.*
5. *Supplément aux Affiches Américaines*, July 5, 1783.
6. The two operas: *Le Peintre amoureux et son modèle (opéra-bouffon*, two acts) and *Gilles, garçon peintre, s'amoureux t' et rival*, a one-act parody of the former work.
7. *Le Tableau parlant*, a *comédie-parade* in one act, was composed by André-Ernest-Modeste Grétry (1741–1813) on a libretto by Louis Anseaume (?1721–1784). The work premiered in Paris on September 20, 1769, at the Comédie-Italienne. It was launched in the colonies on February 12, 1780, at the Cap Français Comédie, and a few months later in Port-au-Prince (December 19, 1780).
8. *Supplément aux Affiches Américaines* 50 and 51 (December 7 and 14, 1779), 41 (October 12, 1782), and 3 (January 18, 1783).
9. Depoix did not actually leave Port-au-Prince in 1784 as he had planned, because the gazettes reflect that for the period 1784–1787 he was still performing in some of the most successful operas produced in that city. See also Moreau de Saint-Méry, *Description topographique . . . partie française*, 2:325; and Fouchard, *Artistes et repertoire*, 26.
10. Two plays were on the program: *Gaston et Bayard, tragédie*, and *Christophe le Rond, comédie.* Authors and performance records of these works were not cited.
11. The operas were *La Servante maîtresse* (a translation of *La serva padrona*, an *intermezzo* in two acts, composed in 1733 by Giovanni Battista Pergolesi [1710–1736]) and *Félix, ou l'enfant-trouvé*, an opera in three acts, composed by Pierre-Alexandre Monsigny (1729–1817) on a libretto by Michel-Jean Sedaine (1719–1797).
12. *Affiches Américaines* 47 (November 20, 1781).
13. *Le barbier de Séville* (1775) was the first play in Beaumarchais's classic Figaro trilogy, followed by *Le mariage de Figaro* (1784) and *La mère coupable* (performed in 1792). The first two were set to music by several composers, notably Rossini (*Il barbiere di Siviglia* [1816, Rome]) and Mozart (*Le nozze di Figaro* [1786, Vienna]).

14. Charles also played violin, bass, and bassoon. In 1783 he was appointed *maître de musique du spectacle*. See below, note 17, for information on Petit.
15. *Supplément aux Affiches Américaines* 27 (July 5, 1783).
16. Composed by A.E.M. Grétry (1741–1813) on a libretto by J. F. Marmontel (1723–1799). It premiered on November 9, 1777, at Fontainebleau and was performed over 220 times at the Comédie-Italienne. Premieres in the colonies occurred on August 30, 1772 (Cap Français), February 17, 1778 (Port-au-Prince), and in 1787 (Guadeloupe and Martinique).
17. Petit was consistently heralded as one of the best violinists in the colony. In the early part of his career (1778–1782), he worked in Cap Français and was appointed *maître de musique au spectacle*. In 1783 he was with the Port-au-Prince Comédie, where he garnered two prestigious positions, *maître de musique* and first violinist, in the orchestra. Petit was a former pupil of Giovanni Mane Giornovichi, 1735–1804 (Jarnovic), Italian composer and violinist, and one of the most popular musicians in Paris during the 1770s. Petit was unquestionably devoted to his teacher, for in the numerous concerts in which he performed, Petit almost always included a Jarnovic concerto.
18. Mr. Acquaire was an important partner in "breaking through the barrier," which will be discussed in greater detail in the following section and also in chapter 6.
19. Composed by Pierre-Alexandre Monsigny (1729–1817) on a libretto by Charles-Simon Favart (1710–1792). It premiered on November 7, 1773, at Fontainebleau and was performed more than 160 times at the Comédie-Italienne. Premieres in the colonies occurred on October 25, 1778 (Port-au-Prince), January 16, 1779 (Cap Français), March 30, 1784 (Les Cayes), and in 1787 (Guadeloupe and Martinique).
20. "Déclarations du Roi, concernant les nègres-esclaves des colonies amenés en France," December 15, 1738, in Moreau de Saint-Méry, *Loix et constitutions*, 3:547–50; and "La Police des noirs sous Louis XVI en France," *Revue de l'histoire des colonies françaises* 21 (1928): 433–46.
21. Jacqueline Rosemain, *La musique dans la société antillaise*, 48.
22. Ibid.
23. In keeping with the French propensity to attach labels to everything and to everyone—and with confusing frequency—some sources describe the sisters as *mulâtresses* while others call them *métives*.
24. *Le théâtre*, 303–7. Fouchard presents a florid account of the early childhood of the two sisters, including conditions under which they met the Acquaires, but he cites no source for this information. However, since Fouchard's voluminous studies on Saint-Domingue society are highly respected historical documents, the biographical sketches of the sisters (prior to Minette's concert debut in 1780) that I provide in this section are excerpted from Fouchard's study.
25. *Affiches Américaines*, January 17, 1776.
26. *Supplément aux Affiches Américaines* 51 (December 19, 1780), 411.

Chapter 5. Breaking through the Barrier

1. Moreau de Saint-Méry grudgingly applauded Saint-Martin's consent to allow the debut of Minette. Although Moreau conceded that Minette's "talents and zeal are still applauded each day," he also viewed Saint-Martin's decision as a matter of arrogance (of an artist) overriding colonial politics. *Description topographique . . . partie française*, 2:329.
2. *Isabelle et Gertrude, comédie mêlée d'ariettes*, was composed by Adolphe Benoit Blaise (d.1772) on a libretto by Charles-Simon Favart (1710–1792). The work premiered at the Comédie-Italienne, had 230 subsequent performances, and remained in the repertoire until 1787.
3. *Le Devin du village* premiered at Fontainebleau on October 18, 1752, and was performed five months later in Paris by the Académie Royale de Musique. The work was extremely popular, with over 400 performances; it remained in the repertoire until 1829. *Le Devin du village* was performed several times in Cap François and in Port-au-Prince.
4. *Silvain, comédie mêlée d'ariettes*, in one act, was composed by Grétry on a libretto by Marmontel. It premiered at the Comédie-Italienne on February 19, 1770, and was performed more than 210 times. *Le Maître en droit, ou le tuteur dupe, opéra-buffon* in two acts, was composed by Pierre Alexandre Monsigny (1729–1817) on a libretto by Pierre René Lemonnier (1731–1796). The work was first performed by the Opéra-Comique, Foire Saint-Germain, on February 13, 1760, and was repeated more than 124 times.
5. The operas were *On ne s'avise jamais de tout, comédie mêlée d'ariettes* (May 1; P. A. Monsigny, composer, M.-J. Sedaine, librettist); *Le Sorcier, opéra comique* (May 6; Philidor, composer, Poinsinet, librettist); *Le Maréchal ferrant, opéra comique* (May 20; Philidor, composer, A. F. Quétant, librettist); *Zémire et Azor, comédie-ballet, mêlée de chants et de danses* (June 5; Grétry, composer, Marmontel, librettist); *La Belle Arsène, comédie féerie mêlée d'ariettes* (August 14; P. A. Monsigny, composer, Favart, librettist); *La Fée Urgelle, ou ce qui plaît les dames, comédie mêlée d'ariettes* (September 11 and December 4; E. Duni, composer, C.-S. Favart, librettist); *Pygmalion, scène-lyrique* (September 11; J.-J. Rousseau, composer, Rousseau and H. Coignet, librettists); *L'Amoureux de quinze ans, ou la double fête, comédie mêlée d'ariettes* (October 2; J.P.A. Martini, composer, P. Laujon, librettist); *Toinon et Toinette, opéra comique* (October 23; F. J. Gossec, composer, J. Desboulmiers, librettist); *Sara, ou la fermière écossaise, comédie* (November 20; P. Vachon, composer, J.-B. Collet de Messine, librettist); and *Le Jugement de Midas, comédie mêlée d'ariettes* (December 18; Grétry, composer, M. D'Hêle, librettist).
6. *Démocrite amoureux*, five acts (Jean-François Regnard [1655–1709], author).
7. *Supplément aux Affiches Américaines*, July 31, 1781.
8. *L'Amoureux de quinze ans, ou la double fête, comédie mêlée d'ariettes*, three acts, premiered at the Comédie-Italienne on April 18, 1771, and was repeated more than 161 times.
9. *Le Jugement de Midas, comédie mêlée d'ariettes*, three acts, premiered at the Comédie-Italienne on June 27, 1778, and was repeated more than ninety times.

10. *Annales* 2:122–24.
11. *1782*: January 5: *Les Trois fermiers, comédie mêlée d'ariettes*, two acts (Nicolas Dezèdes, composer, and J.-M. B. de Monvel, librettist), and *La Nouvelle école des femmes, comédie mêlée de chants et de danses*, three acts (Philidor, composer, Moissy, librettist); March 19: *Orphée et Eurydice, grand opéra*, three acts (Gluck, composer, Moline, librettist); November 26: *L'Isle des fous, comédie mêlée d'ariettes*, two acts (Duni, composer, Anseaume, librettist), and one play, *Jérome Pointu, comédie*, one act (author unknown).

    1783: January 14: *Zémire et Azor*; October 28: *L'Infante de Zamora, opéra-féerie*, three acts (Giovanni Paisiello [1740–1816], composer, on a libretto by Nicolas Etienne Framery [1745–1810]); November 5: *La Fille mal gardée, ou le pendant amoureux, comédie mêlée d'ariettes* (Duni, composer, Favart, librettist); November 15: *Aucassin et Nicolette, ou les moeurs du bon vieux temps, comédie mise en musique*, three acts (Grétry, composer, Sedaine, librettist); November 18: *Les Raccoleurs, opéra comique*, one act (Vadé, music and text); December 9: *Les Souliers mordorés, ou la cordonnière allemande, comédie lyrique*, two acts (Fridzeri, composer, and Ferrières, librettist); and one play, *Malborough, drame burlesque*, two acts.

    1784: December 7: *Acajou, opéra comique* (also called "*grand opéra-féerie*"), three acts (Favart); December 21: *Blaise et Babet, ou la suite des trois fermiers, comédie mise en musique*, two acts (Dezède, composer, Monvel, librettist), and *Les Voyages de Rosine, opéra*, two acts (Augustin de Piis, composer, P. Y. Barré, librettist).

    1785: October 11: *L'Epreuve villageoise, opéra bouffon*, two acts (Grétry and P.-J.-B. Desforges).
12. *Supplément aux Affiches Américaines*, April 10, 1783, and April 11, 1784.
13. Benefits were held on January 14, 1783; October 28, 1783; December 21, 1784; and October 11, 1785.
14. *Supplément aux Affiches Américaines*, October 18, 1783. *L'Infante de Zamora* was a revision of Paisello's *La Frescatana*, which premiered in Venice in 1774. Four years later, it was performed at the Paris Opéra (September 10, 1778), and at Versailles on the following Monday, September 14. *L'Infante de Zamora* premiered at Versailles in 1781.
15. *Les Raccoleurs* premiered at Foire Saint Germain on March 11, 1756. Six years later, it was presented at the Comédie-Italienne, where it had thirty subsequent performances. *Les Raccoleurs* was also performed in Cap Français (February 28, 1765) and in Saint-Marc (March 4, 1769).
16. Fouchard, *Le théâtre*, 323.
17. *Description topographique . . . partie française*, 2:462.
18. *Acajou* premiered at Foire Saint-Germain on March 18, 1744, and was performed at the Opéra a few months later (October). The work was revived on July 19, 1773, and was produced forty-seven times over the next fifteen years.
19. See Fouchard, *Le théâtre*, 317–19.
20. Minette sang one *ariette* and took part in a chorus of singers in a concert in January 1789. *Affiches Américaines*, January 29, 1789.
21. *Supplément aux Affiches Américaines*, July 31, 1781.

22. Ibid. See also *Supplément aux Affiches Américaines*, December 11, 1784; *Affiches Américaines*, October 15, 1785, and October 7, 1786.
23. *Supplément aux Affiches Américaines*, July 31, 1781, and *Affiches Américaines*, October 6, 1785.
24. *1786*: February 6, Saint-Marc: *Les Tonneliers, opéra comique*, one act, composed by François-Joseph Gossec (1734–1829) on a libretto by Nicolas-Médard Audinot (1732–1801); and *Les Amours de Mirabalais, parodie Nègre du Devin du village*.

    1787: February 19, Léogane: *L'Épreuve villageoise, opéra-bouffon*.

    1788: January 22, Léogane: *L'Amant statue*, and *Les Deux tuteurs*; and January 29, Léogane: *Le Faux Lord, opéra comique* (Niccolò Piccinni *père*, composer, and G. M. Piccinni *fils*, librettist).
25. *Le Tonnelier, opéra comique*, one act, was composed by François-Joseph Gossec (1734–1829) on a libretto by Nicolas-Médard Audinot (1732–1801). It premiered at the Comédie-Italienne on March 16, 1765, and subsequently had over 250 performances. Composer and librettist for *Les Amours de Mirabalais* are unknown.
26. See note 3 above.
27. *Affiches Américaines*, January 28, 1786.
28. *Affiches Américaines*, October 1, 1785.
29. *Affiches Américaines*, February 19, 1787.
30. *Le Faux Lord, opéra comique*, in two acts, was composed by Niccolò Piccinni (1728–1800) on a libretto by his son, Joseph-Marie Piccinni (1758–1826). The work premiered at Versailles, December 5, 1783, and then at the Comédie-Italienne six days later. It had 48 subsequent performances.
31. Léandre seeks the aid of his valet (Lafleur), a cunning and wise man. In order to see Irène and to give her a message from Léandre, Lafleur disguises himself as a dealer in secondhand goods. After this is accomplished, he then disguises himself as a "vaporous" village lord (Greidneigh); Léandre accompanies him, disguised as a doctor. Greidneigh (Lafleur) warns Anselme of a pending and horrible danger for all women and proposes to take an apartment in Anselme's home for a very generous sum with the provision that no women enter. The greedy Anselme agrees and tells Irène and her servant (Finette) to disguise themselves as men. Greidneigh, however, seeing this, accuses Anselme of deceit and trickery and threatens to leave if the women are not taken away. Anselme, very embarrassed, says he cannot send them away because one is his daughter and the other is her servant. Greidneigh then strikes a bargain with Anselme. He convinces Anselme that in order to save himself from more embarrassment, he should marry Irène to the doctor (Léandre in disguise); Greidneigh would furnish the dowry with the pretense that it actually comes from Anselme in order to conserve the latter's reputation. Anselme sends for the *notaire* and everyone signs the marriage contract. Then Anselme, noticing the name of Léandre on the contract, learns of the latter's true identity. Anselme is furious and enraged, but everyone advises him to quiet down for fear of making a real fool of himself and looking ridiculous. He finally submits and contents himself with the union of his daughter to Léandre.
32. *Affiches Américaines*, June 5, 1788.

33. *1786*: January 17: *Les Vendangeurs, ou les deux baillis, opéra* (Augustin de Piis, composer, P. Y. Barré, librettist); January 31: *L'Infante de Zamora, opéra-féerie*; July 25: *Les Deux tuteurs, comédie mêlée d'ariettes*, two acts (Nicolas-Marie Dalayrac, composer, A.E.X de La Chabeaussière, librettist); October 10: *Blaise et Babet, ou la suite des trois fermiers*, and *L'Amant statue, comédie mêlée d'ariettes*, one act (Dalayrac, composer, and Desfontaines, librettist); October 24: *La Folle journée, ou le mariage de Figaro, comédie*, five acts (Pierre-Augustin Caron de Beaumarchais, author); November 21: *Alexis et Justine, comédie lyrique mêlée d'ariettes*, two acts (Dezède, composer, Monvel, librettist); and December 5: *L'Amant statue* and repeat of one play, *La Folle journée, ou le mariage de Figaro, comédie.*

1787: January 5: *Orphée et Eurydice* (Gluck, composer, and Moline, librettist); January 30: *La Caravane du Cairo, opéra-ballet*, three acts (Grétry, composer, and E. Morel de Chédeville, librettist); February 19: *L'Épreuve villageoise*; March 6: *Nina, ou la folle par amour, comédie mêlée d'ariettes*, one act (Dalayrac, composer, B.-J. Marsollier des Vivetières, librettist); May 3: *La Belle Arsène, comédie-féerie*, four acts (Monsigny, composer, Favart, librettist); and May 5: *Le Mariage d'Antonio, ou la suite de Richard coeur de lion, comédie mêlée d'ariettes*, one act (L. Grétry and A. Grétry, composers, and Mme de Beaunoir, librettist); *L'Amant statue*, and *L'Épreuve villageoise.*

1788: January 19: *L'Amant statue*; February 16: *La Caravane du Caire.*

1789: September 12: *Renaud d'Ast, comédie mêlée d'ariettes*, two acts (Dalayrac, composer, and Radet and Barré, librettists).

34. See Maurice Nicolas, "Le théâtre de Saint-Pierre au XVIIIe siècle: Les années difficiles," *Annales des Antilles* 1 (1955): 54–55.

35. Madame Marsan's husband died in 1787, and she left Saint-Domingue three or four years later, probably due to the dangers she and her children faced during the slave revolts. She settled in New Orleans, Louisiana, where she had similar success. She died there in 1807 at the age of sixty-one.

36. *Affiches Américaines*, January 2, 1781; May 29, 1782; November 20, 1782; and February 19, 1783.

37. *Affiches Américaines*, March 1, 1787

38. *Supplément aux Affiches Américaines*, January 18, 1783; October 18, 1783; December 21, 1784; *Affiches Américaines*, March 1, 1787; March 10, 1787; and May 3, 1787.

39. *Affiches Américaines*, January 2, 1781; May 29, 1782; November 20, 1782; and February 19, 1783.

40. *Affiches Américaines*, May 3, 1787.

41. In August 1781, she had a minor role in this opera. See *Supplément aux Affiches Américaines*, July 31, 1781.

42. *Affiches Américaines*, May 3, 1787.

Chapter 6. The Escape from Reality Continues

1. This occurred between the third and fourth acts in a Cap Français performance, November 18, 1777. *Supplément aux Affiches Américaines*, November 15, 1777.
2. "Un amateur connu pour imiter parfaitement les gestes et le langage des nègres remplira le role de Figaro, sous le costume d'un valet nègre, avec un divertissement et des couplets créoles." *Supplément aux Affiches Américaines*, May 7, 1785.
3. Cap Français, April 3, 1773; *Supplément aux Affiches Américaines*, March 27, 1773. *Soliman second, ou les trois sultanes, comédie mêlée d'ariettes*, in three acts, was composed by Paul César Gibert (1717–1787) on a libretto by Charles-Simon Favart (1710–1792). It premiered at the Comédie-Italienne on April 9, 1761, and played at the Académie Royale de Musique later that year (December 19). The opera was performed subsequently over 165 times at the Comédie-Italienne.
4. *Affiches Américaines*, January 24, 1788.
5. *Description topographique . . . partie française*, 1:64–65.
6. See Alfred de Laujon, *Souvenirs et voyages* (Bordeaux, 1835), 267–69; Baron de Wimpffen, *Saint-Domingue à la veille de la Révolution*, 120–21; Moreau de Saint-Méry, *Description topographique . . . partie française*, 1:92–97; "La Vie au Cap Français en 1789," *Revue d'histoire des colonies françaises* 36 (1927): 113, 120–21; and Rosemain, *La musique*, 47–48.
7. Moreau de Saint-Méry, *Description topographique . . . partie française*, 1:366; also cited in Fouchard, *Le théâtre*, 286.
8. *Artistes et répertoire des scènes de Saint-Domingue* (Port-au-Prince: Imprimerie de l'État, 1955), 18.
9. *Lundi au Cap, ou les recouvremens, comédie* in three acts. *Affiches Américaines*, March 2, 1779. The work was well acclaimed and, subsequently, was performed several times in Cap Français, Port-au-Prince, and Saint-Marc. See also Moreau de Saint-Méry, *Description topographique . . . partie française*, 1:367.
10. Troubadours were poet-musicians of the twelfth and thirteenth centuries who worked in the south of France. Their songs centered on love and its many associations with joy, despair, deception, idolatry, power of the lady, etc., which led to several genres such as the *canso* (a courtly love song) and the *pastorela* (portrayal of amorous encounters between a knight and a shepherdess).
11. *Blaise et Babet, ou la suite des trois fermiers, opéra-bouffon* in two acts, was composed by Nicolas Dezède (?1740–1812) on a libretto by Jacques-Marie Boutet de Monvel (1745–1812). The work premiered at Versailles on April 4, 1783, and was performed at the Comédie-Italienne over 155 times. Subsequently, it was performed several times in Port-au-Prince and in Cap Français.
12. *Feuille du Cap*, January 26, 1788. *Julien et Susette* premiered in Cap Français on February 7, 1788.
13. *Supplément aux Affiches Américaines*, October 30, 1781.
14. For a linguistic analysis of this work, see Marie-Christine Hazaël-Massieux, "A propos de Jeannot et Thérèse: Une traduction du Devin du village en créole du XVIIIe siècle?" in *Creolica* (September 2005): 1–24.

15. For an excellent, groundbreaking study on the complexities of class, racial, and sexual politics of black minstrelsy, see Eric Lott, *Love and Theft: Blackface Minstrelsy and the American Working Class* (New York: Oxford University Press, 1993). See also Robert Hornback, "Black Shakespeareans vs. Minstrel Burlesques: 'Proper' English, Racist Blackface Dialect, and the Contest for Representing 'Blackness,' 1821–1844," *Shakespeare Studies* 38 (January1 2010); Yuval Taylor and Jake Austen, *Darkest America: Black Minstrelsy from Slavery to Hip-Hop*. New York: W.W. Norton, 2012.
16. "Une comédie en langage et costume Nègres dans la quelle un amateur, connu pour imiter parfaitement les Nègres dans leur idiôme et dans leurs manières, remplit le principal rôle." *Affiches Américaines*, December 24, 1785.
17. "La couleur & le costume des Nègres, ainsi que celui des Cabaretiers Blancs, Reinfort & Tienbon, seront observés avec exactitude. Cette pièce a déjà été jouée plusieurs fois sur des Théatres de la Colonie & a beaucoup amusé les Spectateurs." *Affiches Américaines*, November 4, 1786.
18. *Supplément aux Affiches Américaines*, March 25, 1786.
19. See *Supplément aux Affiches Américaines*, May 4, 1785; March 25, 1786; and August 23, 1786; *Affiches Américaines*, January 28, 1786, and November 4, 1786; and *Gazette de Saint-Domingue*, January 8, 1791.

Chapter 7. Finale: The Beginning of the End

1. *Considérations politiques sur les esclaves des colonies françoises de l'Amérique, et sur leurs gens de couleur libres, présentées d'après les resolutions unanimes de tous leurs Habitans* (Paris, 1791). In *Oeuvres complètes de Condorcet*, 2nd ed. (Brunswick & Paris, 1804–An XIII), 1:101–11.
2. For more information on Abbé Grégoire's contributions to these issues, see his works: *Lettre aux philanthropes sur les malheurs, les droits et les reclamations des gens de couleur de Saint-Domingue, et des autres isles françoises de l'Amérique* (Paris, 1790); *Lettre aux citoyens de couleur et nègres libres de Saint-Domingue et des autres îles françaises de l'Amérique* (Paris, 1791); *Mémoire en faveur des gens de couleur ou sang-mêlés de Saint-Domingue, et des autres îles françoises de l'Amérique, adressé à l'Assemblée nationale* (Paris, 1789); *De la Littérature des nègres, ou recherches sur leurs facultés intellectuelles, leurs qualités morales et leur littérature, suivies de notices sur la vie et les ouvrages des nègres qui se sont distingués dans les sciences, les lettres et les arts* (Brooklyn: Thomas Kirk, 1810); and *De la Noblesse de la peau, ou du préjugé des blancs contre la couleur des Africains et celle de leurs descendans, noirs et sang-mêlés* (Paris, 1826).

   Brissot's works include *Discours sur la nécessité d'établir à Paris une société pour concourir, avec celle de Londres, à abolition de la traité et de l'esclavage des nègres* (Paris, 1788); *Mémoire sur les noirs de l'Amérique septentrionale. Lu à l'assemblée de la Société des amis des noirs, le 9 fev. 1789* (Paris, 1789); *Nouveau voyage dans les Etats-Unis de l'Amérique septentrionale, fait en 1788* (Paris, 1791), 3 vols.; and *Correspondance et papiers* (Paris: Picard et fils, 1912).

3. Gabriel Debien, *Les Colons de Saint-Domingue et la Révolution: Essai sur le Club Massiac* (Paris: Librairie Armand Colin, 1953), 62–63. For more information on the two associations, see Liliane Chauleau, ed., *Archives départementales de la Martinique: La Martinique pendant la Révolution de 1789* (Fort-de-France, 1977); and Léo Elisabeth, *La Société martiniquaise aux XVIIe et XVIIIe siècles, 1664–1789* (Paris: Éditions Karthala, 2003), 437, 447, 449, 464, 467–69.
4. C.L.R. James, *The Black Jacobins: Toussaint l'Ouverture and the San Domingo Revolution*, 2nd ed., rev. (New York: Vintage Books, 1989), 50.
5. For an excellent discussion on antislavery sentiment (with mention of numerous essays, pamphlets, and other publications), see Edward Derbyshire Seeber, *Anti-Slavery Opinion in France during the Second Half of the Eighteenth Century* (New York: Burt Franklin, 1971), 162–72. For more information on the *Exclusif*, see Adrien Questel, "Le Pacte colonial," *La Revue guadeloupéenne*, Nouvelle série 11 (March–April–May, 1947): 27–31; Rosemain, *La musique*, 11–13; Carl Ludwig Lokke, *France and the Colonial Question: A Study of Contemporary French Opinion, 1763–1801* (New York: Columbia University Press, 1932), 27–31; and *s.v.* "colonies," *Encyclopédie, ou dictionnaire raisonné des sciences, des arts et des métiers*, 35 vols. (Paris, 1751–80).
6. This incident is recounted in Maurice Nicolas, *Les Grandes heures du théâtre de Saint-Pierre* (Berger Bellepage, S.A., 1974), 14.
7. Hayot, *Les gens de couleur libres*, 15–16.
8. See above, "Military Power," chapter 2.
9. Rosemain, *La musique*, 78.
10. "Nouvelles diverses," *Affiches Américaines* 81, October 7, 1789.
11. Ibid.
12. Louis XVI departed the Palace of Versailles where the royal family lived and returned to Paris on July 17, 1789, wearing a cockade of three colors (red and blue for Paris and white for the Bourbons), the tricolor that later would become the French national flag.
13. The following summary of events over the eight days is taken from "Nouvelles diverses," *Affiches Américaines* 81, October 7, 1789.
14. "This charming production calls to mind the virtues of the best of kings as well as his goodness and the simplicity of his private life." *Affiches Américaines*, January 7, 1786.
15. *Artistes et répertoire des scènes de Saint-Domingue* (Port-au-Prince: Imprimerie de l'État, 1955), 65, 253.
16. Favart revised and presented the work in 1759 at the same theatre under the title *La Répétition interrompue, ou le petit-maître malgré lui.*
17. See the novel based on the life of Minette by the Haitian writer Marie Chauvet, *Dance on the Volcano*, translated from the French by Salvator Attanasio (New York: William Sloane Associates, 1959). While the work is extremely interesting and well written, the reader must keep in mind that it is a fictionalized account of the lives of the sisters.
18. René J. Le Gardeur Jr., *The First New Orleans Theatre, 1792–1803* (New Orleans: Leeward Books,

1963), 8–14.

19. Gardeur, *The First New Orleans Theatre*, 11.

20. *Le Moniteur de la Louisiane*, November 19, 1806. Cited in Gardeur, *The First New Orleans Theatre*, 13. See also Fouchard, *Artistes et répertoire des scènes de St.-Domingue* (Port-au-Prince: Imprimerie de l'État, 1955), 62–63.

21. *Le Moniteur de la Louisiane*, January 23, 1806. Cited in Gardeur, *The First New Orleans Theatre*, 13.

22. Bernard Camier, "Minette, chanteuse de couleur à Saint-Domingue," *Généalogie et histoire de la Caraïbe*, n° 165 (December 2003): 4023. According to Gardeur, the funeral notice of Mlle Minette Ferrand states her full name as Louise-Elizabeth-Alexandrine-Minette Ferrand.

23. "Minette (1767–1807), artiste de couleur à Saint-Domingue," *Revue de la Société haïtienne d'Histoire et de Géographie*, n° 205 (October–December 2000): 7.

24. Camier, "Minette, chanteuse de couleur à Saint-Domingue," 4023.

25. "Minette: Situation sociale d'une artiste de couleur à Saint-Domingue," *Généalogie et histoire de la Caraïbe*, n° 185 (October 2005): 4638.

26. Ibid.

27. "Les concerts dans les capitales de Saint-Domingue à la fin du XVIIIe siècle," *Revue de musicologie* 93, no. 1 (2007): 81.

28. "Minette: Situation sociale d'une artiste de couleur à Saint-Domingue," 4639.

29. See notes 26 and 29 above.

30. "Minette (1767–1807), artiste de couleur à Saint-Domingue," *Revue de la Société haïtienne d'Histoire et de Géographie,* n° 205 (October–December 2000), 1–11.

31. The Saint-Pierre Comédie continued to prosper for several decades, even under English occupation. Taking advantage of the turmoil in Martinique and in France, and the inability of France to dispatch troops to protect the colony, the English took possession of Martinique in 1794. They maintained control until 1802, at which time France again took possession of the colony. The English also had control of the island in 1809–1814 and a few months in 1815. The last transfer of Martinique between these two powerful enemies occurred in 1816, the year that France took permanent control of the island.

32. For more information on the development, repertoires, and *comédiens* of these two institutions, see Gardeur, *The First New Orleans Theatre*; and Eola Willis, *The Charleston Stage in the XVIII Century, with Social Settings of the Time* (New York: Benjamin Blom, 1968).

33. Willis, *The Charleston Stage*, 234–37.

34. For a discussion on the later development of blackness on the operatic stage in the United States, see Naomi André, Karen M. Bryan, and Eric Saylor, eds., *Blackness in Opera* (Urbana: University of Illinois Press, 2012).

Epilogue

1. "Émancipation des noirs, tel est notre premier voeu. Prospérité des colonies, tel est notre second voeu. Nous demandons l'une au nom de l'humanité, l'autre au nom de la nationalité, toutes deux au nom de la justice." Victor Schoelcher (1804–1893) was the driving force behind the abolishment of slavery in the French Antilles in 1848. Afterwards, he served as deputy in the National Assembly for Guadeloupe and Martinique, where he continued to work tirelessly to eliminate the abuses of colonialism and to fight for the equality of blacks. There is a very impressive monument in Martinique that reflects the importance of this great abolitionist, the Bibliothèque départementale Schoelcher, a library that houses Schoelcher's personal library of more than 10,000 volumes he bequeathed to Martinique. For the people of Martinique, the building symbolizes extremely important events, the struggle for and the final abolition of slavery. It is in this historic institution that I spent several months examining several important documents for the present study.

Appendix 3. Moreau: Effects of Miscegenation

1. Émile Hayot, *Les gens de couleur libres du Fort-Royal* (Paris, 1971), 60–61. See also *Antilles d'hier et d'aujourd'hui: Tout l'univers antillais du début de la colonisation à nos jours* (Fort-de-France, Martinique: Emile Désormeaux, 1978), 6:66; and Nicole Vanony-Frisch, "Les Esclaves de la Guadeloupe à la fin de l'ancien régime d'après les sources notariales (1770–1789)," *Bulletin de la Société d'Histoire de la Guadeloupe* 63–64 (1985): 29–40.

BIBLIOGRAPHY

Colonial Periodicals (1764–1790)

Affiches Américaines

Avis du Cap

Courrier de Saint-Domingue

Feuille du Cap

Gazette du Jour

Gazette de la Guadeloupe

Gazette de la Martinique

Gazette de Saint-Domingue

Journal Général de Saint-Domingue

Journal Historique et Critique des Antilles (formerly, *Gazette des Petites Antilles*)

Supplément aux Affiches Américaines

Additional Archival Materials (rules of conduct and other legal documents)

"Arrêt du Conseil du Cap concernant le loto et les jeux publics," June 23, 1785. In Méderic-Louis-Elie Moreau de Saint-Méry, *Loix et constitutions*, 6:779.

"Arrêt du Conseil du Cap, qui condamne un Negre à porter aux pieds, toute sa vie, chez son maître, une chaîne pesant 15 livres," June 2, 1719. In *Loix et constitutions*, 2:648.

"Arrêt du Conseil du Cap contre un Mulâtre libre qui avoit porté le main sur un Blanc," October 22, 1783. In *Loix et constitutions*, 6:373.

"Arrêt du Conseil du Cap, qui 1°. adjuge à des mulâtres bâtards le legs à eux faits par un blanc leur pere naturel, (de deux habitations contenant, 348 carreaux de terre, 240 negres, 30 mulets, 80,000 pieds de café, etc. etc.); 2°. réduit à l'an et jour la durée de l'execution testamentaire déferée au-delà de ce terme," October 5, 1775. In *Loix et constitutions* 5:609.

"Arrêt du Conseil du Cap, qui fixe à 6 mois l'action rehibitoire pour les Negres attaqués d'epilepsie," January 11, 1773. In *Loix et constitutions*, 5:421.

"Arrêt du Conseil du Cap, sur les affranchissemens," May 25, 1771. In *Loix et constitutions*, 5:190–92.

"Arrêt du Conseil du Cap touchant l'election des tuteurs des esclaves poursuivant leur liberté," October 22, 1783. In *Loix et constitutions*, 6:372.

"Arrêt du Conseil du Cap, touchant les libertés, et la qualification de libre donné aux enfans des Gens de couleur," November 27, 1777. In *Loix et constitutions*, 5:802–3.

"Arrêt du Conseil du Cap, touchant des mulâtresses insolentes, et l'évasion de l'une d'elles des prisons," June 9, 1780. In *Loix et constitutions*, 6:30–32.

"Arrêt du Conseil du Cap, touchant 1°. les Negres, qui après avoir subi des peines, ne sont pas réclamés par leurs maîtres; 2°. les Negres reçus à la chaine publique, par forme de correction; et 3°. les prisons," July 12, 1774. In *Loix et constitutions*, 5:512.

"Arrêt du Conseil du Cap, touchant le service de feu Roi Louis XV," July 21, 1774. In *Loix et constitutions*, 5:513.

"Arrêt du Conseil du Cap, touchant un trouble causé au Spectacle de la même village, et un Décret de prise de corps décerné sans enunciation du désir, June 22, 1785. In *Loix et constitutions*, 6:778.

"Arrêt du Conseil d'Etat, concernant le retour des Noirs, Mulâtres ou autres gens de couleur aux colonies," September 7, 1777. In *Loix et constitutions*, 5:798.

"Arrêt du Conseil d'Etat, sur l'exécution de l'Article quarante-quatrième de la Déclaration du mois de Mars 1685, touchant les Esclaves des Isles de l'Amérique, qui déclare les Negres meubles," August 22, 1687. In *Loix et constitutions*, 1:460.

"Arrêt du Conseil d'Etat, pour le renouvellement des Cartouches des Noirs et autres Gens de couleur qui sont à Paris," March 23, 1783. In *Loix et constitutions*, 6:305.

"Arrêt du Conseil d'Etat du Roi, qui ordonne qu'il ne sera plus envoyé de Vagabonds, Gens sans aveu, Fraudeurs & Criminels à la Loüisianne, que les ordres qui Sa Majesté auroit pû donner à ce sujet seront changez, Et la destination desdits Vagabonds faite pour les autres Colonies Françaises," May 9, 1720. Research Division, New York Public Library (NYPL).

"Arrêt du Conseil d'État du Roi concernant le retour des noirs, mûlatres ou autres gens de couleur aux colonies," September 7, 1777. NYPL and in *Loix et constitutions*, 5:798.

"Arrêt du Conseil d'État du Roi pour la police des noirs, mûlatres ou autres gens de couleur qui sont dans la ville de Paris," January 11, 1778. NYPL.

"Arrêt du Conseil de la Martinique, qui condamne des Vagabonds à server comme engagés," February 16, 1671. In *Loix et constitutions*, 1:220–21.

"Arrêt du Conseil de la Martinique, touchant les esclaves, 7 Octobre 1652." In *Loix et constitutions*, 1:73.

"Arrêt du Conseil du Port-au-Prince, qui confisque au profit du Roi un mulâtre se disant libre," February 7, 1770. In *Loix et constitutions*, 5:290.

"Arrêt du Conseil du Port-au-Prince, qui enjoint de prendre les officiers et praticiens pour assesseurs du Siège de Jérémie en matière criminelle, et à défaut, les officiers du Siège le plus prochain, March 16, 1785. In *Loix et constitutions*, 6:729.

"Arrêt du Conseil du Port-au-Prince, qui 1°. proscrit les enquêtes à futur; et 2°. évoque à soi toutes les contestations relatives aux personnes attaquées pour raison de leur naissance, comme entachées de sang mêlé," January 13, 1770. In *Loix et constitutions*, 5:287.

"Arrêt du Conseil du Port-au-Prince, touchant les affranchissemens," December 29, 1767. In *Loix et constitutions*, 5:149–50.

"Arrêt du Conseil du Port-au-Prince, touchant les plaintes ou demandes des Esclaves contre leurs Maîtres, et les affranchissemens, July 8, 1782. In *Loix et constitutions*, 6:266–67.

"Arrêt du Conseil du Port-au-Prince, touchant les Réglemens de Police," September 23, 1761. In *Loix et constitutions*, 4:412.

"Arrêt du Conseil portant défense de célébrer mariage entre les blancs, noirs, mulâtres et autres gens de couleur, et à tous notaires de passer aucun contrat entre eux," April 5, 1778. In *Recueil general des anciennes lois françaises, depuis l'an 420 jusqu'à la Révolution de 1789* (Paris, 1863): 25:257–58.

"Arrêt du conseil qui défend à tous curés, notaires, arpenteurs et autres officiers publics, de qualifier aucunes gens de couleur du titre de sieur et dame," November 6, 1781. In *Recueil general des anciennes loix françaises depuis l'an 420 jusqu'à la Révolution de 1789*, 27:107.

"Arrêt de Réglemens du Conseil du Port-au-Prince qui enjoint aux Notaires aux Curés d'insérer dans leurs actes les qualités des Negres, Mulâtres, Quarterons, et autres de sang mêlé," September 24, 1761. In *Loix et constitutions*, 4:412–13.

Catalogue des ouvrages du fonds Caraïbe. Basse-Terre: Conseil Général de la Guadeloupe, March 1991. Archives départementales de la Guadeloupe.

Chauleau, Liliane, ed. *Archives départementales de la Martinique: La Martinique pendant la Révolution de 1789*. Fort-de-France, 1977.

———. *Guide des Archives de la Martinique*. Fort-de-France, 1978.

"Code Noir, le, ou, Edit servant de Réglement pour le Gouvernement et l'Administration de la Justice et de la Police des Isles Françoises de l'Amérique, et pour la Discipline et le Commerce des Negres et Esclaves dans ledit Pays. Du mois du Mars 1685." In *Loix et constitutions*, 1:414–24.

Code Noir, le, ou Recueill des reglemens rendus jusqu'à present, concernant le gouvernement, l'administration de la justice, la police, la discipline & le commerce des nègres dans les colonies françaises, et les conseils et compagnies établis à ce sujet. Paris, 1742 and 1767. Stanford University Special Collections (1742 edition) and University of California-Berkeley (1767 edition).

"Déclaration du Roi, concernant les vagabonds & gens sans aveu," March 12, 1719. University of California-Berkeley.

"Déclaration du Roi, contre les Jeux," March 30, 1781. In *Loix et constitutions*, 6:117–18.

"Déclaration du Roi, qui ordonne que la Déclaration du 8 janvier 1719, au sujet des vagabonds gens sans aveu, etc., sera executé selon sa forme et teneur, par tout le Royaume," May 12, 1719. University of California-Berkeley.

"Déclaration du Roi, qui permet d'envoyer les condamnés aux galères, les bannis, les vagabonds & les gens sans aveu aux colonies, pour y server comme engagés," January 8, 1719. University of California-Berkeley.

"Déclaration du Roi, portant Établissement d'un Conseil Supérieur à la Martinique," October 11, 1664. In *Loix et constitutions*, 1:125–27.

"Déclaration du Roi portant établissement d'une Justice Souveraine dans les Isles d'Amérique," August 1, 1645. In *Loix et constitutions*, 1:59–61.

"Déclaration du Roi, pour ne plus envoyer de Vagabonds & gens sans aveu aux Colonies," July 5, 1722. Registered at the Parlement de Paris on August 26, 1722. In *Loix et constitutions*, 3:14–15.

"Déclaration du Roi, touchant les Libres qui recèlent des Esclaves, et les Donations faites aux Gens de couleur par les Blancs," February 8, 1726. In *Loix et constitutions*, 3:159–60.

"Déclaration du Roi, concernant les Négres-Esclaves des Colonies amenés en France, du Décembre 1738." In *Loix et constitutions*, 3:547–50.

"Déclaration du Roi pour la police des noirs, donnée à Versailles le 9 août 1777, registrée en Parlement le vingt-sept août 1777." *Revue de l'histoire des colonies françaises* 21 (1928): 436–41.

"Edit du Roy, concernant les esclaves nègres des colonies," October 1716. In *Le Code Noir, ou Recueill des reglemens rendu, jusqu'à présent*, 192–206.

"Edit servant de Réglement pour le Gouvernement et l'Administration de la Justice, Police, Discipline et le Commerce des Esclaves Négres, dans la Province et Colonie de la Louisiane," Versailles, March 1724. In *Loix et constitutions*, 3:88–95.

État des inventaires des archives départementales, communales et hospitalières au 1er janvier 1983. Introduction by Jean Favier. 2 vols. Paris: Archives Nationales, 1984.

"Extrait de la lettre du Ministre à M. Ducasse, concernant les Negres amenés en France, et la liberté à donner aux Mulâtres," February 5, 1698. In *Loix et constitutions*, 1:579.

Histoire de l'Académie royale de musique depuis son établissement, 1645, jusqu'à 1709, composée et écrite par un des secrétaires de Lully. MS B230, Bibliothèque-Musée de l'Opéra, Paris.

"Instructions données à l'intendant des îles françaises du vent, le 25 août 1716." *Revue de l'histoire des colonies françaises* 17 (1924): 67–92.

Léti, Geneviève, ed. *Il y a 150 ans l'abolition de l'esclavage à la Martinique*. Archives départementales, Martinique, 1998.

"Lettre du Conseil du Port-au-Prince, à M. Bart, sur un duel dont il s'étoit évoqué la connoissance, et réponse de ce Gouverneur Général," September 25, 1761. In *Loix et constitutions*, 4:413.

"Lettre de M. le Général, aux Directeurs honoraires du Spectacle de Saint-Marc, sur sa loge," July 8, 1773. In *Loix et constitutions*, 5:451.

"Lettre de M. l'Intendant à l'Ordonnateur du Cap, qui décide que la Clef de sa loge au Spectacle soit remise à l'Ordonnateur," June 4, 1772. *Loix et constitutions*, 5:389.

"Lettre du Ministre aux Administrateurs, contenant une decision sur trois points relatifs aux Races Noires et Indiennes," January 7, 1767. In *Loix et constitutions*, 5:80–81.

"Lettre du Ministre aux Administrateurs, sur les Négres amenés en France," March 28, 1783. In *Loix et constitutions*, 6:306–7.

"Lettre du Ministre aux Administrateurs, sur les sangs-mêlés," May 27, 1771. In *Loix et constitutions*, 5:356.

"Lettre du Roi à M. de Baas, pour lui dire de laisser entière liberté de conscience au Juifs des Isles, et de les faire jouer des même privileges que les autres habitants," May 23, 1671. In *Loix et constitutions*, 1:225–26.

"Lettres-patentes concernant les Privilèges accordés aux Peres de la Compagnie de Jésus, dans l'une et l'autre Amérique Septentrionale et Méridionale, July 1651 et du 11 March 1658." In *Loix et constitutions*, 1:71–73.

"Lettres-patentes concernant les Juifs," signed April 23, 1615; published May 18, 1615. In *Loix et constitutions*, 1:13–14.

"Lettres-patentes pour l'Etablissement des Religieux Carmes de la Province de Touraine aux Isles d'Amérique," May 1650. In *Loix et constitutions*, 1:69.

"Lettres-patentes, portant Confirmation de l'Etablissement des FF. Prêcheurs dans l'Isle Saint-Domingue," September 7, 1721. Registered at Petit-Goave, January 5, 1724. In *Loix et constitutions*, 2:776–78.

"Lettres-patentes, portant établissement des Religieux de la Compagnie de Jésus dans l'Isle Saint-Domingue, du mois d'Octobre 1704. R. au Conseil du Cap, le 18 Mars 1705." In *Loix et constitutions*, 2:18–20.

"Lettres-patentes, portant que les Religieux établis dans l'Isle de Saint-Domingue, ne pourront à l'avenir faire aucune acquisition, soit en terres ou maisons, sans la permission expresse et par écrit de Sa Majesté, à peine de reunion," August 3, 1721. Registered at Léogane on March 3, 1722, and at Cap Français on March 4, 1722. In *Loix et constitutions*, 2:770–71.

Mémoire concernant l'establissement d'un Spectacle à St. Pierre de la Martinique, August 5, 1780. Colonie $C8^B$ 15, Archives Nationales, Paris.

Mémoire concernant l'establissement d'un Spectacle à St. Pierre de la Martinique, 1780: provides a financial plan and an outline of advantages for all inhabitants. Série C^{8b} 15, 43 bis, Archives Nationales, Paris.

Correspondence confirming that the Mémoire cited above (Série C^{8b} 15, 43 bis) was sent to Mr. Tascher, President of the colony, on August 5th and hopes that he will sign his approval and forward it on to Monseigneur, 1780 (Série C^{8b} 15, 53, Archives Nationales, Paris).

"Mémoire du Roi pour server d'instruction au S. de Ricouart, intendant des îles françoises du vent." *Revue de l'histoire des colonies françaises* 17:67–92 (1924).

"Mémoire du 7 mars 1777 pour servir d'instructions aux Gouverneurs." In *Antilles d'hier et d'aujourd'hui: Tout l'univers antillais du début de la colonisation à nos jours*, ed. Emile Désormeaux. 6:66. Fort-de-France, Martinique: Emile Désormeaux, 1978.

Ordonnance concernant l'établissement du Spectacle, April 1772, signed by Le Comte de Nozière, Governor, and Taskew, General Intendant, regarding an attempt to revive the theatre in Martinique. Conseil Supérieur (1771–1779), Martinique B[13], F°41. Archives départementales de la Martinique.

"Ordonnance de M. de Baas, touchant les Religionnaires, les Juifs, les Cabaretiers et les Femmes de mauvaise vie," August 1, 1669. In *Loix et constitutions*, 1:180–82.

"Ordonnance des Administrateurs, qui affranchit provisoirement, jusqu'aux ordres de Sa Majesté, un Mulâtre confisqué par Arrêt du Conseil du Port-au-Prince," February 26, 1770. In *Loix et constitutions*, 5:290–91.

"Ordonnance des Administrateurs, qui autorise l'Etablissement d'un Spectacle à Saint-Marc, conformément au projet approuvé par leurs Répresentans, le 29 Octobre précédent," November 10, 1779. In *Loix et constitutions*, 5:910.

"Ordonnance des Administrateurs, qui, à la requête de la dame de Silvecanne, declare nulle la liberté accordée à seize esclaves par son mari, sans ratification par les Administrateurs," September 5, 1742. In *Loix et constitutions*, 3:703.

"Ordonnance du Commandant en Chef par interim, concernant l'établissement de cinq Compagnies de Chasseurs-Royaux, tirés des Compagnies de Milices de Gens de Couleur," May 16, 1780. In *Loix et constitutions*, 6:22–30.

"Ordonnance du Gouverneur-Général, concernant les milices," June 30, 1762. In *Loix et constitutions*, 4:471.

"Ordonnance du Gouverneur Général, portant création d'un Corps de Troupes Légeres, désigné sous le nom de *Premiere Légion de Saint Domingue*," January 15, 1765. In *Loix et constitutions*, 4:825–31.

"Ordonnance de M. l'Intendant, qui enjoint à l'Imprimeur du Port-au-Prince d'imprimer les Affiches pour la Comédie du même lieu, à raison de 50 liv. le cent," January 26, 1775. In *Loix et constitutions*, 5:534.

"Ordonnance du Roi concernant l'Affranchissement des Esclaves," October 24, 1713. In *Loix et constitutions*, 2:398–99.

"Ordonnance du Roi concernant les esclaves des îsles françoises de l'Amérique," June 15, 1736, In *Le Code Noir, ou Recueill des reglemens rendu, jusqu'à present*, 476.

"Ordonnance du Roi, concernant la Police des Cabaretiers," September 30, 1766. In *Loix et constitutions*, 5:60–61.

"Ordonnance du Roi, contre les negres libres, qui facilitent aux Esclaves les moyens de devenir marons," June 10, 1705. In *Loix et constitutions*, 2:36–37.

"Ordonnance du Roi contre les vagabonds et les gens sans aveu," November 1718. NYPL.

"Ordonnance du Roi, sur la forme des affranchissemens des Esclaves," July 10, 1768. In *Loix et constitutions*, 5:190–92.

"Ordonnance du Roi portant défenses aux Capitaines de Navires de laisser débarquer aucun Noir, Mûlatre ou autres Gens de couleur, avant d'avoir fait leur rapport à l'Amirauté," February 23,

1778. In *Revue de l'histoire des colonies françaises* 21 (1928): 441–45, and *Loix et constitutions*, 5:814.

"Ordonnance du Roi, au sujet des Places et Rangs dans les Eglises, Processions, Marches et autres Cérémonies publiques," September 30, 1713. Registered at Cap Français on January 7, 1714. In *Loix et constitutions*, 2:392–95.

"Ordonnance du Roi touchant la Police des Bals des Gens de Couleur libres, et celle des Spectacles," March 11, 1785. In *Loix et constitutions*, 6:727–28.

"Ordonnance générale des Milices," January 15, 1765. In *Loix et constitutions*, 4:812–24.

"Ordre du Roi, portant exemption en faveur des officiers des compagnies de Milices de Gens de Couleur," August 2, 1743. In *Loix et constitutions*, 3:761.

"Ordre du Roi pour la translation du Conseil Supérieur de Léogane au Port-au-Prince," October 23, 1750. Registered at Léogane on March 14, 1752. In *Loix et constitutions*, 4:33–34.

"Ordre du Roi pour porter des Engagés aux Isles," February 19, 1698. In *Loix et constitutions*, 1:581.

"La Police des noirs sous Louis XVI en France," In *Revue de l'histoire des colonies françaises* 21 (1928): 433–46.

"Provisions pour M. le Comte de Blénac, de Gouverneur-Lieutenant-Général des Isles sous le Vent, dont le Gouvernement est déclaré independant de celui des Isles du Vent, du 1er Janvier, 1714." In *Loix et constitutions*, 2:408–9.

Recueil general des anciennes lois françaises, depuis l'an 420 jusqu'à la Révolution de 1789. Paris, 1863.

"Réglemens du Conseil de la Martinique, touchant la Police des Esclaves," October 4, 1677. In *Loix et constitutions*, 1:306–7.

"Réglement du Gouverneur-Général pour la Police des Spectacles, March 25, 1785. *In Loix et constitutions*, 6:734–35.

Répertoire de l'Opéra-Comique depuis 1731 jusqu'à 1899. C.9781, Bibliothèque-Musée de l'Opéra, Paris.

"Saint-Pierre, ville d'art et d'histoire." *Guides Archéologiques de la Martinique* (Martinique: Ministère de la Culture et de la Communication sous direction de l'Archéologie, 1990), B.6108, Archives d'Outre-mer, Aix-en-Provence.

Série Colonies C^{8A}: 19, F° 388, June 23, 1713; 37, F° 307, April 17, 1727; 56, F° 289, January 30, 1746; 58, F° 24, January 12, 1718; 58, F° 249, April 15, 1749; 60, F° 123, March 1753; 60, F° 127, June 30, 1753; 60, F° 129, January 24, 1746; 60, F° 131, January 16, 1751; 85, F° 302–6, 1785; and C^{8A} 94, F° 31, January 20, 1790. Archives Nationales, Paris, France.

Taillemite, Étienne, ed. *Inventaire de la Série Colonies C^{8a}, Martinique (Correspondance à l'arrivée)*. 3 vols. Paris: Imprimerie nationale, 1967.

Libretto Collections and Performance Records

Music and libretto sources consulted for the present study and housed at the Bibliothèque Nationale, Paris, are indicated by the initials "BN". The remaining items are located at the Bibliothèque-Musée de l'Opéra, Paris, unless stated otherwise.

Collection of French Plays and Librettos. 203 vols. Paris, 1731?–1851. Bancroft Library, University of California-Berkeley.

Journal des Spectacles représentés devant leurs majestés sur les Théâtres de Versailles & Fontainebleau, depuis 5 janvier 1764, jusqu'au 30 décembre de la même année. Paris, 1764. (BN)

Journal des Spectacles représentés devant leurs majestés sur les Théâtres de Versailles & Fontainebleau, pendant l'année 1765. Paris, 1766. (BN)

Journal des Spectacles donnés devant leurs majestés depuis leur retour de Fontainebleau, jusqu'au jeudi 17 mars 1763. Paris, 1763. (BN)

Journal des Spectacles représentés devant leurs majestés sur les Théâtres de Choisy, Fontainebleau & Versailles depuis 13 juin 1763, jusqu'au 29 décembre de la même année. Paris, 1764. (BN)

Journal des Spectacles représentés devant leurs majestés sur les Théâtres de Choisy & de Fontainebleau, pendant l'année 1769. Paris, 1769. (BN)

Parodies du Nouveau Théâtre Italien, Nouvelle Édition. Geneva: Slatkine Reprints, 1970. (BN)

Recueil des comédies et ballets représentés sur le Théâtre des Petits Appartemens pendant l'hiver de 1747 à 1748. 4 vols. n.d. (BN)

Recueil general des opéras représentez devant Sa Majesté, depuis leur établissement. 2 vols. Paris: Christophe Ballard, 1703. (BN)

Recueil general des opéras représentez par l'Académie Royale de Musique depuis son établissement. 16 vols. Paris: Christophe Ballard, 1703–1745. Reprint, Geneva: Slatkine Reprints, 1971. (BN)

Recueil des opéras, des balets [sic], & des plus belles pièces en musique, qui ont été représentées depuis dix ou douze ans jusques à present devant Sa Majesté très-chretienne . . . suivant la copie de Paris. Amsterdam, 1684 [1686]–[1746]. 13 vols. (BN)

Théâtre de l'Opéra, Journal. Usuel 201, Bibliothèque-Musée de l'Opéra, Paris.

Individual Librettos

Acajou, opéra-comique en trois actes. Par Monsieur Favart. Représenté sur le Théâtre du Fauxbourg Saint Germain. Avignon, 1767.

Acis et Galathée, pastorale héroïque en musique. Représentée pour la première fois dans le Château d'Anet devant Monseigneur le Dauphin, par l'Académie Royale de Musique. Paris, 1686.

Acis et Galathée, pastorale héroïque. Représentée pour la première fois par l'Académie Royale de Musique le janvier 1686, & remise 31 mai 1704, le 3 septembre 1709, le 18 août 1718, le 13 Septembre 1725, le 9 août 1734, le 18 août 1744, et remis au théâtre le mardi, 7 septembre 1762. Paris: Lormel, 1762.

Acis et Galathée, pastorale héroïque, mis en musique par J.-B. Lully. Texte de 1686, avec onze illustrations et une introduction par Henry Prunières. Amsterdam and Paris: Éditions de la Revue Musicale, 1933.

Amours champestres, pastorale, Les. Parodie de l'acte des *Sauvages*, quatrième entrée des *Indes galantes.* Représenté pour la première fois par les Comédiens Italiens ordinaires du Roi, le jeudi, 2 septembre

1751. Paris: Delormel & fils, 1751. Includes vocal airs and a *divertissement*.

Amours champestres, pastorale, Les. Représentée pour la première fois, par les Comédiens Italiens ordinaires du Roi, le jeudi, 2 septembre 1751. Troisième édition. Paris: Duchesne, 1759. Includes vocal airs. (BN)

Aristote amoureux, ou, le philosophe bridé, opéra comique, en un acte & en vaudevilles. Représenté pour la première fois par les Comédiens italiens ordinaires du Roi, le vendredi 11 août 1780. (University of California-Berkeley)

*Arlequin sauvage, comédie, Par le Sieur D****. Représentée pour la premiere fois par les Comédiens Italiens ordinaires du Roi, le 17 juin 1721. In *Le Nouveau théâtre italien ou recueil général des comédies*. Nouvelle édition. Geneva: Slatkine Reprints, 1969.

Aucassin et Nicolette; ou les moeurs du bon vieux tems, comédie remise en trois actes et en vers, dont une partie est en musique. Représentée, pour la premiere fois, devant leurs Majestés à Versailles, le 30 décembre 1779 par les Comédiens Italiens ordinaires du roi, & à Paris, le 3 janvier 1780, & reprise le 7 janvier 1782. Le drame est de M. Sedaine; la musique de M. Grétry. Paris, 1782.

Azemia, ou les sauvages, comédie en trois actes et en prose, melée d'ariettes. Représentée à Fontainebleau devant leurs Majestés le 17 Octobre 1786, & à Paris, le 3 Mai 1787. Paris, 1788.

Ballet royal de Flore, dansé par sa Majesté, le mois de Fevrier 1669. Paris: Robert Ballard, 1669.

Belle esclave, ou Valcour et Zeila, La, comédie en un acte et en prose, mêlée d'ariettes. Musique de M. Philidor. Paris: Prault, 1787.

Bienfaisance de Louis XVI, ou les fêtes de la paix, La, drame lyrique en deux actes et en vers, mêlé de français & de provençal, composé à l'occasion de la paix glorieuse de 1783. Marseilles, 1783. (BN)

Cadmus et Hermione, tragédie. Représenté pour la première fois en 1674, devant le Roi. Ensuite en 1678 par l'Académie Royale de Musique; remise au Théatre en 1703, en 1711, au mois d'aoust, et le jeudi vingt-deuxième aoust 1737. Paris: Jean-Baptiste-Christophe Ballard, 1737.

Corsaire, Le, comédie en trois actes et en vers, mêlée d'ariettes. Représentée pour la première fois à Versailles devant leurs Majestés & la famille royale, le 7 mars 1783, par les Comédiens Italiens ordinaires du Roi, & à Paris le 17 du même mois. Paris, 1783.

Devin du village, Le, intermède par J. J. Rousseau. Représentée pour la première fois à Fontainebleau sur le Théâtre de la Cour, devant leurs majestés, les 18 & 24 octobre 1752, et à Paris par l'Académie Royale de Musique, le 1 mars 1753. Geneva, 1760. Includes vocal airs and ensembles. (University of California-Berkeley)

Europe galante, L', ballet. Représenté par l'Académie Royale de Musique le vingt-quatrième d'octobre 1697. Repris en années 1703, 1715, & 1724. Remis au Théâtre le jeudi quatorze juin 1736. Paris: Jean-Christophe-Ballard, 1736.

Idylle sur la paix, 1685. In *Oeuvres complets de Jean Racine*, 6:79–89. 1803.

Indes dansantes, Les, parodie des Indes galantes. Représentée pour la première fois par les Comédiens Italiens ordinaires du Roi, le lundi, 26 juillet, 1751. The Hague: Pierre Gosse Junior, 1756. (BN)

Indes galantes, Les, ballet héroïque. Représenté par l'Academie Royale de Musique pour la premiere fois, le mardi 23 Aoust 1735. Remis avec la nouvelle entrée des Sauvages, le samedi, le dixième mars

1736. Paris: Jean-Baptiste-Christophe Ballard, 1736.

Négresse; ou le pouvoir de la reconnaissance, La, comédie en un acte & en vaudevilles, mêlée de divertissements. Représentée pour la première fois par les Comédiens Italiens Ordinaires du Roi, le vendredi 15 June 1787. Paris, 1787. (BN)

Romans, Les, ballet héroïque. Représenté par l'Académie Royale de Musique pour la première fois le jeudi 23 d'aoust 1736. "Le Roman merveilleux," nouvelle entrée, ajoutée aux trois précédents, le 23 septembre 1736. Paris: Jean-Baptiste-Christophe Ballard, 1736.

Zémire et Azor, comédie-ballet, en vers et en quatre actes; mêlée de chants & de danses; Représentée, devant Sa Majesté, à Fontainebleau, le 9 Novembre 1771. Les paroles sont de M. Marmontel, de l'Académie Française. La musique est de M. Gretry. Paris: Robert-Christophe Ballard, 1771.

Zémire et Azor, comédie-ballet, en vers et en quatre actes; mêlée de chants & de danses. Représentée devant Sa Majesté, à Fontainebleau, le 9 Novembre 1771, & sur le Théâtre de la Comédie Italienne, le lundi 16 décembre suivant. Par Marmontel, de l'Académie Française. La musique est de M. Gretry. Paris, 1772.

Scores

Acis et Galathée, pastorale héroïque, mise en musique par Monsieur Lully, Sur-Intendant de la musique du Roy. Paris: Christophe Ballard, 1686.

Amitié à l'epreuve, L', comédie en deux actes, mêlée d'ariettes. Représentée devant Sa Majesté, à Fontainebleau, le 13 novembre 1770, et à Paris le 17 janvier 1771. Dédiée à Madame La Dauphine par M. Grétry de l'Académie de Boulogne. Lyon, France: M. Castaud, n.d. (BN)

Amitié à l'epreuve, L', comédie en deux actes, mêlée d'ariettes. Représentée devant Sa Majesté, à Fontainebleau, le 13 novembre 1770, et à Paris le 17 janvier 1771. Dédiée à Madame La Dauphine par M. Grétry de l'Académie de Boulogne. Paris, 1771.

Amoureux de quinze ans, ou la double fête, L', comédie en prose et en trois actes mêlée d'ariettes. Par M. Laujon. La Musique est de M. Martini. Paris, 1777.

Aucassin et Nicolette, ou les moeurs du bon vieux tems, comédie en trois actes. Représentée pour la premiere fois devant leurs Majestés à Versailles le 30 décembre 1779 par Les Comédiens Italiens Ordinaires du Roi, et à Paris le 3 janvier 1780, et reprise le 7 janvier 1782. Paris, 1782.

Azémia, ou, les sauvages, comédie en trois actes. Paris: Le Duc, 1787?

Ballet du temple de la paix, dansé devant Sa Majesté à Fontainebleau. Par Monsieur de Lully, Conseiller Secretaire du Roy, Maison, Couronne de France et de ses finances, & Sur-Intendant de la musique de Sa Majesté. Paris: Christophe Ballard, 1685. (Stanford University).

Ballet royale de Flore. Dansé par Sa Majesté le mois de fevrier, 1669. Recueilly [*sic*] et copié par Philidor laisné [*sic*] en 1690. (Stanford University)

Cadmus et Hermione, tragédie mise en musique par Monsieur de Lully, Escuyer, Conseiller de ses Finances

& Sur-Intendant de la musique de Sa Majesté. Représenté pour la première fois devant le Roy à Saint-Germain-en-Laye, en l'année 1674. imprimée pour la première fois de Jean-Baptiste-Christophe Ballard. Paris, 1719. (BN)

Caravane du Caire, La, ballet en trois actes. Representé à Fontainebleau devant leurs Majestés le 30 octobre 1783, et pour la premiere fois sur le Théâtre de l'Académie de la Musique le lundi 12 janvier 1784. Paris: Huguet, musicien de la Comédie Italienne, n.d. (Jean Gray Hargrove Music Library, University of California-Berkeley)

Caravane du Caire, La, opéra-ballet in three acts. In *Chefs-d'oeuvre classiques de l'opéra français* 12 (1971).

Carnaval du Parnasse, Le, ballet héroïque. Dedié à Madame La Marquise de Pompadour. Mis en musique par Monsieur Mondonville, maître de musique de la Chapelle du Roy. Représenté par l'Académie Royale de Musique pour la première fois le 23 septembre 1749. Paris, n.d.

Diane et Endimion, pastorale héroïque, Année 1690. Manuscript, Paris, Bibliothèque de l'Arsenal.

Festes, ou le triomphe de Thalie, Les, ballet en musique. Par Monsieur Mouret, Ordinaire de la musique de S.A.S. Madame la Duchesse de Maine. Représentée pour la première fois par l'Academie Royale de musique le mardi quatorzième aoust 1714. Paris: Christophe Ballard, 1714. (BN)

Idylle sur la paix, avec l'Eglogue de Versailles et plusieurs pieces de symphonie, mises en musique par Monsieur de Lully, Escuyer, Conseiller, Secrétaire du Roi, Maison, Couronne de France & de ses Finances, & Sur-Intendant de la musique de Sa Majesté. Paris: Christophe Ballard, 1685. (BN)

Indes galantes, Les, ballet, reduit à quatre grands concerts avec une nouvelle entrée complete. Par Monsieur Rameau. Paris, n.d. (BN)

Négresse; ou le pouvoir de la reconnaissance, La, comédie en un acte, en prose & en vaudevilles, mêlée de divertissements. Par MM. Radet et Barré. Les airs arrangés par M. Lescot, musicien du Théatre Italien. Représentée pour la première fois au Théatre Italien le vendredi 15 June 1787. Paris: Imbault, 1787. (BN)

Roland, tragédie mise en musique par Monsieur Lully, Escuyer, Conseiller Secrétaire du Roy, Maison, couronne de France & de ses Finances & Sur-Intendant de la musique de Sa Majesté. Paris: Christophe Ballard, 1685.

Romans, Les, ballet héroïque, par M. Niel. Représenté pour la Ière fois par l'Académie Royale de Musique le XXIII aoust MDCCXXXVI. Paris: N. Baillieul, n.d. (BN)

Serva padrona, La (*The Maid Mistress*), intermezzi. Giovanni Battista Pergolesi, composer. English translation and adaptation by Joseph Furgiuele. New York: Ricordi, 1955.

Titon et l'Aurore, pastorale héroïque. Dédié à Monseigneur le Prince de Soumise. Mis en musique par Monsieur Mondonville, maitre de musique de la chapelle du Roy. Representée par l'Académie Royale de Musique pour la première fois le 9 janvier 1753. Paris, n.d.

Théagéne et Caraclée, tragédie, mise en musique par Monsieur Desmarets, pensionnaire ordinaire du Roi. Paris, 1695. (BN)

Tom Jones, opéra comique en trois actes. Revised by Michel-Jean Sedaine, edited by Nicolas McGegan and Adrian Salter. London: Boosey & Hawkes, 1978. (Jean Gray Hargrove Music Library,

University of California-Berkeley)

Triomphe de l'Amour, Le, ballet royal, mis en musique par Monsieur de Lully, Sur-Intendant de la musique du Roi. Paris: Christophe Ballard, 1681. (BN)

Zémire et Azor, opéra-comique en 4 actes, paroles de Marmontel, musique de Grétry. Partition pour Piano et Chant par Auguste Bazille. Paris: E. Girod, c.1862. (University of California-Berkeley)

Other Publications

Abenon, Lucien, Jacques Cauna, and Liliane Chauleau. *La Révolution aux Caraïbes*. Paris: Éditions Nathan, 1989.

André, Naomi, Karen M. Bryan, and Eric Saylor, eds. *Blackness in Opera*. Urbana: University of Illinois Press, 2012.

Anthony, James. *French Baroque Music from Beaujoyeulx to Rameau*. Rev. ed. New York: W.W. Norton & Co., 1978.

Antilles d'hier et d'aujourd'hui: Tout l'univers antillais du début de la colonisation à nos jours. 9 vols. Fort-de-France, Martinique: Emile Désormeaux, 1978.

Aucassin and Nicolette (Aucassin et Nicolette). Edited by Anne Elizabeth Cobby, translation and introduction by Glyn S. Burgess. Garland Library of Medieval Literature 47, Series A. New York: Garland Publishing, 1988.

Austen, Jake, and Yuval Taylor. *Darkest America: Black Minstrelsy from Slavery to Hip-Hop*. New York: W.W. Norton & Co., 2012.

Bachaumont, Louis Petit de. *Mémoires secrets pour servir à l'histoire de la république des lettres en France depuis 1762 jusqu'à nos jours, ou Journal d'un observateur contenant les analyses des pièces de théâtre qui ont paru durant cet intervalle*. 36 vols. London: John Adamson, 1777–1789.

Bangou, Henri. *La Guadeloupe 1492–1848, ou l'histoire de la colonisation de l'île liée à l'esclavage noir de ses débuts à sa disparition*. Paris: Éditions du centre, 1962.

Benot, Yves. *Diderot de l'athéisme à l'anticolonialisme*. Paris, 1970.

Bernabé, Jean, Patrick Chamoiseau, and Raphaël Confiant. *Éloge de la Créolité, Édition bilingue français/anglais*. Translated by M. B. Taleb-Khyar. Baltimore: Johns Hopkins University Press, 1990.

Bernardin de Saint-Pierre, Jacques Henri. *Paul and Virginia*. Translated by Helen Maria Williams. Oxford: Woodstock Books, 1989.

———. *Paul and Virginia*, with a Critical and Biographical Introduction by Andrew Lang. New York: Howard Fertig, 1987.

———. *Voyage à l'Ile de France*. In *Oeuvres de Jacques-Henri-Bernadin de Saint-Pierre*. Paris, 1840.

Biondi, Carminella. *Ces esclaves sont des hommes*. Lotta abolizionista e letteratura negrofila nella Francia del Settecento. Pisa: Editrice Libreria Goliardica, 1979.

Bjurström, Per. *Giacomo Torelli and Baroque Stage Design*. Figura, Uppsala Studies in the History of Art,

New Series 2. Stockholm: Almquist & Wiksel, 1961.

Blaise, J. *Culture et politique en Guadeloupe et Martinique*. Culture et politique aux Antilles. Paris: Karthala: Alizes, 1981.

Boisvert, Jayne. "Colonial Hell and Female Resistance in Saint-Domingue." *Journal of Haitian Studies* 7, no. 1 (Spring 2001): 61–76.

Bonnet, Jacques, and Pierre Bourdelot. *Histoire de la musique et de ses effets depuis son origine jusqu'au présent*. Paris, 1715.

Boucher, Philip, and Gabriel Debien. "Chronique bibliographique de l'histoire des Antilles françaises (1979–1982)." *Bulletin de la Société d'histoire de la Guadeloupe* 59 (1984): 3–75.

Bougainville, Louis de. *Voyage autour du monde par le frégate de roi la Boudeuse et la flûte l'Etoile; en 1766, 1767, 1768 et 1769*. Paris, 1771. *A Voyage Round the World*. Translated by John Reinhold Forster. London, 1772. Reprint, New York: Da Capo Press, 1967.

Brainard, Ingrid. "New Dances for the Ball: The Annual Collections of France and England in the Eighteenth Century." *Early Music* 14, no. 2 (1986): 164–73.

Brenner, Clarence D. *A Bibliographical List of Plays in the French Language, 1700–1789*. Berkeley, CA, 1947.

———. *The Theatre Italien: Its Repertory, 1716–1703*. Berkeley: University of California Press, 1961.

Brown, Jonathan. *The History and Present Condition of St. Domingo* (1837). Reprint, London: Frank Cass and Company, 1971.

Brumfitt, J. H. *The Age of Louis XIV and Other Selected Writings*. New York: Washington Square Press, 1963.

Buffon, George Louis Leclerc, Comte de. *The History of Man and Quadrupeds*. Vol. 4, *Natural History, General and Particular*. Translated by William Smellie with notes and observations. London, 1812.

Cabon, le, R. P. Adolphe. *Histoire d'Haïti: Cours professé au Petit-Seminaire-college, Saint-Martial*. Port-au-Prince: Édition de La Petite Revue, 192_?–1937?

Cale, John G. "French Secular Music in Saint-Domingue (1750–1795) Viewed as a Factor in America's Musical Growth." PhD diss., Louisiana State University and Agricultural and Mechanical College, 1971.

Cally, Sully. *Musiques et danses Afro-Caraïbes*. Gros-Morne, Martinique: Sully-Cally/Lezin, 1990.

Camier, Bernard. "Les concerts dans les capitales de Saint-Domingue à la fin du XVIIIe siècle." *Revue de musicologie* 93, no. 1 (2007): 75–98.

———. "Minette, artiste de couleur à Saint-Domingue." *Revue de la Société haïtienne d'Histoire et de Géographie*, no. 205 (October–December 2000): 1–11.

———. "Minette, chanteuse de couleur à Saint-Domingue." *Généalogie et histoire de la Caraïbe*, no. 165 (December 2003): 4023.

———. "Minette: Situation sociale d'une artiste de couleur à Saint-Domingue," *Généalogie et histoire de la Caraïbe*, no. 185 (October 2005): 4638–40.

Camier, Bernard, and Laurent Dubois. "Politiques et pratiques coloniales (XVIIIe–XXe siècles): Voltaire et Zaire, ou le théâtre des Lumières dans l'aire atlantique française." *Revue d'histoire moderne et contemporaine* 54, no. 3 (2007): 41–69.

Camier, Bernard, and Marie-Christine Hazaël-Massieux. "Jeannot et Thérèse, un opéra-comique en créole à Saint-Domingue au milieu du XVIIIème siècle." *Revue de la Société haïtienne d'Histoire et de Géographie*, no. 215 (April–September 2003): 135–66.

Camus, Michel. "Au début des Français à Guadeloupe: Lettre du P. Pélican au P. Carré (18 août 1635)." *Bulletin de la Société d'histoire de la Guadeloupe* 52 (1982): 5–19.

Capécia, Mayotte. *I Am a Martinican Woman & The White Negress: Two Novelettes of the 1940s by Mayotte Capécia.* Translated by Beatrice Stith Clark. Pueblo, CO: Paseggiata Press, 1997.

Cauna, Jacques, Lucien Abenon, and Liliane Chauleau. *La Révolution aux Caraïbes.* Paris: Éditions Nathan, 1989.

Césaire, Aimé. *Notebook of a Return to the Native Land.* Translated and edited by Clayton Eshleman and Annette Smith. Middletown, CT: Wesleyan University Press, 2001.

Chamoiseau, Patrick. *Texaco.* Translated from the French and Creole by Rose-Myriam Réjouis and Val Vinokurov. New York: Vintage International, 1998.

Chanvalon, Thibault de. *Voyage à la Martinique, contenant diverses Observations sur la Physique, l'histoire naturelle, l'Agriculture, les moeurs & les usages de cette Isle, faites 1751 & dans les années suivantes.* Paris, 1761.

Chapman, Hester W. *Privileged Persons: Four Seventeenth-Century Studies.* New York: Reynal/ William Morrow, 1966.

Châtillon, Marcel. "Sucreries au Brésil et aux Antilles à la fin du XVII siècle (d'après Antonil et Labat)." *Bulletin de la Société d'histoire de la Guadeloupe* 55 (1983): 15–49.

Châtillon, Marcel, Camille Fabré, and Jacqueline Rosemain. "Messe en cantiques pour les esclaves (1763)." *Bulletin de la Société d'histoire de la Guadeloupe* 52 (1982): 39–63.

Chauleau, Liliane. *La Société à la Martinique au XVIIe siècle (1635–1713).* Caen: Comité d'études historiques et juridiques, 1966.

Chauleau, Liliane, Lucien Abenon, and Jacques Cauna. *La Révolution aux Caraïbes.* Paris: Éditions Nathan, 1989.

Chauvet, Marie. *Dance on the Volcano.* Translated from the French by Salvator Attanasio. New York: William Sloane Associates, 1951.

Chefs d'oeuvre classiques de l'opéra français. New York: Broude Brothers Ltd., 1971.

Chinard, Gilbert. *L'Amérique et le rêve exotique dans la littérature française au XVIIe et au XVIIIe siècle.* Paris, 1913. Reprint, Geneva: Slatkine Reprints, 1970.

———. *L'exotisme américain dans la littérature française au XVIe siècle d'après Rabelais, Ronsard, Montaigne, etc.* Paris, 1911. Reprint, Geneva: Slatkine Reprints, 1978.

Cohen, William B. *The French Encounter with Africans: White Response to Blacks, 1530–1880.* Foreword by James D. Le Sueur. Bloomington: Indiana University Press, 2003.

Condorcet, Antoine-Nicolas de. "Réflexions sur l'esclavage des nègres." In *Oeuvres complètes de Condorcet.* 21 vols. Paris, 1804–AN XIII.

Contour, Solange. *Saint-Pierre, Martinique.* Paris: S. Contour, 1988.

Cottrel, René, and Théodore Baude. *Tricentenaire des Antilles, Guadeloupe-Martinique, 1635–1935*. Fort-de-France, Martinique, 1935.

Cordier, Henri. "Voyages de Pierre Poivre de 1748 jusqu'à 1757." *Revue de l'histoire des colonies françaises* 6 (1918).

Correspondance littéraire, philosophique et critique par Grimm, Diderot, Raynal, Meister, etc. (1754–1813). 16 vols. Paris: Garnier Frères, 1877–1882.

Crain, Timothy M. "Music in the Colonial Charleston, South Carolina Theatre: 1732–81." PhD diss., Florida State University, 2002.

Cranston, Maurice. *The Noble Savage: Jean-Jacques Rousseau, 1754–1762*. Chicago: University of Chicago Press, 1991.

Crause, Nellis M. *French Pioneers in the West Indies, 1624–1664*. New York: Columbia University Press, 1940.

———. *French Struggle in the West Indies, 1665–1713*. New York: Octagon Books, 1966.

Créole, Coeur. *Saint-Pierre-Martinique, 1635–1902*. Paris: Berger-Levrault & Cie, 1905.

Curtin, Philip D. *The Atlantic Slave Trade: A Census*. Madison: University of Wisconsin Press, 1969.

Dacier, Emile. "Les Caractères de la danse: Histoire d'un divertissement pendant la première moitié du XVIIIe siècle." *La Revue Musicale* 5 (1905): 324–35, 365–67.

D'Alembert, Jean le Rond. *Mélanges de littérature, d'histoire, et de philosophie*. 5 vols. Amsterdam, 1767.

D'Aquin de Chateau-Lyon, Pierre Louis. *Siècle littéraire de Louis XV, ou Lettres sur les hommes célèbres*. Paris, 1754.

D'Auberteuil, Michel-René Hilliard. *Considérations sur l'état present de la colonie française de Saint-Domingue*. Paris, 1776.

Dauphite, Maïotte. *Saint-Pierre, avant et après*. Anse Turin, Martinique: Centre d'art Musée Paul Gauguin, 1983.

Debbasch, Yvan. *Couleur et liberté*. Paris: Librairie Dalloz, 1967.

Debien, Gabriel. *Les esclaves aux Antilles françaises, XVIIe–XVIIIe siècles*. Basse-Terre, Guadeloupe: Société d'histoire de la Guadeloupe, and Société d'histoire de la Martinique, 1974.

Debien, Gabriel. *Les colons de Saint-Domingue et la révolution: Essai sur le Club Massiac (Août 1789–Août 1792)*. Paris: Librairie Armand Colin, 1953.

Dechamps, Leon. *Histoire de la question coloniale en France*. Paris: E. Plon, Nourrit & Co., 1891.

Diderot, Denis. *Oeuvres complètes de Diderot, revues sur les éditions originales comprenant ce qui a été publié à diverses époques et les manuscrits inédits conservés à la Bibliothèque de l'Ermitage. Notices, notes, Table Analytique étude sur Diderot et le mouvement philosophe au XVIIIe siècle*. Edited by J. Assézat. 20 vols. Paris: Garnier Frères, 1875. Reprint, Nendeln, Liechtenstein: Kraus Reprint Ltd., 1966.

———. "Court essai sur le caractère de l'homme sauvage." In *Oeuvres complètes de Diderot*, ed. J. Assézat. Paris, 1875. Reprint, Nendeln, Liechtenstein, 1966.

———. *Écrits sur la musique: Textes choisis et présentés par Béatrice Durand-Sendrail*. Paris: J.C. Lattés, 1987.

———. *Supplément au voyage de Bougainville* (1772). In *Oeuvres complètes de Diderot*. Paris, 1875. Reprint, Nendeln, Liechtenstein, 1966.

———. *Supplément au voyage de Bougainville.* Edited by Herbert Dieckmann. Geneva: Droz, 1955.

Dieckmann, Herbert. "Les contributions de Diderot à la 'Correspondance littéraire' et à 'l'Histoire des deux Indes'," *Revue d'histoire littéraire de la France* 51 (October–December 1951): 417–40.

———. *Inventaire du fonds Vandeul, et inédits de Diderot.* Geneva: Droz, 1951.

Dorvigny. *Le Nègre Blanc, comédie en un acte et en prose.* Représentée à Versailles devant Leurs Majestés et à Paris sur le Théatre des Variétés Amusantes, le 28 Juin 1780. Paris, 1783.

[Dubuc, Jean Baptiste.] *Lettres et politiques sur les colonies et le commerce des villes maritimes de France, addressées à G.T. Raynal.* Geneva, 1785.

Duchêne, Albert. *La politique coloniale de la France: Le ministère des colonies depuis Richelieu.* Paris: Payot, 1928.

Dumerve, Etienne Constantin Eugène Moise. *Histoire de la musique en Haïti.* Port-au-Prince: Imprimerie des Antilles, 1968.

Dunham, Katherine. *Dances of Haiti.* Photographs by Patricia Cummings. Los Angeles: Center for Afro-American Studies, University of California, Los Angeles, 1983.

———. *Island Possessed.* Garden City, NY: Doubleday, 1969.

Durey de Noinville, Jacques-Bernard. *Histoire du théatre de l'Académie royale de musique en France, depuis son établissement jusqu'à present.* 2nd ed. Paris: Duchesne, 1757.

Du Tertre, R.P.J.B. *Histoire générale des Antilles, habitées par les François, contenant l'histoire naturelle, enrichy de cartes & de figures.* Paris, 1667.

Elie, Louis E. *Histoire d'Haïti: Les origines du peuple haïtien.* Port-au-Prince: n.p., 1945.

Elisabeth, Léo. "The French Antilles." In *Neither Slave nor Free*, ed. David W. Cohen and Jack P. Greene. Baltimore: Johns Hopkins University Press, 1972.

———. *La Société martiniquaise aux XVIIe et XVIIIe siècles, 1664–1789.* Paris: Éditions Karthala, 2003.

Encyclopédie, ou dictionnaire raisonné des sciences, des arts et des métiers. 35 vols. Paris, 1751–80.

État des inventaires des archives départementales, communales et hospitalières au 1er janvier 1983. Introduction by Jean Favier. 2 vols. Paris: Archives Nationales, 1984.

Exoticism in French Literature. French Literature Series 13. Columbia: University of South Carolina, 1986.

Fabre, Camille. "Dans le sillage des caravelles." *Annales d'église en Guadeloupe, 1635–1970.* St.-Pierre-de-Colombier, Burzet, 1976.

Fanon, Frantz. *Black Skin, White Masks.* Translated by Charles Lam Markann. New York: Grove Press, 1967.

"Fête-Dieu à la Martinique en 1753, la." *Revue de l'histoire des colonies françaises* 20 (1927): 600–603.

Fouchard, Jean. *Artistes et répertoire des scènes de Saint-Domingue.* Port-au-Prince: Imprimerie de l'État, 1955.

———. *Les marrons du syllabaire.* 1953; Port-au-Prince: Éditions Henri Deschamps, 1988.

———. "Minette et Lise . . . deux actrices de couleur sur les scènes de Saint-Domingue." *Revue d'histoire des colonies françaises* 42, no. 147 (1955): 186–219.

———. *Plaisirs de Saint-Domingue.* Port-au-Prince: Imprimerie de l'État, 1955.

———. *Le théâtre à Saint-Domingue.* Port-au-Prince: Imprimerie de l'État, 1955.

Fournel, Victor. *Les Contemporains de Molière, recueil de comedies, rares ou peu connues, jouées de 1650 à 1680 avec l'histoire de chaque théâtre*. Paris: Firmin Didot Frères, Fils et Cie, 1866.

Franko, Mark. *Dance as Text: Ideologies of the Baroque Body*. New York: Cambridge University Press, 1993.

Gardeur, René J., Jr. *The First New Orleans Theatre, 1792–1803*. New Orleans: Leeward Books, 1963.

Garrigus, John D. *Before Haiti: Race and Citizenship in French Saint-Domingue*. New York: Palgrave Macmillan, 2006.

Garraway, Doris Lorraine. "Race, Reproduction and Family Romance in Moreau de Saint-Méry's *Description . . . de la partie française de l'Isle Saint-Domingue*." *Eighteenth-Century Studies* 38, no. 2 (2005): 227–46.

Geggus, David Patrick, and Norman Fiering, eds. *The World of the Haitian Revolution*. Bloomington: Indiana University Press, 2009.

Gerstin, Julian. "Musical Revivals and Social Movements in Contemporary Martinique: Ideology, Identity, Ambivalence." In *The African Diaspora: A Musical Perspective*, ed. Ingrid Monson (New York: Garland Publishing, 2000), 205–327.

Gherardi, Evaristo. *Théâtre Italien de Gherardi, ou le recueil general de toutes les comedies et scenes françoises jouées par les comédiens italiens du roy, pendant tout le temps qu'ils ont été au service de Sa Majesté*. 8 vols. London: J. Tonson, 1714.

Gisler, Antoine. *L'esclavage aux Antilles françaises, XVIIe–XIXe siècles: Contribution au problème de l'esclavage*. Fribourg, Switzerland: Éditions Universitaires, 1965.

Glissant, Edouard. *Caribbean Discourse: Selected Essays*. Translated and with an introduction by J. Michael Dash. Charlottesville: University Press of Virginia, 1989.

Grannis, Valleria Belt. "Dramatic Parody in Eighteenth Century France." PhD diss., Columbia University, 1931.

Grégoire, Abbé Henri. "On behalf of the Jews in France and On the Status of the Colored People in Saint-Domingue and other French Islands in America." In *Two Rebel-Priests of the French Revolution*, trans. and with intro. by Raymond L. Carol. San Francisco: R and E Research Associates, Inc., 1975.

Grimm, Friedrich Melchior. *Correspondance littéraire, philosophique et critique, par Grimm, Diderot, Raynal, Meister, etc., 1754–1813*. 16 vols. Paris: Garnier Frères, 1877–1882.

Hall, Gwendolyn Midlo. "Saint-Domingue." In *Neither Slave Nor Free*, ed. David W. Cohen and Jack P. Greene. Baltimore: Johns Hopkins University Press, 1972.

Hayot, Émile. *Les gens de couleur libres du Fort-Royal, 1679–1823*. Paris: Société française d'histoire d'outre-mer et Librairie orientaliste Paul Geuthner, 1971.

Hazaël-Massieux, Marie-Christine. "A propos de Jeannot et Thérèse: Une traduction du Devin du village en créole du XVIIIe siècle?" *Creolica* (September 2005): 1–24.

Hearn, Lafcadio. *Two Years in the West Indies*. New York: Harper & Brothers, 1890.

Herskovits, Melville Jean. *Life in a Haitian Valley*. New York: A.A. Knopf, 1937.

———. *The Myth of the Negro Past*. 1941; reprint, Gloucester, MA, 1970.

Hilton, Wendy. *Dance of Court and Theater: The French Noble Style, 1690–1725*. Princeton, NJ: Princeton

Book Company, 1981.

Hornback, Robert. "Black Shakespeareans vs. Minstrel Burlesques: 'Proper' English, Racist Blackface Dialect, and the Contest for Representing 'Blackness,' 1821–1844." Report. *Shakespeare Studies* 38 (January 1, 2010).

Hurston, Zora Neale. *Tell My Horse: Voodoo and Life in Haiti and Jamaica*. New York: Harper & Row, 1938.

Isert, Paul Erdman. *Voyage en Guinée et dans les Iles Caraïbes en Amerique*. Paris, 1793.

Isherwood, Robert M. *Farce and Fantasy: Popular Entertainment in Eighteenth Century Paris*. New York: Oxford University Press, 1986.

———. *Music in the Service of the King: France in the Seventeenth Century*. Ithaca, NY: Cornell University Press, 1973.

Jaenen, Cornelius J. *Friend and Foe: Aspects of French-Amerindian Cultural Contact in the Sixteenth and Seventeenth Centuries*. New York: Columbia University Press, 1976.

Jailier, Maurice, and Yollan Lossen. *Musique aux Antilles: Mizik bô kay*. Paris: Éditions Caribéennes, 1985.

James, C.L.R. *The Black Jacobins: Toussaint L'Ouverture and the San Domingo Revolution*. 2nd ed., rev. New York: Vintage Books, 1989.

Jones, P. M. *The Peasantry in the French Revolution*. Cambridge: Cambridge University Press, 1988.

Journal du Marquis de Sourches sur le règne de Louis XIV, 1686–1700. 6 vols. Paris, 1882.

Kenton, Edna, ed. *Black Gown and Redskins: Adventures and Travels of the Early Jesuit Missionaries in North America (1610–1791)*. With a New Preface by David B. Quinn. Introduction by Reuben Gold Thwaites. London: Longmans, Green and Co., 1956.

King, Stewart R. *Blue Coat or Powdered Wig*. Athens: University of Georgia Press, 2001.

Koehler, Winston Haverland. "The Operatic Repertoire of Madame de Pompadour's Théâtre des Petits Cabinets (1747–1753)." PhD diss., University of Michigan, 1971.

Labat, Jean-Baptiste. *Nouveau voyage aux isles de l'Amerique, contenant l'histoire naturelle de ces pays, l'origine, les moeurs, la religion & le gouvernement des habitans anciens & modernes*. Paris, 1722.

Lagrave, Henri. *Le Théâtre et le public à Paris de 1715 à 1750*. Paris: Librairie C. Klincksieck, 1972.

Lagrave, Henri, and Philippe Rouyer. *La Vie théâtrale à Bordeaux des origines à nos jours*. Paris: Éditions du Centre national de la recherche scientifique, 1985.

Lahontan, Baron de. *New Voyages to North America*. Reprint from the English edition of 1703, with facsimiles of original title pages, maps, and illustrations, and the addition of Introduction, Notes and Index by Reuben Gold Thwaites. Chicago: A. C. McClurg & Co., 1905.

Lajarte, Théodore de. *Bibliothèque musicale du Théâtre de l'Opéra: Catalogue historique, chronologique, anecdotique rédigé*. 2 vols. Paris, 1878. Reprint, Hildesheim: Georg Olms Verlag, 1969.

Langellier-Bellevue, Richard. "Le concept d'exotisme chez Rameau: Un exemple, 'Les Sauvages' des *Indes galantes*." *Recherches sur la musique française classique* 21 (1983): 158–60.

La Porte, Joseph de, and J.-M.-B. Clément. *Anecdotes dramatiques. Contenant toutes les pièces de théâtre, tragédies, pastorales . . . jouées à Paris et en province depuis l'origine des spectacles en France jusqu'en 1775. Tous les ouvrages dramatiques imprimés ou manuscrits dans quelques bibliothèques, un recueil d'anecdotes, faits curieux auxquels ont donné lieu les représentations de la plupart des pièces de théâtre, les noms de tous les auteurs, poètes ou musiciens qui ont travaillé pour nos théâtres, de tous les acteurs ou actrices célèbres avec an abrégé de leur vie, etc.* (1775). Reprint, Geneva: Slatkine Reprints, 1971.

Largey, Michael D. "Musical Ethnography in Haiti: A Study of Elite Hegemony and Musical Composition." PhD diss., Indiana University, 1991.

Laujon, Alfred de. *Souvenirs et voyages*. Bordeaux, 1835.

Launay, Denise, ed. *La Querelle des Buffons, Paris (1752–54): Texte des pamphlets avec introduction, commentaires et index*. 3 vols. Reprint, Geneva: Menkoff Reprints, 1973.

Lebeau, Auguste. *De la condition des gens de couleur libres sous l'Ancien Régime*. Paris: Guillaumin & Cie, 1908.

Le Brun, Antoine Louis. *Théâtre lyrique*. Paris, 1712.

LeCerf de la Viéville, Jean Laurent. *Comparaison de la musique italienne et de la musique française*. Vols. 2–4, *Histoire de la musique et de ses effets depuis son origine jusqu'au présent*, ed. Jacques Bonnet and Pierre Bourdelot. Paris, 1715.

Le Jeune, Paul. "Brief Relation of the Journey to New France, made in the month of April Last by Father Paul le Jeune of the Society of Jesus. August 28, 1632." In *The Jesuit Relations and Allied Documents: Travels and Explorations of the Jesuit Missionaries in North America (1610–1791)*, ed. Edna Kenton, introduction by Reuben Gold Thwaites, preface by Dr. George N. Shuster. New York: Vanguard Press, 1954.

Léris, Antoine D. *Dictionnaire portatif historique et littéraire des théâtres*. Paris, 1763.

Le Sage, Alain René. *Théâtre*. Edited by Maurice Bardon. Paris: Éditions Garnier Frères, 1948.

———. *Le Theâtre de la foire, ou l'opéra-comique: Contenant les meilloeurs pieces qui ont été représentées aux foires de S. Germain & de S. Laurent*. 10 vols. Paris: P. Gandouin, 1724–37.

"Letters of Toussaint Louverture and of Edward Stevens, 1798, 1800." *American Historical Review* 16 (1910): 64–101.

Lister, Martin. *A Journey to Paris in the Year 1698*. Edited, with Annotations, a Life of Lister, and a Lister Bibliography, by Raymond Phineas Stearns. Urbana: University of Illinois Press, 1967.

Little, Meredith E. "Dance under Louis XIV and XV." *Early Music* 3 (1975): 331–40.

Lokke, Carl Ludwig. *France and the Colonial Question: A Study of Contemporary French Opinion, 1763–1801*. New York: Columbia University Press, 1932.

Lott, Eric. *Love and Theft: Blackface Minstrelsy and the American Working Class*. New York: Oxford University Press, 1993.

Lough, John. *Paris Theatre Audiences in the Seventeenth and Eighteenth Centuries*. 1957; London: Oxford University Press, 1972.

Louis XIV, King of France and of Navarre: Mémoires for the Instruction of the Dauphin. Edited and translated by Paul Sonnino. New York: The Free Press, 1970.

Lowenthal, David. "Free Colored West Indians: A Racial Dilemma." In *Studies in Eighteenth-Century Culture 3: Racism in the Eighteenth Century*, ed. Harold E. Pagliaro. Cleveland: Case Western Reserve University Press, 1937.

Lully, Jean-Baptiste. *Oeuvres complètes de Jean-Baptiste Lully (1632–1687)*. Edited by Henry Prunières. Paris, 1930–39. Reprint, New York: Broude Brothers Ltd., 1966.

Mably, Gabriel Bonnot, Abbé de. *Lettres à Madame la Marquise de P. . . sur l'opéra*. Paris, 1741.

Machard, Roberte. *Jean-Joseph Cassanéa de Mondonville, virtuose, compositeur et chef d'orchestre*. Paris: Société de musicologie du Languedoc, 1980.

Madiou, Thomas. *Histoire d'Haïti*. Port-au-Prince: A. A. Héraux, 1923.

Marionneau, Charles. *Victor Louis, architecte du Théâtre de Bordeaux, sa vie, ses travaux et sa correspondance*. Bordeaux: Imprimerie G. Gounouilhou, 1881.

Marmontel, Jean François. *The Trial of Friendship* (Translation of *L'Amitié à l'épreuve*). Boston: Gilbert and Dean, 1802.

Martin, Gaston. *Nantes au XVIIIe siècle, l'ère des négriers (1714–1774), d'après des documents inédits*. Paris: Librairie Félix Alcan, 1931.

Martin, Isabelle. *Le Théâtre de la Foire: Des tréteaux aux boulevards*. Oxford: Voltaire Foundation, 2002.

Martineau, A., and L.-Ph. May. *Trois siècles d'histoire antillaise Martinique Guadeloupe*. Paris: Société de l'histoire des colonies françaises, 1935.

Mason, Amelia Ruth Gere. *The Women of the French Salons*. New York: The Century Co., 1891.

Masson, Chantal. "Journal du Marquis de Dangeau, 1684–1720." In *Recherches sur la musique française classique*, vol. 2. Paris: Éditions A. & J. Picard, 1961–1962.

Masson, Paul-Marie. "Lullistes et ramistes, 1733–52." *L'Année musicale* 1 (1911): 187–211.

———. *L'Opéra de Rameau*. Paris: Henri Laurens, 1930.

Mather, Betty Bang. *Dance Rhythms of the French Baroque: A Handbook for Performance*. Bloomington: University of Indiana Press, 1987.

McGowan, Margaret M. *L'Art du ballet de cour en France, 1581–1643*. Paris: Éditions du Centre national de la recherche scientifique, 1963.

Mélèse, Pierre. *Le Théâtre et le public à Paris sous Louis XIV, 1659–1715*. Paris: Librairie E. Droz, 1934. Reprint, Geneva: Slatkine Reprints, 1976.

Memoirs of Marguerite de Valois, Queen of France, Wife of Henri IV; of Madame de Pompadour of the Court of Louis XV; and of Catherine de Medici, Queen of France, Wife of Henri II. New York: P.F. Collier & Son, 1910.

Mémoires du Duc de Luynes sur la cour de Louis XV (1735–1758). 17 vols. Paris, 1860.

Menestrier, Claude-François. *Des ballets anciens et modernes selon les règles du théâtre*. Paris: René Guignard, 1682.

Mercier. "La vie au Cap Français en 1789." *Revue d'histoire des colonies françaises* 26 (1933): 101–30.

Mercier, Louis-Sébastien. *Jenneval, ou le Barnevelt François, drame*. In *Théâtre complèt de M. Mercier*. Amsterdam, 1778.

Mercier, Roger. "Image de l'autre et image de soi-même dans le discours ethnologique au XVIIIe siècle." *Studies on Voltaire and the Eighteenth Century* 154: 1417–35, ed. Theodore Besterman. Oxford: The Voltaire Foundation and the Taylor Institution, 1976.

Michel, Marianne Roland. "Représentations de l'exotisme dans la peinture en France de la première moitié du XVIIIème siècle." *Studies on Voltaire and the Eighteenth Century* 54: 1437–57, ed. Theodore Besterman. Oxford: The Voltaire Foundation and the Taylor Institution, 1976.

Mintz, Sidney W., and Sally Price, eds. *Focus: Caribbean.* Washington, DC: Latin American Program, Woodrow Wilson International Center for Scholars, 1984.

Mitford, Nancy. *Madame de Pompadour.* New York: E.P. Dutton, 1984.

———. *The Sun King.* New York: Harmony Books, 1966.

Montaigne, Michel de. "Des cannibales." In *Essais de Michel de Montaigne.* Paris, 1865.

Montesquieu, Charles de Secondat, Baron de. *Lettres persanes* (1721). Edited by Laurent Versini. Paris: Imprimerie Nationale, 1986.

———. *Persian Letters* (Paris, 1721). Translated by John Ozell. Introduction by William Graves. 2 vols. New York: Garland Publishing, 1972.

Montesquieu, The Spirit of the Laws. Translated and edited by Anne M. Cohler, Basia Carolyn Miller, and Harold Samuel Stone. Cambridge: Cambridge University Press, 1989.

Mooney, Carolyn J. "On Martinique: Elevating the Status of Creole." *Chronicle of Higher Education,* June 9, 2000, B2.

Moreau de Saint-Méry, Médéric-Louis-Elie. *Dance: An Article Drawn from the Work by M.L.E. St.-Méry Entitled: Repertory of Colonial Information, Compiled Alphabetically* (1796). Translated and with an introduction by Lily and Baird Hastings. Brooklyn, NY: Dance Horizons, 1975.

———. *Description topographique, physique, civile, politique et historique de la partie française de l'isle Saint-Domingue.* 2 vols. Philadelphia, 1797–1798.

———. *Loix et constitutions des colonies françaises de l'Amérique sous le vent.* 6 vols. Paris, 1784–1790.

———. *Voyage aux Etats-Unis de l'Amérique, 1793–1798.* Edited by S. L. Mims. New Haven, 1913.

Mousnier, Roland E. *The Institutions of France under the Absolute Monarchy, 1598–1789: The Organs of State and Society.* Translated by Arthur Goldhammer. Chicago: University of Chicago Press, 1984.

Munford, Clarence J. *The Black Ordeal of Slavery and Slave Trading in the French West Indies, 1625–1715.* 3 vols. Lewiston, NY: Edwin Mellen Press, 1991.

Netton, Ian Richard. "The Mysteries of Islam." In *Exoticism in the Enlightenment,* ed. G. S. Rousseau and Roy Porter. New York: Manchester University Press, 1990.

Nicolas, Maurice. *La Guadeloupe.* Basse-Terre, Guadeloupe: Librairie populaire, 1965.

———. *Les Grandes heures du théâtre de Saint-Pierre.* N.p.: Berger Bellepage, 1974.

———. *St.-Pierre, Martinique.* Fort-de-France, Martinique: Bezaudin, 1971.

———. "Le théâtre de Saint-Pierre au XVIIIe siècle: Les années difficiles." *Annales des Antilles* 1 (1955): 53–64.

Nouveau théâtre italien ou recueil général des comedies représentées par les comédiens italiens ordinaires du Roi, le. Nouvelle Édition, corrigée & très augmentée, & à laquelle on a joint les Airs graves des Vaudevilles à la fin de chaque volume. 10 vols. Paris: Chez Briasson, 1743.

Observations sur les écrits modernes. 34 vols. Paris: Chaubert, 1735–43.

Origny, Antoine D'. *Annales du Theâtre Italien, depuis son origine jusqu'a ce jour.* 3 vols. Paris, 1788. Reprint,

Geneva: Slatkine Reprints, 1970.

Pagliaro, Harold E., ed. *Studies in Eighteenth Century Culture.* Vol. 3, *Racism in the Eighteenth Century.* Cleveland: Case Western Reserve University Press, 1973.

Palmer, R. R. "The Declaration of Independence in France." *Studies on Voltaire* 154: 1569–79, ed. Theodore Besterman. Oxford: The Voltaire Foundation and the Taylor Institution, 1976.

Parallèles 4 (1965); 11 (1965); and 24 (1967).

Pellison-Fontanier, Paul. *Histoire de l'Académie Française.* Paris, 1858.

Petitjean-Roget, Jacques. *Le Gaoulé: La révolte de la Martinique en 1717.* Fort-de-France: Société d'histoire de la Martinique, 1966.

Peyronnet, Pierre. "L'Exotisme américain sur la scène française au XVIIème siècle." *Studies on Voltaire and the Eighteenth Century* 154: 1617–27, ed. Theodore Besterman. Oxford: The Voltaire Foundation and the Taylor Institution, 1976.

Peytraud, Lucien. *L'esclavage aux Antilles françaises avant 1789 d'après des documents inédits des Archives coloniales.* Paris, 1897. Pointe-à-Pitre, Guadeloupe: Emile Désormeaux, 1973.

Pluche, Noël Antoine. *Le spectacle de la nature.* 7 vols. Paris, 1756.

Poivre, Pierre. *Voyages d'un philosophe.* Paris, AN5–1797.

"Police des noirs sous Louis XVI, la." *Revue de l'histoire des colonies françaises* 21 (1928): 433–45.

"Port-au-Prince (1749–1750)." *Revue de l'histoire des colonies françaises* 36 (1927): 225–37.

Powers, David M. "French Caribbean Colonial Society: Dance, Otherness, and the Social Hierarchy under the Bourbon Monarchy." *Journal of Caribbean Studies* 12, nos. 2 & 3 (Fall 1997/Spring 1998): 241–57.

———. "The French Musical Theater: Maintaining Control in Caribbean Colonies in the Eighteenth Century." *Black Music Research Journal* 18, no. 1–2 (Spring/Fall 1998): 229–40.

———. "The *pastorale héroïque*: Origins and Development of a Genre of French Opera in the Seventeenth and Eighteenth Centuries." 2 vols. PhD diss., University of Chicago, 1988.

———. "The *pastorale héroïque*: Problems of Definition and Classification." *Recherches sur la musique française classique* 29 (1996–1998): 53–66.

———. "Perceptions of Non-Europeans in Early French Music Dramas: Parisian Society and the African *Other*." *Opera Journal* 30, no. 1 (March 1997): 2–13.

Présence africaine 121–122 (1982).

Prod'homme, Jacques-Gabriel. "The Economic Status of Musicians in France until the French Revolution." *Musical Quarterly* 16 (1930): 83–100.

Prunieres, Henry. *Le Ballet de cour en France avant Benserade et Lully.* Paris: E. Champion, 1914.

———. *Lully.* Paris: Librairie Renouard, 1909.

———. *L'Opéra italien en France avant Lulli.* Paris: E. Champion, 1913.

Pucci, Suzanne Rodin. "The Discrete Charms of the Exotic: Fictions of the Harem in Eighteenth-Century France." In *Exoticism in the Enlightenment*, ed. G. S. Rousseau and Roy Porter. New York: Manchester University Press, 1990.

Questel, Adrien. "Le Pacte colonial." *La Revue guadeloupéenne.* Nouvelle série 11 (March-April-May,

1947): 27–31.

Ravel, Jeffrey Scott. *The Contested Parterre, Public Theater and French Political Culture, 1680–1791*. Ithaca, NY: Cornell University Press, 1999.

———. "The Police and the Parterre: Cultural Politics in the Paris Public Theater, 1680–1789." PhD diss., University of California at Berkeley, 1991.

Raynal, Guillaume Thomas. *Histoire philosophique et politique des établissements et du commerce des Européens dans les deux Indes*. 4 vols. Geneva, 1780.

Rennard, J. *Histoire religieuse des Antilles Françaises*. Paris: Société de l'histoire des colonies françaises et Librairie Larose, 1954.

———. *Tricentenaire des Antilles: Guadeloupe-Martinique, 1635–1937* (Fort-de-France, Martinique: René Cottrel, 1935).

Revolution française et l'abolition de l'esclavage, la. 12 vols. Paris: Éditions d'histoire sociale, 1968.

Revue de l'histoire des colonies françaises (formerly *Revue d'histoire des colonies françaises* [1933–1958] and *Revue française d'histoire d'outre-mer* [1959–1966]). 53 vols. Paris: La Société de l'histoire des colonies françaises, 1913–1966.

Rice, Paul F. *The Performing Arts at Fontainebleau from Louis XIV to Louis XVI*. Ann Arbor, MI: UMI Research Press, 1989.

Richter, Melvin. *The Political Theory of Montesquieu*. Cambridge: Cambridge University Press, 1977.

Ritter, Alan, and Julia Conaway Bondanella, eds. *Rousseau's Political Writings*. Translated by Julia Conaway Bondanella. New York: W.W. Norton & Co., 1988.

Roberts, John Storm. *Black Music of Two Worlds*. New York: Praeger Publishers, 1972.

Romain, Rolland, André Maurois, and Edouard Herriot. *French Thought in the Eighteenth Century: Rousseau, Voltaire, Diderot*. Introduction by Geoffrey Brereton. New York: David McKay Co., 1953.

Rosemain, Jacqueline. *La musique dans la société antillaise, 1635–1902: Martinique, Guadeloupe*. Paris: Éditions L'Harmattan, 1986.

Rousseau, G. S. "Le Cat and the Physiology of Negroes." In *Studies in Eighteenth-Century Culture*, vol. 3, *Racism in the Eighteenth Century*, ed. Harold E. Pagliaro. Cleveland: Case Western Reserve University Press, 1973.

Rousseau, Jean-Jacques. *Dictionnaire de musique*. Paris, 1768.

———. *Discours sur l'économie politique (1755)*. In *Oeuvres complètes de Jean-Jacques Rousseau*, vol. 3. Paris: Éditions Gallimard, 1964.

———. *Discours sur l'origine et les fondements de l'inégalité*. In *Oeuvres complètes de Jean-Jacques Rousseau*, vol. 3. Paris: Éditions Gallimard, 1964.

———. *Du Contrat social* (1762). In *Oeuvres complètes de Jean-Jacques Rousseau*, vol. 3. Paris: Éditions Gallimard, 1964.

———. *Lettre sur la musique française* (1753). In *Oeuvres complètes de J. J. Rousseau*. Nouvelle édition. Paris, 1793.

Sala-Molins, Louis. *Le Code Noir, ou la calvaire de Canaan*. Paris: Presses universitaires de France, 1987.

Schoelcher, Victor. *Des Colonies françaises: Abolition immédiate de l'esclavage*. Paris: Pagnerre, 1842.

——— *Esclavage et colonisation*. Paris: Presses universitaires de France, 1948.

———. *Vie de Toussaint Louverture*. Paris, 1889.

Scott, R.H.F. *Jean-Baptiste Lully*. London: Peter Owen Ltd., 1973.

Seeber, Edward Derbyshire. *Anti-Slavery Opinion in France during the Second Half of the Eighteenth Century*. New York: Burt Franklin, 1971.

Semmens, Richard. *The* Bals publics *at the Paris Opéra in the Eighteenth Century*. Hillsdale, NY: Pendragon Press, 2004.

Shackleton, Robert. *Montesquieu: A Critical Biography*. Oxford: Oxford University Press, 1961.

Shelley, Henry Charles. *Old Paris: Its Social, Historical, and Literary Associations, Including An Account of the Famous Cabinets, Hôtels, Cafes, Salons, Clubs, Pleasure Gardens, Fairs and Fêtes, and the Theatres of the French Capital in Bygone Times*. Boston: L.C. Page & Co., 1912.

Souriau, Maurice. *Bernadin de Saint-Pierre, d'après ses manuscrits*. Paris, 1905.

Stranahan, Clara Cornelia (Harrison). *A History of French Painting from its Earliest to its Latest Practice; including an account of the French Academy of Painting, its salons, schools of Instruction and Regulations*. New York: C. Scribner's Sons, 1888.

Taylor, Yuval, and Jake Austen. *Darkest America: Black Minstrelsy from Slavery to Hip-Hop*. New York: W.W. Norton & Co., 2012.

Teilhard de Chardin, Joseph. *La Guinée supérieure et ses missions: Etude géographique, sociale et religieuse des contrées évangélisées par les missionnaires de la Société des Missions Africaines de Lyon* (1889). 2nd ed. Holland: Keer-lez-Maastricht, 1910.

Thomas, Downing A. *Aesthetics of Opera in the Ancien Régime, 1647–1785*. Cambridge: Cambridge University Press, 2002.

Thwaites, Reuben Gold. *The Jesuit Relations and Allied Documents: Travels and Explorations of the Jesuit Missionaries in New France, 1610–1791*. Vols. 58–59. New York: Pageant Book Co., 1959.

Tocqueville, Alexis de. *The Old Régime and the French Revolution*. Translated by Stuart Gilbert. Garden City, NY: Doubleday & Co., 1955.

Todorov, Tzvetan. *On Human Diversity: Nationalism, Racism, and Exoticism in French Thought*. Translated by Catherine Porter. Cambridge, MA: Harvard University Press, 1993.

Tramond, J. "Saint-Domingue en 1756 and 1757 d'après la correspondance de l'Ordonnateur Lambert." *Revue de l'histoire des colonies françaises* 20 (1927): 161–200.

Van der Cruysse, Dirk. "L'Exotisme pluriel de Raynal: Le discours exotique dans l'Histoire des deux Indes." *Exoticism in French Literature*. French Literature Series 13 (1986): 13–27.

Vanony-Frisch, Nicole. "Les esclaves de la Guadeloupe à la fin de l'Ancien Régime d'après les sources notariales (1770–1789)." Extrait du *Bulletin de la Société d'Histoire de la Guadeloupe*, nos. 63–64 (1985).

Verba, Cynthia. *Music and the French Enlightenment: Reconstruction of a Dialogue, 1750–1764*. Oxford: Oxford University Press, 1993.

Vilaire, Jean-Joseph. *4 Causeries sur "Boisrond Tonnerre: Nos Duels Historiques. Notre Créole. l'Esprit et les moeurs des Affranchis de St.-Domingue.*" Edited by Maurice Vilaire. N.p.: Imprimerie du Séminaire Adventiste, 1974.

Vilaire, Maurice, ed. *L'Esprit et les moeurs des Affranchis de St.-Domingue.* N.p.: Imprimerie du Séminaire Adventiste, 1974.

Vincent, Leon. *The French Academy.* Boston: Houghton, Mifflin & Co., 1901.

Voltaire, François-Marie Arouet. *Alzire, ou les Américains, tragédie* (Paris, 1736). In *Oeuvres complètes de Voltaire*, vol. 3. Paris, 1823.

———. *Candide, ou l'optimisme* (1759). In *Oeuvres complètes de Voltaire*, vol. 43. Paris, 1820.

———. "Esclaves." In *Dictionnaire philosophique par Voltaire*, vol. 5. Paris: J.N. Barba, 1828.

———. *Essai sur les moeurs et l'esprit des nations.* In *Oeuvres complètes de Voltaire*, vol. 15. Paris, 1820.

Willis, Eola. *The Charleston Stage in the XVIII Century with Social Settings of the Time.* New York: Benjamin Blom, 1968.

Wimpffen, François Alexandre Stanislaus, Baron de. *Saint-Domingue à la veille de la Révolution: Souvenirs du Baron de Wimpffen (1788–1790).* Edited by Albert Savine. Paris: Louis-Michaud, 1911.

Wolpe, Hans. *Raynal et sa machine de guerre: "l'Histoire des Deux Indes" et ses perfectionnements.* 1957; reprint, New York: AMS Press, Inc., 1967.

Wroth, Lawrence Counselman. *Acts of French Royal Administration Concerning Canada, Guiana, the West Indies, and Louisiana prior to 1791.* A list compiled by Lawrence D. Wroth and Gertrude L. Annan. New York: New York Public Library, 1930.

Yolton, John W., Roy Porter, Pat Rogers, Barbara Maria Stafford. "Race." *The Blackwell Companion to The Enlightenment.* Introduction by Lester G. Crocker. Oxford: Blackwell Publishers, 1992.

Zweig, Stefan. *Marie Antoinette: The Portrait of an Average Woman.* Translated by Eden and Cedar Paul. Garden City, NY: Garden City Publishing Co., 1933.

INDEX